119 - good eg's of how SBC enforces ban on
clergy —

A Still Small Voice

Women and Gender in North American Religions
Amanda Porterfield and Mary Farrell Bednarowski
Series Editors

A Still Small Voice
*Women, Ordination,
and the Church*

Frederick W. Schmidt, Jr.

With a Foreword by
The Reverend Betty Bone Schiess

Syracuse University Press

First Edition 1996
96 97 98 99 00 01   6 5 4 3 2 1

The paper used in this publication meets the minimum requirements of American National Standard for Information Sciences—Permanence of Paper for Printed Library Materials, ANSI Z39.48-1984. ∞™

Library of Congress Cataloging-in-Publication Data

Schmidt, Frederick W.
    A still small voice : women, ordination, and the church /
Frederick W. Schmidt, Jr. ; with a foreword by the Reverend Betty
Bone Schiess. — 1st ed.
      p.   cm. — (Women and gender in North American religions)
    Includes bibliographical references and index.
    ISBN 0-8156-2683-5 (alk. paper).
    1. Women clergy—United States—History—20th century.
2. Christian sects—United States—Controversial literature.
I. Title. II. Series.
BV676.S34   1995
262'.14'082—dc20   95-19950

And, behold, the Lord passed by, and a great and strong wind rent the mountains, and break in pieces the rocks before the Lord; but the Lord was not in the wind; and after the wind an earthquake; but the Lord was not in the earthquake. And after the earthquake a fire; but the Lord was not in the fire; and after the fire a still small voice.

—1 Kings 19:11b–12 (King James Version)

Frederick W. Schmidt, Jr., a professor of religious studies, received his doctoral degree from the University of Oxford. He is a contributor to a number of journals, including *The Scottish Journal of Theology* and *Feminist Theology*.

Contents

Foreword

The Reverend Betty Bone Schiess

A good friend often quotes theologian and moralist Reinhold Niebuhr to the effect that nothing worth doing can be done in one lifetime. That may be solace for some of us who see history slipping away and our part in it overlooked. We can pretend that someday our wise action will make its mark, at least nudging our grandchildren's generation a little closer to the kingdom of heaven.

The trouble with this sort of dreaming is that this has seldom happened to women. Even when we intentionally review our past, it is slim going. If we stay with the church hoping for the best, clutching at biblical stories of women, we find for every Deborah a Jael, for every Mary a Martha.

If we discard biblical stories altogether, we wind up digging up ancient goddesses, goddesses too often stuck in some primordial mud, not only forgotten but forgettable. Our models of brave behavior (in my tradition I think of Josephine Butler and Maude Royden) are not in the church calendar, and most Episcopalians have never heard of them. In every generation we must start over. That which is worth doing gets lost. This result is not only forgetful, it is tragic.

Bless Frederick Schmidt. In "A Still Small Voice: Women, Ordination, and the Church," he makes the tragedy clear by drawing us into the experiences of women clergy. By listening carefully to women's voices, by recording and interpreting them with insight and sensitivity, he makes sure that we will not lose them, in this generation or the next. And what voices, what stories!

Writing as a seminary-trained sociologist, Schmidt knows that the
church is often, if not always, hiding behind what he calls a "facade,"
saying one thing and, especially where women are concerned, acting
otherwise. What he reveals is what many of us have suspected all along:
in spite of much effort during the last two decades to include women in
the church as full participants, women clergy and would-be women clergy
(Roman Catholics) are not happy—are, in fact, limited by the churches
they serve, their voices muffled by those who should be listening, their
talents badly used by those who should know about sloth. This is powerful stuff, important beyond church walls and stained glass ceilings. These
voices, as Schmidt concludes, are "the voice of God."

In addition to a sociological overview, here we have an opportunity
to empathize with real live women and to revel in it as we read: the
Episcopal woman denied a job because she was too short; the Methodist
woman burdened with that old saw about women preachers being like
dogs walking on hind legs; the Evangelical Lutheran who did not trust
her denomination's trickle-down reform and who camped outside her
bishop's office until he paid attention to her legitimate complaints; the
Baptist woman whose hero was Lottie Moon, a misunderstood hell raiser;
and the Roman Catholic women who are almost to be envied because
their position is so clearly awful—not much facade there.

For those who tune out when descriptions of virtuous women test
our interest, this book is not only rip-roaring entertainment, more fun to
read than any of us could expect from observations about our feminist
reformation and its importance, it also quickens us, in some cases revives
us, and finally moves us to "Come, Labor On," as that grand old Episcopal hymn goes.

In addition to the actual voices of women, we also learn about that
which we only half knew and should never forget. We are reminded that
the church influences society whether society acknowledges it or not. In
fact, it has often been suggested that no permanent social change takes
place without a religious dimension. And so, what the church does makes
more impact than what General Motors does. Bad enough when GM
diminishes women. When God, as interpreted by church action, says that
women are the second order of creation, we are in real trouble.

Demanding more and more effort to maintain their facade and becoming more and more exhausted by the effort, our churches lose the
capacity to do good. Or if they continue to enjoy influence and continue
to encourage the religious backlash spawned in part by women's ordina-

tion, they will continue to do damage to women and to men in and out of the church.

If my liberal agnostic friends think they escape any of the problems of women clergy and if our major denominations think they have heard the last of our feminist reformation, as my two-year-old granddaughter Zoe would put it, "NO WAY!"

There are other things in this book to be grateful for. By paying attention to those still small voices, this report moves me emotionally because I was, and am, one of those still small voices. I suspect that I am not alone.

As the author points out, much observation about women clergy has been a case of the marginal studying the marginalized. When this happens, it leaves the victims trapped, forever rebels with a narrowly defined cause, unsure and even unaware of their own power. It is a sad old story that women often submit to victimization as if it were a Christian virtue. Reading Schmidt we conclude that this need not be, must not be.

One of Schmidt's most important contributions is his enlarging the concern about women's ordination to include men. In doing so, he not only includes men but he also challenges the feminist movement to pay attention. This focus is a brave and absolutely necessary adventure because the feminist movement has been hiding behind its own facade (unwilling or unable to include men) and because men have often experienced the feminist movement as a war between the sexes.

Schmidt helps us understand the need for his qualitative analysis. Even those of us unfamiliar with his sociological grid easily understand that to depend on denominations to study themselves quantitatively is not the whole story.

As we say in the trade, it is a miracle, a miracle that Schmidt has so clearly explained church polity. When trying to explain my own, the Episcopal Church, I often find myself either tongue-tied or verbose (and in all cases unclear) as I try to describe our history and our canon (church) law—how we work (or do not work) and what social stratification and regionalism have to do with the way we behave. This is a real bonus and one which should draw the attention of any would-be ecumenist, as well as all feminists, male and female, who need to understand one another's ways of behaving, who need to note what similarities there are in the move to ordain women, and who need to learn from one another how reform takes place.

In reading this book and noting its implications, I predict that many more of us, men and women, will swell the chorus so that women's voices will no longer stay small. We will do this for our own sakes, for the sake of the churches we presume to represent and, more grandly, for a society gone astray for want of moral suasion—enough, at least, to satisfy Niebuhr and anyone else struggling to give meaning to her or his life now.

Acknowledgments

I would like to thank Dr. Catherine Wessinger at Loyola University, New Orleans, and Dr. Martha Ice at Concordia College, Moorhead, Minnesota, for their extensive critical input. A special word of thanks is due colleagues Drs. Wilma Bailey, Steve Cobb, Rhonda Jacobsen, Linda Parkyn, Susie Stanley and Robert Wright who critiqued the project at various stages of its preparation, and Pauline R. Schmidt, who produced verbatim manuscripts of the interviews. I would also like to acknowledge the assistance of Dr. Linda M. Givens, who helped in conducting the interviews on which this study is based.

Throughout the process, Dr. William Vance Trollinger, Jr., has provided valuable advice and much-needed encouragement. He has read the manuscript at more than one stage, and the final product, whatever its limitations, is better as a result.

I would also like to thank those at Syracuse University Press who have given my work tireless and painstaking attention. In particular I would like to thank Cynthia Maude-Gembler, Theresa Litz, Rebecca Salome Shaw, and John Fruehwirth. I am honored and delighted that the Reverend Betty Bone Schiess was willing to contribute the foreword. The energy of her observations makes it the kind of piece that will add to the perspectives described in the book.

The study would not exist at all, of course, without the cooperation of the fifty women who responded to my request for an interview. I was struck by their integrity and thoughtful commitment to their respective ministries, and I am grateful to them for the candor that characterized their responses. Ultimately, it is their voices that give this study its significance.

I am particularly indebted to my wife, Dr. Elaine Melotti Schmidt, who provided valuable input at every stage of the study, helping to shape the questionnaire, the interview protocol, and the final manuscript itself. As always, she proved an insightful critic and resource. This book is dedicated to her and to our daughter, Lindsay.

Abbreviations

In order to give the reader some sense of the "spread" of opinion within each group of interviewees, a simple system of abbreviations has been used to document the source of the quotations used from the interview material. The page number that appears after the abbreviation corresponds to the page number on a verbatim transcript of the conversations. This system is used throughout chapters two through six. The abbreviations are as follows:

E	Episcopal Church
ELCA	Evangelical Lutheran Church of America
RC	Roman Catholic Church
SBC	Southern Baptist Convention
UM	United Methodist Church

A Still Small Voice

1

Behind the Facade

Organizations are the facade that covers individual intention and will; they are the marionette show that dazzles and
deceives an audience—an audience of people who will
themselves to believe the performance. But behind the facade
are human actors who do what they want to do. As spectators
we can choose to be enchanted or duped by the show or we
can ask to see behind the facade and to discover who pulls the
strings. Human effort creates organizations, but we usually
choose to forget the effort and to focus on its outcome.
We admire the achievement and deal with it as a detached,
objective reality that is independent of the individuals who
created it.

—Thomas B. Greenfield, "Leaders and Schools"

As a young seminarian I read vol-
ume after volume of theological literature, which described the church as
an agent of not only personal, but social change.[1] What was all but
completely missing from the curriculum, however, was any concerted
attempt to evaluate the church's success in effecting change within its
own walls. Unlike those of my counterparts in so many other fields of
endeavor, my impressions of the "real world" of the church were shaped
by the abstractions of a semester's reading and the random anecdotes provided by our small circle of acquaintances and mentors (the
one ill-formed, the latter often increasingly out of touch with current
developments).

Rarely, if ever, did we see behind the facade. Indeed I often labored under the impression that it was evidence of bad faith to ask questions suggesting that the church is an organization at all. Rhetoric and reality hung suspended in air, the one often uninformed by the other. Today, most discussions about the church *within* the church continue to be similarly schizophrenic, or as Webster's would have it, they are "characterized by loss of contact with the environment" (1990, 1050).

Undoubtedly, there are a number of reasons behind this state of affairs. Churchgoers often infer that much of what the Bible teaches about the evils of judging others also forbids criticism. Similarly, the presence of disagreement or debate is taken to be evidence of spiritual miscarriage.

Above all, however, the reticence of the church to bring its own real-world conduct face to face with its rhetoric may lie in the running battle which the church has fought for centuries with its own theology of incarnation. Applied in the first place to the person and work of Christ, this is the doctrinal view that Jesus was God in human form. Understanding it more broadly as a way of characterizing the activity of God in the mundane world, Christians have historically argued that the theology of the church can be distinguished in its contention that God is active in human history. Having established this beachhead in the war of religious ideology, however, the church has found it far easier to make the claim than to live with it.[2] Having argued that God is at work in and through the mundane, the church has grown to fear that what it believes and what it cherishes might ultimately be explained as a product of the mundane.[3] Hence, there is not a little fear that the church might ultimately prove to be nothing more than the product of people doing what they want or need to do.

The widespread failure to see behind the facade is especially perilous for women. Although they have begun to attend seminaries in record numbers, women continue to serve churches in much smaller numbers than men and (as we shall see) are still locked out of most positions of significant leadership (Carroll and others 1981, 3–7, 137–38; and Charlton 1987). This situation is made all the more perilous given the widespread, but mistaken assumption that on every front in American life, "Women have 'made it' " (Faludi 1991, ix). One is tempted to see parallels both in the plight of African Americans, who, having achieved equal rights under the law, have in reality suffered a net loss of social freedom over the course of the last two decades, and in the church's belated and halfhearted response to that challenge (Russell 1968). Indeed, one might argue that women have experienced an ecclesiastical version of what writer Susan Faludi describes as "backlash" (Faludi 1991).

This is not to suggest that there is no literature on the subject of women, the church, and ordained ministry; there are, in fact, four significant kinds. The first is what I would describe as theological literature, some of it devoted to protest, some of it devoted to the construction of a feminist alternative to Christian theology.[4] Such literature is extremely valuable, and, indeed, one might argue that if significant change is ever to mark the church, such literature is an absolute necessity. As Thomas Greenfield notes, organizations are a product of the imagination (1984). If the church is to change, a new set of symbols will be needed to describe it. By and large, however, this literature is still the abstract alternative to so much of what has dominated the church's conversation about itself. Alone, theological literature is not capable of ameliorating the effects of the church's schizophrenia.

A second category of literature explores the history of women's struggle for ordination.[5] Developed for a variety of journals and some lengthier treatments, this body of literature can provide valuable perspective on the debate, but it cannot replace a discussion of the organizational dynamics that continue to shape the experience of women in the church.

A third kind of literature consists of quantitative (i.e., statistical) studies by some denominations. Such studies are better suited to bridging the gulf between rhetoric and reality, and, indeed, where it is appropriate I have drawn on those findings. By definition, however, such studies are usually conducted within individual denominations and as such lack a vision of developments in the larger church, as well as a larger audience.[6] To the church's discredit these studies are also usually conducted by committees and task forces of the marginalized studying the marginalized.

The fourth body of literature is an ever-growing number of studies conducted mainly by sociologists.[7] Committed to the discussion of a whole host of dynamics surrounding the inclusion of women in the work of the church, this literature is potentially the most helpful in dealing with the challenges described above. It figures prominently in this book and confirms much of what is said here using other methods. As helpful and as varied as the literature is, however, it also has certain limitations. Sociological studies are often couched in language that is less accessible to a lay audience and, for that reason, they appear primarily in academic journals and books published by academic presses. They are also largely

quantitative in nature, and, as important as such work is, it lacks the
narrative content that might help to amplify our understanding of people's
experience of the church as organization.[8] Where the researchers do rely
on interviews, the focus of their efforts lies in areas other than those
addressed here, even though they are of unquestionable relevance.[9]

Purpose

I use the term "voice" in the title to emphasize the importance of
contemplating women's experience in the church as told in their own
words. Relying upon organizational theory to classify and describe the
attitude taken by churches toward the ordination of women and their
ministry, this book identifies and assesses the significance of bureaucratic
and cultural linkages that either mitigate against or facilitate the inclusion
of women. As such it takes its place alongside the other four kinds of
work, as a complement to them, not as a replacement for them. In the
pages that follow the theoretical underpinning of this study will recede
into the background, but a word or two of definition is necessary.

Definitions

The word "linkage" refers to any mechanism in an organization that
"serve[s] to coordinate the activity of people who work there" (Firestone
and Wilson 1985). It is a dynamic term, however, suggesting more than
simply the image of people at work. It also implies that there are varying
levels of coordination when people are engaged in a common task.[10] In
some organizations the level of coordination is "tightly" linked. Com-
mands are given, directives issued, and activities performed. In theory,
the armed forces operate on this model. Other organizations are "loosely"
linked. Directives may be issued by "superiors," but much of the day-to-
day life of the organization is carried on at other levels with relative
independence. The university classroom operates on this model. The fact
of the matter is, of course, that most organizations include elements of
both tight and loose coordination, and any characterization of a specific
group will be only more or less accurate in describing the activity in
which people are engaged.

Within either kind of organization there are two kinds of "linkage,"
one "bureaucratic," the other "cultural." The label "bureaucratic" refers

to such mechanisms as the rules, roles, official procedures, and authority relations that shape organizational life. The influence of bureaucratic linkages is widely acknowledged among students of organizational theory (Firestone and Wilson 1985). Indeed, for a long time sociologists assumed that much, if not all of what occurred in an organization could be explained in bureaucratic terms, and there are still those who would emphasize this dynamic in their descriptions of organizational life.[11]

Widely acknowledged, but often neglected in studies of this kind, are the cultural linkages that shape the meanings participants give to organizational activity (Firestone and Wilson 1985).[12] Referred to as both "the subjective side of organization" and "the glue that holds [them] together," culture consists of shared meanings and the symbols, stories, and rituals that communicate those meanings. Some would argue, in fact, that culture is a more important factor in determining the behavior of a group than is its bureaucratic structure (Deal and Kennedy 1982, 5–7, and Schein 1985, 2). Indeed, there are those who would argue that even an organization's bureaucracy is a part of its culture.

Assumptions

In choosing the language, "bureaucratic and cultural linkages", I am opting for one view (among many) of organizational life. As I have already noted, some thinkers continue to champion sociologist Max Weber's characterization of organizations almost entirely in terms of formal (or bureaucratic) structures. At the opposite end of the spectrum, others argue that organizations have a distinguishable bureaucracy but that such a structure has little to do with the day-to-day life of an organization. By contrast, this study sides with those who find that reality is infinitely more complex than either of these propositions would appear to suggest.

Every organization consists of not only a dominant culture, but alternative cultures as well. At any one time, the tensions between those understandings are negotiated within the boundaries fixed by distinguishable bureaucratic structures. In turn, however, the formal structures can be circumvented and reshaped by the meanings that an organization's members give to it. As a result, the character of the whole is a product of the complex interplay of both kinds of linkage. And the more loosely "linked," or "coupled" an organization is, the richer the texture of that interplay.[13]

As Karl Weick notes, much of what takes place in an organization is far less "rational" than we are prepared to admit. The image that best characterizes what happens is not one of a tightly regimented, linear activity, but one of "an unconventional soccer match: the field for the game is round; there are several goals scattered haphazardly around the circular field; people can enter and leave the game whenever they want to; they can throw balls in whenever they want to, as many times as they want to; the entire game takes place on a sloped field; and the game is played as if it makes sense" (Weick 1976, 1).

Weick applies this model to educational organizations, but the model applies equally well to the contemporary church. With weak bureaucratic ties and local ministries, which are decoupled from one another on a day-to-day basis, even the most structured denominations are loosely not tightly linked. They are also correspondingly dependent upon the cultural linkages that make organizational coherence possible.

Methods

If these assumptions are granted, then the virtues of qualitative research techniques become all the more evident. It may be possible to measure the impact of an organization's culture, but it is difficult to recover the texture of that experience in statistical terms.[14] Furthermore, the random character of organizational life suggested by Weick's model makes it difficult if not impossible to predict the impact of even bureaucratic measures.

Instead, therefore, interviews and questionnaires were used to gather insights from forty ordained females from four mainline denominations (the Episcopal Church, the Evangelical Lutheran Church in America, the United Methodist Church and the Southern Baptist Convention[15]) and ten female seminary graduates from a mainline denomination that does not sanction the ordination of women (the Roman Catholic Church).[16] In three cases a random selection of names was made available by agencies of the denominations being studied.[17] One of those denominations simply provided a directory of names and addresses belonging to both men and women engaged in pastoral ministry from which a random selection was made.[18] In the other two cases I was referred to administrators charged with the specific responsibility of overseeing the activity of women in ministry, and they provided the necessary sample.[19] In the two remaining cases it was necessary to acquire the names from outside the official structures of the denominations being studied.[20] In making my selections I strove for a geographical spread, but in this first, exploratory study I did not attempt to control for differences in either age, race, or ethnic origin.

Respondents were asked to complete a written questionnaire and were then interviewed by telephone, following a basic protocol, which provided the basis for making comparisons between the denominations. The interviewees were supplied with a copy of the protocol in advance of the interview.[21] The average interview lasted seventy-five minutes, and I completed the interview process itself over a period of two months during the summer of 1992.

Broadly speaking the protocol consisted of two parts. The first half of the interview dealt with cultural linkages. There is almost certainly some measure of continuity between the culture of a denomination and the larger regional and national cultures in which a given church is located. Nonetheless, I crafted the protocol on the assumption that each denomination not only "*has*" a culture, but "*is*" a culture with characteristics of its own (Smircich 1983, 347).

Accordingly, respondents were asked to reflect on the degree to which the stories, language, icons (or symbols), and rituals of their denomination had a specific gender orientation. They were also asked to identify which of those traditions had either helped them to identify with their religious tradition or may have alienated them. Realizing that I might run the risk of straitjacketing the interviewees, I also gave them the opportunity to identify other dimensions of their tradition, which were not covered by my choice of categories.

I also examined less formal dimensions of denominational culture as it touches on attitudes toward gender. I asked respondents to answer questions that probed the impact of parishioners' attitudes on their career; the impact of attitudes toward women on their professional relationships with both male and female colleagues; and the effect of the same attitudes on the shape of membership in denominational in-groups. I also asked respondents to describe what if any impact their spouse's employment has had on their career. In those cases in which a respondent served as an associate or assistant, I explored the nature of her relationship with the leader on her staff.

Without assuming that there is any hard and fast line between cultural and bureaucratic linkages, I devoted the second half of the interview protocol to concerns that are, nonetheless, more clearly bureaucratic in nature. I began by asking whether the church polity, discipline, or canon law of the respondents' denominations provide for the involvement of women in the ordained ministry of their church. Depending upon the response, I then determined whether the interviewees believed that these provisions were effectively administered at the local, state (district, conference, or diocesan), and national levels. I also inquired as to whether women were involved in the decision-making process and in worship on all three levels.

Again, in order to avoid straitjacketing the respondents, I closed each interview by asking the participants to add anything of relevance that they believed my inquiry had failed to isolate. A number took this opportunity to elaborate on the responses they had given, and some used the opportunity to focus my attention on a theme they believed was central to the views they had expressed. But none of my interviewees appeared to believe that the process had failed to probe the issue thoroughly.

Validity and Reliability

I would readily describe myself as a feminist. I favor the ordination and full involvement of women in the church's ministry. I have also had connections with three of the denominations studied. Recognizing the need to be as balanced as possible in both my collection and assessment of the data, I have employed a number of strategies.

I used questions that suggested the possibility that the respondents would evaluate their experiences in both positive and negative terms. If a respondent expressed dissatisfaction with the terms I chose, I invited the interviewee to use terms of her own choosing.[22] I scrupulously avoided steering evaluations of my respondents' experiences and allowed them to define the terms used in the protocol as they saw fit. On the rare occasion when an interviewee asked me to clarify the nature of a question, I attempted to clarify the intention of my question by drawing on the content of the interviewee's responses. In addition, I used the same set of questions for all denominations, even though this required some of the participants to adapt the questions to their own setting. This practice kept me from asking questions that pre-judged the possible responses, particularly in the case of the one denomination that does not sanction the ordination of women. As a further precaution, I was assisted by a colleague in conducting the actual interviews. I also tape-recorded the interviews, had transcripts created, took cursory notes, and spent considerable time sifting through the results in order to avoid making observations without clear basis in the content of the interviews. As a final precaution I mailed copies of an early draft to each interviewee, inviting both comment and criticism.

Limits Inherent in the Nature of the Study

On the one hand, it would seem unnecessary to outline the limitations inherent in this study. There is a considerable amount of literature describing both the strengths and the weaknesses of qualitative research.[23] Furthermore, practitioners in the field are well aware that such research offers a different kind of insight into the dynamics of organizational life.

On the other hand, the widespread misapplication of such research, especially as it pertains to the experiences of American women, have been well documented by authors such as Susan Faludi (1991, 327–30). A few words, then, on the limits inherent in the nature of my study are necessary and will permit me to avoid using excessively circumspect language throughout the report of my findings.

Three observations will suffice. First, this study describes the experiences of *some* women and it *may* provide a key to the larger experience of women in the church. But that is by no means certain. The study has a narrow focus, and I make no claims for it of either a statistical or longitudinal character. Second, even where I refer to the number of interviewees who responded in a particular way, I am not implying that those observations are of statistical significance. Such observations are only meant to underline the significance of certain responses in relationship to the specific sample interviewed here. Third, my analysis is self-consciously heuristic, a search for clues as to how women actually experience the church as organization and " 'insights into how things get to be the way they are' " (Merriam 1988, 13).

"The Way Things Are"

The way things are behind the facade may come as something of a surprise. The popular picture of life in the American church is one of a two-party structure.[24] According to that picture, one party endorses a conservative ideology and an ethos to match. Women are unlikely to be involved in the church's ministry, and a largely male leadership prides itself on the argument that women really do run the church, albeit from behind the scenes.

This point of view is clearly reflected in a recent conversation between journalist Bill Moyers and Southern Baptist Minister W. A. Criswell:

> *Moyers:* No recent issue of scriptural interpretation has proved more divisive to Southern Baptists than the ordination of women. Pastors and editors can face censure or the loss of jobs if they publicly support women's ordination. Fundamentalists say women can serve in the church, but the Bible does not permit them to have authority over men. (interviewing) What is the biblical base for your position on the ordination of women?
>
> *Dr. Criswell:* Bill, let me sarcastically answer that, if I can be forgiven.
>
> *Moyers:* I'll forgive you, but I'm not sure . . .
>
> *Dr. Criswell:* The scripture says, you know, in I Timothy, chapter three, "For the bishop, the preacher, the elder, is to be the husband of one wife", "and I say sarcastically, facetiously, if a woman can be the husband of one wife, ordain her, that'll be fine. Just go ahead."
>
> *Moyers:* Now, is that a literal reading of scripture?
>
> *Dr. Criswell:* That's a literal reading of the scripture.
>
> *Moyers:* Some people tell me that it's because they read the Bible to say man was the first to be created, and woman was the first to fall. But you don't hold to that, I gather.
>
> *Dr. Criswell:* Oh, no. Plainly, Bill that is written in the Bible for the preacher, your pastor, is to be the husband of one wife.
>
> *Moyers:* Should women not be ordained, then?
>
> *Dr. Criswell:* No, sir, they should not be ordained.
>
> *Moyers:* Should they not be in authority over men?
>
> *Dr. Criswell:* No.
>
> *Moyers:* What should a young woman do if she sincerely believes she's been called by God to be a pastor in the Southern Baptist Convention?
>
> *Dr. Criswell:* She is mistaken. God never called her. Her own personal ambition, or longing for recognition, or a thousand other things led her into that persuasion.
>
> *Moyers:* What should she do? I've talked to some women who believe they have been called to be pastors.

Dr. Criswell: There are 10,000 ways that women can serve, and serve effectively and beautifully. They do here in this church. The women actually run the church there's no doubt about that. My wife, these women, gracious alive, if I don't get along with the women, I couldn't pastor the church, I wouldn't have a church. They exert an enormous influence in it, but they ought not be the pastor and the preacher up there in the pulpit (Moyers 1987, 9–10).

The other party is, by contrast, progressive and socially engaged and ostensibly nurtures an inclusive way of life that by definition insures the full involvement of women. It is a deceptive picture that had no real basis in fact, even in the forties and the fifties when it gained currency, and few people asked directly about its legitmacy are tempted to endorse it. Nonetheless, it is a powerful picture, which to some degree has been used by those who "pull the strings."

On this basis, one might think that a comparative study of women's experience of the church could be charted in a fairly predictable fashion. Supposedly the largely disenfranchised women live in denominations affiliated with the first of these parties. Those women who enjoy a greater measure of involvement live in denominations belonging to the second. In fact, however, the two-party understanding of the church is no more reliable as a means of summarizing the involvement of women than it is as a guide to the larger realities governing the church's theology and ethos.

The sense of alienation experienced by women cannot be charted in such a clear fashion and persists as strongly in denominations considered mainline and liberal as it does in denominations considered conservative and outside the mainstream. The voices of those women who continue to live within the orbit of all five denominations provide us with an opportunity "to see behind the facade" in an attempt to understand who pulls the strings, why they do it, and how.

Notes

1. For example, Hennelly 1989; Hillyer 1990; and Snyder 1991.
2. Note the recent flap surrounding the film, "The Last Temptation of Christ," on which see Anker 1988. Similar battles have been fought by the church with astronomy, sociology, psychology, and biblical criticism, among others.

3. Sociologists refer to this as a fear of "reductionism."

4. Ground-breaking examples include Daly 1968 and Ruether 1972 on whose work, see Porterfield 1987. Since then far more has been written than can be cited here.

5. See, for example, Ruether and Keller 1986, whose treatment is wide-ranging; Prelinger 1992a, whose focus is the Episcopal Church; and Field-Bibb 1991, whose work is devoted to the Methodist, Anglican, and Roman traditions in England. For other treatments, see the bibliography.

6. See, for example, "Report of Executive Council's Committee on the Status of Women" (1991c); and Pellauer 1990. Two studies of a more expansive nature are Euzenas 1989 and Darling 1987. Even these, however, focus on single denominations.

7. See, for example, Carroll and others 1981, whose work compares the experiences of female and male ministers, "in seminary, the job market, the parish, and balancing their careers with their personal lives." See also Lehman 1985, whose work focuses on "the ways in which church members responded to women serving their congregations as ordained clergy." For numerous other examples, see the bibliography at the end of this work.

8. As Martha Ice notes, "We have attitude studies and behavior studies. . . . We have probability statistics; . . . but they tell us nothing of the experience of flesh-and-blood women and men who make up the numbers. This is not a failure of those studies; they are not designed to do so. Still they leave us with only a fragment of knowledge. Therefore, we need . . . qualitative studies that can capture the fullness of experience, the richness of living" (Ice 1987, x).

9. See, for example, Kleinman 1984, whose focus is seminarians; Ice 1987, whose work deals with the world views of clergywomen, including "(1) self-image, (2) notions of ministry, (3) views of institutional settings, and (4) ultimate preoccupations"; and Wallace 1992, whose focus is "priestless parishes" in the Roman Catholic Church where women serve as pastors.

10. Compare Weick 1976; and Firestone and Wilson 1985.

11. Sociologists will immediately recognize the influence of Max Weber (1946). For a discussion of Weber's ongoing influence on students of organizational life, see Ranson and others 1980.

12. Compare Greenfield 1984, 152 with whose observations the chapter opens.

13. Using the jargon of the discipline, Stewart Ranson, Bob Hinings, and Royston Greenwood argue much the same thing: "Three abstract and interdependent conceptual categories are integral to a theoretical model that seeks to articulate the way in which the process of structuring itself defines and mediates organizational structures: (1) Organization members create *provinces of meaning* which incorporate interpretive schemes, intermittently articulated as values and interests, that form the basis of their orientation and strategic purposes within organizations. (2) Since interpretive schemes can be the basis of cleavage as much as of consensus, it is often appropriate to consider an organization as composed of alternative interpretive schemes, value preferences, and sectional interests, the resolution of which is determined by *dependencies of power* and domination. (3) Such constitutive structuring by organizational members has, in turn, always to accommodate *contextual constraints* inherent in characteristics of the organization and the environment, with organizational members differentially responding to and enacting their contextual

conditions according to the opportunities provided by infrastructure and time" (Ranson and others 1980).

14. Compare Ranson and others 1980.

15. The Southern Baptist Church provides a special opportunity to study the impact of both cultural and bureaucratic linkages, since its polity permits local congregations to ordain women, even though the national convention has taken a formal stand against the practice. Further observations are made below.

16. The sample included both sisters and non-vowed women.

17. These were the Episcopal Church, the Evangelical Lutheran Church in America, and the United Methodist Church.

18. The Evangelical Lutheran Church in America provided a copy of its 1992 *Yearbook.*

19. The Episcopal Church referred me to the Reverend Katherine Ragsdale, Advocacy Coordinator for Women in Mission and Ministry at the Episcopal Church Center in New York, N.Y. The Reverend M. Lynn Scott, Director of Support Systems and Spiritual Formation, at the Board of Higher Education and Ministry in Nashville, Tenn., helped to identify United Methodist ministers who might be willing to participate.

20. I was assisted by the Reverend Amanda Hiley, Center Administrator of Southern Baptist Women in Ministry, based in Louisville, Ky. and by Ms. Ruth McDonough Fitzpatrick, National Coordinator of the Women's Ordination Conference, based in Fairfax, Va.

21. A sample copy of both the questionnaire and the protocol appear in the appendices.

22. One out of fifty participants did, but in connection with the same word in only two questions.

23. See, for example, Lofland and Bogdan 1984; Merriam 1988; Schwartz and Jacobs 1989; and Taylor and Bogdan 1984.

24. I am dependent upon the analysis provided in a recent article by Jacobsen and Trollinger 1994, 682–84.

2

The Episcopal Church
A Hierarchical and Male-Dominated Culture

> Organizations are abstractions. They are symbolic ..., but
> they are also important. They hold the power of life and death
> over us as, for example, in the questions of whether the foetus
> has the right to life and whether a person whose unconscious
> life depends on an artificial life-support system has a right to
> die. But these questions and all that lie between them are
> answered not by abstractions, but by other people. As Sartre
> said, hell has no need of brimstone and turning on a spit. Hell
> is other people. It exists here and now. We ourselves make it.
> Once made, we call the resulting order organization.
>
> —Thomas B. Greenfield, "Leaders and Schools"

Among some outside observers, the
Episcopal Church enjoys a reputation for inclusivity. According to others,
it labors under a lamentable lack of theological direction. It is surprising,
then, that the vast majority of women asked to describe their church
contend their denomination is "hierarchical" and, therefore, "male-
dominated."[1]

Bureaucratic Linkages

There is much about the hierarchical character of the Episcopal
Church that is mandated by its *Constitution and Canons* (1991). It is this
body of legislation that dictates the division of the church into dioceses,

14

or geographical units, and places bishops in positions of leadership over each of those dioceses. It is also canon law that delegates the ongoing conduct of the church's life to a presiding bishop and a bicameral legislative structure consisting of the House of Bishops and the House of Deputies.[2]

Defined more by its approach to worship than any other dimension of its life, very often the rubrics[3] found in the church's *Book of Common Prayer* apply where canon law does not. For example, the prayerbook dictates that only a bishop or a priest can preside over the Eucharist. The rubrics also dictate that it is the "prerogative" of the Bishop, when present, to preside (Book of Common Prayer 1979, 322). Indeed, the church's constitution, canons, and prayerbook are, more or less, precisely what one would expect from a tradition heavily informed by its English and monarchical origins, as well as by its more immediate roots in the eighteenth century and the Enlightenment.

Sitting Atop the Pyramid

On the bureaucratic plane, women lodge two kinds of criticisms against the church. One body of criticism might be described as procedural or performance-based. Canon law now provides for the ordination of women, but all of the women interviewed are dissatisfied with the rate at which they are being admitted to positions of leadership, the extent to which some parts of the church remain resistant to their involvement, and a pattern of selective inclusion that leaves men largely in charge of the church.

> I think by and large women are not included representatively. There are some women, but they tend to be people who have other connections rather than just their stellar intellect or wonderful personality. (E1:25)

> I believe [we have] the most open ordination process that we've ever had right now—it's got a way to go. There's still a double standard. The yardstick with which women are measured for the ordination process is still a harsher yardstick. . . . At the diocesan level women [who] are involved are involved in a minority sense of the term. The decision-making is still largely white males over fifty. (E2:28–29)

Well, women are heavily involved in things which are perceived to be women's work. It has been more difficult to incorporate women into the decision-making body. And the body in the diocese which shares ecclesiastic authority with the bishop is called the Standing Committee; and it took a very long time to get [female] clergy elected at that level. I think that there's been two, one that was originally appointed to fill a vacancy and was elected later when the term ended and now, more recently, a second woman has managed to be elected to the Standing Committee, but it is not routine. I think the other position which is considered a pretty powerful one is the position of Deputy to the General Convention. We have one woman priest who's been part of an eight member delegation for some years. We've never been able to elect a second. (E5:29)

Right, it [i.e., the impact of gender on the extent to which women are included in the decision-making process] has both of those aspects, as I told you. Often women are sought after because they need to have a woman on one of those positions [in] decision-making bodies. The other part is that there is always that insidious feeling that the real decisions are made by the in-crowd which are the old boys. (E6:20)

For these interviewees, the piecemeal inclusion of women—wed to the hierarchical character of the church—helps to explain why some women identify the structure of the church as intrinsically male and oppressive. One interviewee described the dynamic quite clearly: "The assumption is, when we gather, that the person who sits atop the pyramid will be the presider and the preacher-teacher roles and that means that we are usually hearing from white males" (E3:37).

The Demons of Patriarchy

On another level, however, Episcopal priests find the hierarchical character of the church itself alienating. Here the distinctions between bureaucracy and culture are all but transparent.[4]

I'm in the process of moving from one parish to another parish. I think about polity and government and the pastor/parish relationship, and in a kind of existential way, that in some ways I think is still the most possessed by the demons of patriarchy and male dominated. Shall I use the jargon and say, patriarchal oppression and male hierarchy? . . . Well, you know about canon law. . . . And, you know, this is all stuff from the middle ages refined through enlightenment and fiddled around with for the last couple of hundred years and it certainly reflects a structured society in which the men are in charge and the ways in which decisions are carried out, the ways in which authority is distributed. Those, I think, are all fundamentally very oppressive. . . . I think there are some real difficulties with the mechanics, the structure and the government. (E1:7–8)

Yeah, I think that it factors into me feeling like an outsider when I deal with the more routine ways of getting things done, because the church is very hierarchical and because the hierarchy is modeled after male ways of doing business. Being female and not trying to be—not interested in being an honorary male makes me an outsider, because I don't communicate in the good-old-boy style, and if the men that I work with identify power and respectability by how well you can do the old-boy thing, then I am very much an outsider. (E4:12)

A Mixed Bureaucratic Message

The disenchantment felt by the interviewees is further exacerbated by the way in which the church decided to ordain women in 1976 and by the compromise struck between the church's episcopal leadership and those who objected to the decision.[5] Advocates had pressed for the ordination of women in 1970 and 1973 without success, and the "irregular" ordination of eleven women in 1974 met with swift rejection at an emergency meeting of the House of Bishops (Huyck 1982, 390–91). As a result, the National Coalition for the Ordination of Women to the Priesthood and Episcopacy and others opted in 1976 to move for a change in canon law, rather than attempt to change the constitution of the church, which would have required successful votes at two consecutive General Conventions. They also decided to modify canon law, not by changing the wording of all the canons dealing with ordination, but by introducing a new canon that would permit (not require) the episcopal leadership of each diocese to interpret the male pronouns used in canons dealing with ordination.[6]

When, at the General Convention of 1976, women were finally given access to full ordination, the ground had also been laid for a constitutional battle. Almost immediately some argued that the canonical changes did not and could not take precedence over the constitution of the church. There are those who continue to make this argument, and, to date, no constitutional change has been made (Wantland 1987).

> Interestingly enough, the way in which we provide for the involvement [of women] through canon law, we interpret the word "he" in the canon law to mean "he/she." In other words, we . . . went at [it] by changing the canons, by inserting this canon that said we interpret the "he" to mean "he/she," but we did not change the constitution. So there are still people who argue that the constitution does not allow us to ordain women. So the legal foundations are still in dispute. (E3:28)

The bureaucratic picture was further complicated shortly after the General Convention when, at a meeting in Port St. Lucie, Fla., the House of Bishops passed a "conscience clause." The conscience clause was designed to avoid schism and to strike the kind of compromise that is more a hallmark of Episcopal culture than its bureaucratic procedures.[7] It also recognized the relative autonomy of each diocese and its bishop.[8] Specifically, the clause exempts its members "from any compulsion to ordain women beyond the diaconate, should it be that any bishop has serious theological reservations on that matter" (Dennis 1981, 138). Then, in the 1988 General Convention, both the House of Bishops and the House of Deputies passed a motion providing for "Episcopal Visitors." This provision makes it possible for the rector of a parish, who objects to the consecration of women as bishops to invite a male bishop to baptize, confirm the members of his church, and celebrate the Eucharist, in the event that his own bishop is a woman (Frizzell 1988).[9] Emboldened, perhaps by the decision to provide for episcopal visitors, the dioceses that refused to ordain women took the further step of forming what they describe as "missionary dioceses," i.e., non-regional dioceses united in their opposition to the changes in canon law.[10] One interviewee put the creation of missionary dioceses in historical and organizational perspective: "The best way to understand Episcopal polity is the people who put the United States together also put the Episcopal Church together. So they are almost identical. So it would be like if one of the provinces in Canada suddenly said, 'We are a state of the United States.' They could not be there unless there was a vote in our Congress and they were accepted as a state, but they are declaring that they are a state" (E3:32).

Selling Out to Political Fears

There can be little doubt that this mixed bureaucratic message has had an impact on the reception women have received in the church. There is considerable variation from diocese to diocese, and the "permissive" character of the changes made to canon law are, according to interviewees, an important factor in creating that variation.[11]

Again, it's where you are that makes the big difference. I mean, it's very different in San Francisco and Washington and Connecticut and New York than it is here—and this is relatively benign—or in some of the dioceses who do not ordain women at all, such as San Joaquin, you know, something like that. (E9:25–26)

I think there is less [affirmation of the ministry of women] on a diocesan level than on a national level but, again, it depends on which diocese you're in. Some dioceses are very good about affirming women and women's ministries. Some dioceses simply do not accept women at all and some dioceses are very slow and they're letting it happen rather slowly. They give more lip service to it than actual action to it. So, I'd say it varies a great deal from one diocese to another. (E10:16)

Well, I think we know that one and the answer is, it varies. I think in most cases, in most dioceses, yes, but the way the legislation is written it is permissive, not mandatory. (E1:22)

To my knowledge there has not been a diocese within an Episcopal election where the bishop elected did a turn-around and opposed women's ordination, but there's certainly been elections where the bishop elected—Well, in the case of the diocese that I'm going to, _____, the bishop there, was totally opposed to the ordination of women except to the diaconate. And even then, wasn't really thrilled about that. He was succeeded by _____, the present bishop, who is very much in favor, _____, who is bishop of _____ is now—he hasn't moved to the point of ordaining women, but he is allowing and licensing ordained women to settle in the Diocese of _____. That's change. The change is up to this point—has always been in the direction of including women in the ordained ministry, not excluding them and driving them out. (E1:22–23)

Nonetheless, the vast majority of dioceses do ordain women, and, as more than one of the respondents observed, "conversion," where it occurs, favors women's ordination.

In light of that pattern of conversion, the impact the decision has had on the women I interviewed is all the more striking. Familiar with the Episcopal bent toward compromise and the niceties of canon law, they continue to be morally outraged by the mixed bureaucratic message the church is sending its membership and, they suggest, the implications of the changes to canon law could have been interpreted differently.

The national church has not to date taken any action to force those seven dioceses to make a choice about ordaining [women]. I mean, they've left that option open and we do have these other "wonderful" regulations in place at the moment. "Wonderful" with quotes around it, obviously, that says, for example, "If a diocese elects a woman as bishop and a congregation is opposed to her ministry in their congregation, to come and do confirmations, they can request that a male bishop be sent to them from another diocese. And that was a national decision and is sort of considered by many to be a temporary measure to allow people to get used to the idea of women as bishops, and, of course, there are people who are hoping that it will be a permanent provision. Then there were other movements which have taken that one step further. A number of those seven dioceses and people in other dioceses have gone together and formed what they call a missionary diocese of the Episcopal Church that would, among other things, not ordain women. It's a non-geographic diocese. The national church has not given that diocese, that entity, any recognition, official recognition of any sort. The other side is the national church also does not take any kind of economical punitive action, or say to them, "Now, you all, either decide you're in or out and, if you aren't going to follow the canons of this church, you're out." (E3:31)[12]

The Episcopal Church really sells out to its political fears [on the national level]. Right now we have this strange division going on with these arch-conservative dioceses who are splitting off from the church because of the issue of the ordination of women to the priesthood, which was really brought to a head with the consecration of Barbara Harris as the first woman bishop. And I just think if the church leadership believes that the ordination of women to the priesthood and to the episcopate is an issue of justice and equality, then it needs to stand there and affirm that in ways that don't invite a kind of wishy-washy stance by saying, "Well, we'll leave it up to diocesan decision about what you're going to do about the ordination of women." I think that's a real, to be blunt, "chicken-shit position." And I think it undermines any kind of theological argument that they are trying to make for the ordination of women, because basically what they're saying is "Well theologically we believe that women can be full participants in all levels of leadership in the church, but politically we are afraid of losing members in the church, so we'll let you deal with that 'hot potato.' " That, to me, is not a sound position to take, if you really believe that it is a matter of justice.... It's manifest concretely because the Presiding Bishop and the House of Bishops will not say, "Because we are now ordaining women to the priesthood and because we are now consecrating women as bishops and believe that this is a theologically sound position to take, all bishops in the United States are expected to ordain women to the priesthood. This is not a diocesan decision. This is a decision made by the House of Bishops, the General Convention. This is now something that belongs in the canons and constitutions and, if you refuse, then you can be brought up on charges." They don't say that and because they don't say that, I really seriously question the depth of commitment to women in leadership positions in the church. (E4:25)[13]

Organizational Culture

None of what has been said above, however, means that the ongoing protests of the women I interviewed are rehearsals of past grievances, without contemporary justification. Not only are the compromises made in 1976 still in place,[14] but the culture of the church also appears to have subverted to some degree the intention of the changes made to canon law.[15] Out of ten respondents, five mentioned only the adverse affects that their gender had on their career. Three described their gender as having had both positive and negative impact. The remaining respondents characterized themselves as fortunate, the beneficiaries of gender concerns. But they also maintained that their experience was exceptional. When asked whether gender had an impact on her career, one respondent replied, "Anybody who thinks it hasn't is absolutely nuts, blind, dumb, or stupid" (E1:13).

Ordination Is One Thing

The way in which this dynamic is felt varies. The process of looking for a parish usually requires more time for women than it does for men —in most cases, three years "at least," as opposed to two for men (E3:22). Some women were denied posts and one indicated that she had also been denied assignments that would have naturally been a part of her job description, had she been a male. Five of the respondents described "vertical movement" as "difficult."[16]

> Again, I live by stories. One story is of interviews I've had with people who were considering me for an appointment or a position who said that I was too strong or too articulate. . . . I don't believe that I'm any stronger or more articulate than my male counterparts, but coming from a woman it's disconcerting. So when I've done interviewing, I've often asked for feedback from my interviewing team and that's something that's consistently said "We would call you, _____, except you intimidated the male members of our search committee, and some of the female members [too]—I should be fair—make that statement. So, in terms of sort of vertical movement up the traditional career ladder, I have found myself essentially judged by a double standard. That's a kind of summary for all of that. I've obviously been not even considered for various kinds of opportunities, either career changes, or added work within my own career, or other responsibilities that could fall to me. Even in my present position I've been disqualified from those merely because of being female. (E2:15)

Others used the phrase, "glass ceiling," noting that many women have been forced to move "sideways . . . into secular careers or into administrative [positions]" (E3:21).

> Well . . . the primary thing I would say was . . . [that] I hit the glass ceiling. I've probably interviewed in some forty congregations in about a three-year-period. I would say that in thirty of those, I came out second and invariably the response I would get when they called me was, "We just don't think the congregation is ready for a woman." And I don't know whether they were or weren't. I mean, first off my response to that always is, "Of course, they're not ready for a woman; you can't be ready for a woman. You've got to do it and then you'll

adjust." But the attitude that the congregation couldn't somehow survive this phenomenon made it real hard to get a job and was part of the reason why I ended up leaving and going into a secular position at that point. (E3:14–15)

As a result, the pool of available candidates tends to be younger and less experienced, adding to the reasons that some parishes give for declining to call a woman (E3:21).

Three of the interviewees noted that even when women are hired, they are hired more often in parishes with large staffs. There they are rarely in charge, particularly when there are men.[17]

> But I am aware, especially around issues of call, and maybe some other issues, committee activities and so on, women are not perceived as having the same authority that their male colleagues would have. It is much easier, for instance, for women to get jobs as assistants, than to get jobs where they are the in-charge person; and it's even more uncommon for a woman to be in charge if there is a man on staff. The women who are in charge are usually, not always, but usually, solo. If there is a multiple staff arrangement the in-charge person will not be female. . . . The idea of women having authority over men is difficult. (E5:12)

Such patterns, of course, have a direct impact on the size of the parishes served by women and, therefore, an impact on the salaries they receive. Nor is the problem of pay differentials to be found in parish ministry alone. One of the admittedly more dramatic stories involving chaplaincy work revealed not only stunning differences in pay, but crass sexism as well (Morgan 1985; Lehman 1993c).

> I came on as the first new staff member of my boss's—the beginning of his tenure here. . . . The following year my colleague was hired under circumstances which I thought were suspect in terms of equality and pay . . . I asked around, trying to fill in the blanks without asking someone blatantly to get me information that I wasn't supposed to have and pieced together what I thought was a fairly reliable picture—that my colleague was hired at probably close to $10,000 more than I was. This is [a] person who is younger than me and less experienced, but he was male and in this situation he is black and that was an issue which I believe my boss was willing to pay more for, if that makes any sense.

And I took that information and basically played a hunch, because I didn't have any concrete information, because that information is confidential. But I played a hunch and I went in to talk to my boss about the fact of this colleague—of this colleague's hiring—and basically went down the list of qualifications and asked him if in any of those areas I was less qualified than the person he had just hired; and he, to his credit, answered honestly and said, "no." And I said, "Then I expect to be brought up to equity in terms of salary and benefits with this person you've just hired, because there is nothing in my résumé that justifies me being paid so much less than him." Now I had no idea what he had offered this guy. I just had a really strong feeling that it was a heck of a lot more than what he paid me. During that conversation my boss kept trying to say, "But, _____, we're friends"; and at one point he had the audacity to say, "Do you wonder if you're liked or appreciated? You know I love you." He used those words and I looked at them and I said, "This is not a discussion about any personal relationship that might develop out of my job here." He was really stunned that I was that direct and, to his credit, he took that confrontation and moved to do something about it. I mean, he couldn't rectify the salary and equity in one year, which tells me that my hunch was right. That there was a huge discrepancy that it's taken him nearly three years to correct. (E4:14–15)

In other cases, patterns of discrimination circumscribe the future as well as the present. One interviewee in her forties, who holds two graduate degrees and serves as an associate, observed:[18]

How does gender affect my career? . . . I am extremely cognizant that who I am, what I am and where I am, here, my next step is very limited—if, indeed, there will be a next step. . . . So, I need to be very realistic. . . . That's part of my reality. I got into this knowing that I am the first generation of what I am and I did not want to be a priest. I did not wake up one morning and say, "God, I love church, I really want to go and be a priest!" There were many things I liked about it, but it was one of those things that I'd never been able to explain to a department of ministry—and I can't explain now—but here I am. But I just know that whatever path I am supposed to walk (and I'm doing it; and the first generation of what you are is never easy), there's a way that I have to say, "That's alright too." Not that I won't keep trying. (E9:16)

In addition to the dynamics cited above, the respondents also reported occasions on which they encountered sex role stereotypes and trivial complaints about hair, clothing, and the use of makeup.[19] One respondent was even (ostensibly) denied employment because she was "too short" (E7:8–10).

> When I graduated from seminary there was a position open at the _____ for a [school] chaplaincy. The bishop thought I was the right person for that position [and] I thought I was the right person for that position. Unfortunately, the headmaster at that time was leaving for a new job elsewhere and so the incoming headmaster did not want to do something as radical as hiring the first woman to ever be a chaplain. And then after two years this person they hired left and so the position was open again. Again the bishop said, "I still think you're the right person for the job" and the canon presenter who was on the search committee agreed. So I submitted all of my papers again. The reason the bishop and I and the canon presenter all agreed that I would be a good person for that job was that I had nineteen years experience in the classroom before and during seminary. So I was putting my teaching background with theological education, if I were to be the chaplain there. Well, apparently there were some roadblocks and the bishop said he went to the board meeting to say something and someone finally burst out and said, "Oh, but we can't have her." They couldn't say, "No, we don't want her because she's a woman," or "We don't want her because she's oriental." So they said, "Oh, but she's too short" (I'm only 4′ 11″). . . . I didn't realize the bishop had gone to plead my case, but at the fall clergy conference after all this had been said and done, he said, "I want to tell you something. Come take a walk with me around the grounds." And he told me the story and he said, "I am sorry to say that sexism and racism are alive and well in this diocese." (E7:9)

As more than one interviewee observed, "Ordination is one thing, deployment is another."[20]

Intentions

It is difficult in the Episcopal church to distinguish the experiences women have in the parish from the experiences they have in a given diocese. In many cases, the dynamics described above are, in some measure, the product of the climate in a given diocese. Both parishes and clergy have considerable latitude in the selection process, but both serve in any diocese at the pleasure of the bishop, and it is hardly surprising to find, therefore, that the "spotty" reception women have received depends in large part upon the bishops (E2:27). Supportive, benignly neglectful, or openly hostile, bishops differ greatly in the support they provide (E9:25–26).

Where women feel that their dioceses are supportive, bishops are public and intentional in their attempts to include women.

> Where there is a desire for inclusion and having broad representation, women in some senses have a much better shot at leadership roles because we constitute about ten percent of the clergy and that means that for every one of us there are nine men standing in line for the two slots on the committee. So your chances of getting in are much higher. But if there is no intentional policy, then your ability to rise naturally is much more limited. (E3:34)[21]

Even in supportive dioceses, however, sex-role stereotypes can continue to shape the way women are involved, particularly when elections are the means by which a given position is filled. Women are still often chosen to do "women's work" and on the rare occasion when a woman is elected or appointed to do other kinds of work, she often finds herself in the minority.

> The bishop put together what he called a kind of financial summit and he got together the leaders of all the committees of the diocese that have some piece of the financial pie. The diocesan treasurer was there, I was there for the Stewardship Committee, the Budget Committee, the Finance Committee, the Investment Committee, the Development Committee. I mean, that's the kind of picture it was and I was the only woman in the room. I thought that was very interesting. Now don't think he chose me to be there. I mean, he chose me because of the Stewardship Committee, not because of my role, but it does say to me on the other hand, that gender does continue to be a factor, that women are not perceived as people who deal with money. (E5:34)

"Assistant" Bishops

If there appears to be a level at which change is taking place more rapidly, it is on the national level. Nine out of ten of the interviewees are convinced that at the national level the ordination of women is supported. These women spoke of "comfortable evolution" (E9:27) and a much "brighter" picture (E2:29).

Two factors are clearly at work. One factor is the leadership provided by the presiding bishop (Edmond L. Browning), whose support for women's ordination has been unqualified and public. The other factor has been "quotas" or "commitment" made to include women in the church's ministry. Although the latter appears to be part of an informal under-standing (again, largely underwritten by the presiding bishop), the assurance that concrete, measurable progress is being made has helped to foster a much more positive view of developments on the national level (E2:29, 31–32).

Nonetheless, the picture given by the respondents is not unqualified. The church's national leadership has made no effort to eliminate the mixed bureaucratic message created by the conscience clause and the provision for episcopal visitors.[22] And while women are much more in-volved in the decision-making process at the national level, more than one interviewee characterized the change as "slow" (E10:15), with "a strong standard of deviation" (E2:28).

In this respect, the House of Bishops is symbolic of the marginaliza-tion women experience.[23] Out of some 280 bishops, only three are women. Of those three, two are suffragans. That is, they are assistants or associates. They possess liturgical authority, but they are without primary jurisdiction over a diocese, and they lack any right of succession.[24] It was not until June 5, 1993 that the first female diocesan (i.e., a bishop with full administrative powers) was elected.[25] Notably, soon afterward three men were elected bishop coadjutor (i.e., bishop-elect) to the dioceses of West Tennessee, New Jersey, and Texas ("It Took Just," 1993b). The dynamic that shapes women's experience in the parish also appears to shape life in the cathedral (E5:12).

The Old-Boy Network

In addition to the male domination of formal organizational struc-tures, there was little doubt in the minds of the women with whom I spoke that there are other influential alliances shaping the life of the church. When asked about these in-groups, all ten reported that on at least one or more levels those groups, too, are male dominated.

Three went further, identifying one of the in-groups with national influence as not only male, but southern in origin.

> Yes, there is [an in-group]. Actually, there are probably several in-groups. . . . There are several circles that overlap that are more in the center of the power. . . . One circle is people who influence and control the legislative process in the church and they have traditionally been white, male, even southern. That's shifting. . . . There are more women coming in, more people of color. So, there is movement but it is still . . . white, male and clergy. (E3:25)

Still another interviewee described the in-group as one with a base of influence in the east, rather than in the south.

> The in-groups in the Episcopal Church are white men over 45 who are safely liberal, or safely Republican. They usually have some significant experience with the church on the East coast. They are upper middle class, if not wealthy, or they have such a strong desire to be in that economic class that they will make sure that their lower class background is not known. They don't marry interracially. They don't rock the boat. They are very learned in the old-boy's network and how to play it and they watch each other's back and are very careful about who they let in and out. (E4:21)

The product of a network of relationships developed over a period of time, the members of these groups reputedly attended the "right" prep schools, colleges, and seminaries. It is this dynamic, and the fact that women are denied access to so-called cardinal parishes, that effectively excludes many of them from their membership.

> *Interviewer:* Do you perceive there to be an in-group in your denomination?
> *Respondent:* Yes, it's becoming lessened, but there's what we call an old-boy network.
> *Interviewer:* Could you be more specific?
> *Respondent:* I'm talking about rectors of what we call cardinal parishes, that is, parishes that have substantial numbers as well as substantial budgets that are sought after throughout the country. [As yet] none of those has [called] a woman. Then in the lay order there are men who make decisions that women never know about. (E6:14)

Where (against the odds) women are involved in in-groups, it often appears to be a function of either an affirmative action initiative or the office one holds.[26] Even the few women who perceive themselves to be a part of an in-group on some level view their role with a measure of detachment, if not cynicism. Their membership is a practical consideration, a necessary evil. Asked if membership in such groups is important, one interviewee responded:

> Only if you want to get something done. It's playing with fire. It always is with any organization. If you're not interested in any impact on the institution, and if you want to stay pure, then you obviously don't want to have anything to do with that group, but if you want to have an effect on the church as an institution, and if you're willing to try to move it a short distance rather than get everything you want, then, yes, you need to be involved with that group. That doesn't mean join it and they won't believe you [are one of them]. . . . They know I'm not a Southern male. (E1:19–20)

By and large, respondents describing in-groups used largely negative categories and used the phrase, "old-boy network" repeatedly. One respondent, however, argued that on at least one level, she is reassured, rather than repelled by their existence.

> Yeah, there's kind of an in-group at every stratum wherever you look. It seems to me that power tends to concentrate in the hands of individuals, particularly in hierarchical structures. Nationally my sense is that the in-group of individuals are people who are liberal in their political attitudes, actively working to combat the sexism and homophobia and racism. That those people tend to hold a kind of liberal, inclusive kind of mentality and that they are kind of the in-group in the Episcopal Church and I like that, actually. That is a comfort to me. I have a sense that the in-group has fostered some of the changes that I understand to be positive. (E2:22)

Monkeys and Marauding Terrorists

There were, as I have already noted, more positive patterns as well. Four of the respondents described themselves as the beneficiaries of affirmative action, particularly later in their careers. And two women noted that they had been able to turn sex-role stereotypes to their own advantage, reaching people (particularly women) who would not readily discuss some of their concerns with a male priest. In some cases the stereotypes of women have even begun to soften, but one can hardly say they have disappeared.

> Yeah, I think things are different now. Early in my career there was an assumption on the part of the church that all women going into the ministry were, by definition, angry, militant feminists with a cause. I mean we used to sort of kid about being treated as marauding terrorists because that was kind of the hostile defensive responses we would get from churches. Now I never get that any more. People are much more likely to simply accept me for who I am and to evaluate my gifts and limitations accordingly, the one exception being the sort of tricky issue of authority. I think women are still often screened out by churches because they're perceived as not having sufficient authority to be able to lead a congregation. (E5:17)

Interviewees also noted some modest improvements during their tenure. Four observed that they are no longer considered "unusual," an "oddity" (E1:15), a "curiosity" (E2:18), or "the monkey in the zoo" (E3:17), and this development has freed them for a more effective ministry. The increased number of women engaged in ministry has provided a model that is more accessible to the new generation of students. And three women have been elected bishop. But each of the five women who argued that things had improved also qualified the progress made. They clearly felt that not all of the improvements represented an unbegrudging change, or one for which the denomination could take complete credit.

> Yes [thing's are different]. I think that the call forward continues. When I started out, she said—feeling very elderly—when we were in our twenties . . . feminist theology was something that almost had no content. Well, now it does. . . . A tradition has built up, some common issues, a framework, something that we can talk about—an approach to the world, an epistemology. Now, there are people who don't like it, but there it is. In the Episcopal Church the ordination of women to the presbyterate was approved in '76. Now I am no longer an oddity as a woman rector. That's a major change. Even the people who opposed me . . . toe the line. . . . Five years ago, they wouldn't have even given me the time of day. We now have two women bishops. There is a movement forward. We are at least tolerating the official use of inclusive language liturgies, with enormous restrictions, but still it's being toler-

ated, it's moving forward, it's being worked on. For Episcopalians that's major change. So, yes there is change, there is regression. It's not as quick as I'd like. I suppose it never is, but there is major change. (E1:14–15)

Glorious Queen Bess

The hierarchical and male-dominated character of the Episcopal church may be structural in origin, but the more clearly cultural dimensions of the denomination reinforce and give added depth to the church's chauvinism. As a result, perhaps, stories from the denomination's own history are mentioned less often than are other stories, and when they are, they are more likely to be described in a negative light. Some women explained their frustration at length.

> I think if you look at the whole storyline of the Episcopal tradition, it is very male-dominated and clericalized. We begin with Thomas Cranmer [the first Archbishop of Canterbury] and we come down to today, when there's a big fight over Barbara Harris and Jane Dixon [the first women to be elected as bishops]. So the storyline is dominated by women with frustration who step out of line. Queen Elizabeth, I suppose, is the great exception. You know you go back to the Elizabethan compromise and there's glorious Queen Bess setting the limits. So there are some cautionary notes in our storyline. Maybe ten years ago I would have been more horrified by some of it than I [am] now. Now I'm just distressed enough to want to make a difference. (E1:1–2)

Others simply dismissed the church's history as one with a single message. To paraphrase slightly: Women cannot, do not and should not govern. "Stories out of the Episcopal tradition—well, it's just very highly male, of course, starting from the founding of the Anglican Communion and because we do have bishops and, until Barbara Harris, they've all been male. I mean, it's just highly male" (E7:2). When interviewees did describe the church's stories in a positive light, they invariably focused on the contributions made by women. They told the stories of Li Tim Oi, the first woman to be ordained a deacon (Hiatt, forthcoming); the stories of the eleven women ordained to the priesthood in 1974 in violation of canon law (Huyck, 1982); and the story of Barbara Harris, the first woman to be ordained a bishop (Walker, 1989). More importantly, these stories illustrate the plight they and other women face and, as such, serve as examples for their own lives.

Stories of a similar nature were also told involving women less well known to the larger church:

> There's one other story, too, and this is more of a contemporary thing and that was the story of _____ when she was ordained to the priesthood. _____ was one of my professors in seminary and she was one of the women who was ordained in sort of the first batch, not *the* first, not the very first ones, but . . . within the first year or so of ordination. And she talked about how they had to clear the church the day before her ordination and search the church for any bombs. They had a dog go through to make sure that there was nothing there. . . . And she was prepared for the objections when they were asked [for] during her ordination . . . I thought, "Oh, my goodness!" She had such tremendous courage to go through with ordination that it just touched me very, very deeply and I thought, "Well, if she could do that, then there's a lot that I must be able to do by being ordained." (E10:2)

In discussing stories, Episcopal priests drew at much greater length on the biblical text and, in fact, when asked, nine out of ten mentioned biblical stories first. For some, the preference appeared to be a product of upbringing and education. On another level, however, I sensed that the interviewees found the chauvinism of the text more easily explicable.

This is not to say that they viewed the Bible with an uncritical eye. Indeed, many of the biblical stories were described in an entirely negative light. The creation narrative, stories of the patriarchs, the brutality with which women were treated in the Old Testament, and the call issued by Jesus to twelve males. All of these figured prominently in the conversations with Episcopalians. More than one priest observed that still other stories "cut both ways" (E1:1; E5:1). Jesus, for example, was a male and far from being "a twentieth-century feminist". His behavior, however, was surprisingly inclusive for the day and the age in which he lived (E1:1).

Over and against such accounts, the stories respondents identified with most strongly were those in which women figured prominently, including some women the respondents felt commentators had treated unfairly. Mary, Elizabeth, Sarah, Esther, Ruth, and Judith were among those mentioned. Mary Magdalen also figured prominently in the conversation with one interviewee:

> Some of these are examples of things that may cut both ways. Both help me identify or have been in some ways alienating. . . . The story of [Mary] Magdalen, for instance, [is] hurtful in that the Episcopal Church, at least, has always referred to the legend of her being a harlot, and so she has never been able to function as a very effective role model. On the other hand, [her story] may be helpful because having had the opportunity to study, I have a more scriptural picture of Mary Magdalen. And so, the story of Mary Magdalen was helpful for me to sort of get clear that the Scripture describes her as the person from whom seven demons were driven out, rather than someone who was a harlot; and [I put that] together with Joanna and Susanna being responsible for having provided for Jesus and his followers. I mean, in today's society we would talk about someone like that as being a benefactor, and we would see those women in a very different light, if they were the people who paid the bills for a ministry like that. . . . Certainly the empty tomb narratives have been important and I think maybe last of all, realizing that for the Eastern Church she [Mary Magdalen] has been the apostle of the apostles. (E5:1,3)

Three of the women with whom I spoke volunteered that it was seminary that had alerted them to the sexism of the biblical text. For all of the women, however, their recourse to the Bible had been spurred on by the use others had made of it in arguing that women should not be ordained.

An Act of War

Language and ritual are not easily separated in the Episcopal church, given the denomination's dependence upon *The Book of Common Prayer,* which brings the two into close proximity to one another and provides the context for worship on a regular basis (1979). The book was revised as recently as 1979, and the women I interviewed find the ongoing process of liturgical revision a reassuring feature of life in their church. Nonetheless, three of them were quick to describe the language of the latest revision as only fractionally improved over its 1928 predecessor, and all ten insist that God-language and the language used to describe the church remain heavily "masculinized" (E2:7).

The new prayerbook is only a hair better than the old one. I mean, they got rid of the purification of women after childbirth, which is a ridiculous rite, and I'm glad it's gone, and they got rid of some of the more offensive language in the marriage ceremony and in the Eucharist; but they haven't changed the exclusive language and, so, the symbols about divinity are still male. . . . I'm really at the point now where using the exclusive term of Father, Son and Holy Spirit to talk about God or the Trinity is just not acceptable to me. I can do it, if it's mixed with other symbols, but because a prayerbook, the current prayerbook, doesn't mix the symbols at all, it's making a very clear statement about its belief theologically that God is male and that's not just theologically sound to me, nor is it spiritually healthy. (E4:3–4)

The power that such language has was given its most poignant expression by one of the interviewees, who observed:

I am, at this point, real alienated by all male-specific language. I am alienated when I hear words like Father, Son—when I hear masculine pronouns about the divine—when I hear masculinized imagery about the believers. "Christ came to save all mankind," for example. . . . I feel increasingly, painfully alienated by masculine imagery. . . . This experience that I just described about alienation has been an evolution and I have resisted that evolution as much as possible, because I have a consciousness that I am moving toward the fringes of my denomination and that's frightening to me. But I am simply unable, with any integrity, to use male-specific language about God or the church without feeling it inside. (E2:7–8)

The strategies women employ in response vary. One woman takes some satisfaction from the fact that she is a central figure in the church's ceremony and she differentiates between the contexts in which such language is used.

No, [the use of language] depends on the place, and I'll be real concrete as far as that's concerned. If I went into . . . an Episcopal Church and the rector there would rather have those under him [be] males than have me celebrate the Eucharist at his altar, that's just the way it is. The male language there, because it is all male orientation, the power structure of that particular church is very male, then it would offend me. My church . . . is a Rite One church, which probably doesn't mean anything to you, but it is the old Episcopal language and so on, and it's all male language. But the reality is that I'm up there saying these words and that these people are very, very inclusive in their orientation, so far as women or races or sexuality [is concerned]. And so what they are speaks more loudly to me than the words they choose to use. So, it depends upon the setting. (E9:2–3)

Others have begun to change the vocabulary of the prayerbook itself, a practice at least one priest was encouraged to use beginning in seminary.

Of the ten priests I surveyed, eight of the respondents described the ritualistic acts of the church as alienating; one described them in positive terms; and another described herself as "unaffected, but aware that many of her colleagues are" (E10:3–4). The Eucharist is a particularly problematic ritual. None of the women considered the ritual itself as having an intrinsically male orientation. Indeed, three of the interviewees contended that, along with baptism, the Eucharist is "at bottom" a feminine ritual. "The two central rituals of our church are deeply affirming for me, the ritual of the Eucharist and the ritual of baptism. Both of those sacraments, at very bottom to me, are utterly female, feeding and washing. I really think of those as [primarily] female activities and, so participating as an ordained woman in those rituals is extremely affirming to me. It probably is the one thing that keeps me going when nothing else does" (E2:9).

The problem, the women argue, is that a fundamentally female activity has been "moved to a masculine domain" where, at times, it is performed as if it were "an act of war" (E3:6; E1:7). In a broader reflection on the question, one interviewee put it this way:

You see, we have had people who would say that even the notion of ritual and the notion of God and the notion of worship, in the sense of assuming a real relationship to a deity who is not an eminent force, that is oppressive. And that's something that I simply don't agree with. So, within my framework, we say, "Yes, there is God who is revealed through Scripture and in tradition and in human experience and all that Anglican stuff." Yes, there is a God. This God is not male according to the articles of religion, has [neither] body parts [nor] passion. At the same time, the structure of the rituals has been very sexist, very oppressive and very patriarchal. You've had a male clergy doing stuff at [the] congregation. So, there have been ways the rituals have been done, especially when the people leading the worship are all males, [it] certainly can be repellently reinforcing of all the nasty stereotypes. And I think that, for me, is very often not what is written down and what ought to be done, but the way things get acted out can sometimes be the most objectionable feature of the rituals. The rituals which don't have to be . . . sexually . . . oppressive (E1:6).

As with the language of worship, the other great source of frustration with the church's ritualistic acts is, quite simply, the absence of women in visible roles.

As I say, my consciousness was raised. I mean, I had been all these years going through this and it never occurred to me that women should or ought to be there. I just had been very passive about that, and when these two women came to be seminarians in my home parish and they began to be up front—at first, I was stunned by it. It seemed foreign to me, and all of a sudden I realized that a whole half of the created order was missing. (E6:4–5)

One Up, One Down

Episcopal priests—like their Roman Catholic counterparts—would be expected to mention iconography. But, strikingly, only three of the respondents had much to say about icons, and many of the examples supplied by all ten respondents are not strictly speaking icons at all. This oddity may be due to the fact that, as a rule, anglo-catholics (whose tradition relies more heavily on the use of icons) have been largely opposed to the ordination of women (Walker 1989). As a result, women interested in ordination are less likely to come from anglo-catholic parishes and are less likely to be attracted to an anglo-catholic ethos later in life. However, women may also be engaged in a process of redefining the nature of male-dominated icons.

Nonetheless, nine out of the ten interviewees had something to say about icons, as they understood them. The interviewees tended to gravitate toward feminine images or images without gender association. They found male images of God, Jesus, and the disciples—as well as the Trinity—among the more problematic symbols in their tradition. Even here, interviewees detected the hierarchical culture they found throughout the church: "Shepherds and sheep, fathers and sons, things that reflect one up, one down relationships and, therefore, sort of reinforce themes of domination and subordination" (E5:6).

The Hymns Stink

Episcopal priests identified still other features of their culture, which they argued had an alienating gender orientation. Those elements included the lectionary and the church's hymnal. These observations were made by two of the interviewees:

> The hymns stink. . . . There are—you know, I'm not saying the whole hymnal is terrible—because there are some hymns that I absolutely have to sing at Christmas and Easter to feel like I've been to church. But they are hard for me to use here because we require inclusive language in the service and in the hymns and so . . . a lot of them I just can't use because they have exclusive language in them. (E4:6)

> Another issue that I find an alienating one is the relative invisibility of women in the lectionary. It is an ongoing issue, and we know that the church is trying to do better, but the relative invisibility of women in the lectionary is alienating for me, and I will sometimes substitute other readings for the day. (E5:9)

It's So Much More

It would be easy, it seems, to take the view that the dynamics experienced by women in the Episcopal Church are primarily bureaucratic in origin. Certainly, the male-dominated and hierarchical character of the church is deeply imbedded in its history and in the documents that history has produced. Nor can anyone doubt that the "mixed" message the church has sent to its membership, largely in the form of legislative resolutions, has helped to fuel the anger and sense of injustice these interviewees and others clearly feel.

It would be a mistake to assume, however, that the situation is so simple. The lines between bureaucracy and culture are so thin as to be transparent; and at times, during the interviews and the process of writing, I have sided—more often than not—with those who view bureaucratic structures as simply one more expression of an organization's culture, alongside its stories, rituals, and language. It also seems clear that the kind of "willful action" Thomas Greenfield argues shapes organizational life determines the way leaders think, evaluate, and act —even when the activities in which they are engaged are not, strictly speaking, actions taken in their official capacity as leaders (Greenfield 1984).

Bureaucratic change, therefore, can foster inclusivity—or, perhaps at best, create an occasion for it. But there are limits to what can be accomplished, and bureaucratic initiatives are in some sense extraordinarily fragile, contrary to much of what we might assume. We often take bureaucracies to be the hard, unyielding machinery by which certain ends (good, bad, or indifferent) can be accomplished, if there is a will to do the job. The last phrase, however, is the operative one: "If there is a will."

Edward Lehman, in studying a sample of the English laity,[27] has established that much of the sexism expressed in opposition to involving women fully in the life of the church is rooted neither in theological considerations,[28] nor even in the provincialism of its members,[29] but in a desire to maintain the organization itself. The ordination of women is seen as "a radically new concept of ministry" and, therefore, a potential occasion for discord. With voluntary memberships and limited resources, many fear that the ordination of women will drive both away (Lehman 1987b, 274–75, 280).

It is not difficult to identify evidence of the same concerns in the conduct of the House of Bishops, which, while wielding the authority granted it by canon law, is at the same time prepared to wave its requirements as they apply to the ordination of women. The prior consideration, then, is not bureaucratic, but instead, a question of will. It turns out that bureaucratic provisions are not only fragile, but are the children of far more fundamental considerations. Any potential, then, for broad-based and effective change may well lie in first reevaluating the culture of the Episcopal Church.

My own thinking on this subject was provoked by one of the interviewees (herself, a bureaucrat!), who kindly read and responded by letter to an earlier draft of this chapter. She writes:

> I want to lift up something which is hinted at in your material, but seems to hover just below the surface. That has to do with the men-in-power whom I will call the "angels" (I could use the secular term "mentor," but their role seems larger than the significance that secular term could ever convey). Such men-in-power not only stand as the

stewards of the denominational position ("I support the ordination of women"), but they actively and publicly seek to share their power with their women colleagues. These "angels" are generally men with a high sense of self-esteem who see leadership as an empowering function. There are far too few of such men-in-power.

As I look at my own ministry, I can identify several such men who have empowered me. They did so first by taking me seriously, without patronizing or competing. In ways large and small, they have asked for my input, referred power to me when they could, quoted me when I had something smart to say, credited me when it was my work / idea / project that enhanced their ministry, and had the integrity to tell me directly when they felt I was off-base. An interesting spin here is that all these men have told me that our teamwork (theirs and mine) has given them a new understanding of the truth of collegiality, such that they have not enjoyed with their male colleagues. And there was about none of these bondings any hint of sexualizing, of paternalism or of self-aggrandizement (as in, "See how liberal I am? I have lots of women working for me.").

In this matter, the potential role of "bureaucracy" in fostering the ministry of women needs to be explored. It's so much more than just making sure one's staff—or circle—or clergy team—has a female presence. It's something to do, I would aver, with a vision of full equality and inclusivity that has captured the spirituality of these angels, and is lived out almost unselfconsciously. And a clear vision of servant leadership—that leadership which values the full expression of the gifts of those whom one leads.

Notes

1. The Protestant Episcopal Church gained its autonomy from the Church of England in 1789. The church has a bicameral legislature, consisting of the House of Bishops and the House of Clerical and Lay Deputies. A forty-member Executive Council provides administrative guidance between legislative sessions. A presiding bishop is elected and serves as the church's primate. In turn, the church is divided into dioceses, each with its own bishop.

2. The former is, as the name suggests, a legislative body in which bishops alone are seated. The latter consists of both elected lay and ordained representatives. See "Constitutions and Canons" (1991a).

3. Put simply, rubrics are the rules governing the conduct of worship.

4. See chapter 1 above.

5. On the events leading up to the General Convention of 1976, see Hewitt and Hiatt

1973; and Huyck 1982. On the far more torturous history of women's ordination in the Episcopal Church, as well as the larger Anglican communion, see Suzanne R. Hiatt's article, "Women's Ordination in the Anglican Communion: Can this Church be Saved?" soon to be published by the Univ. of South Carolina Press under the editorial leadership of Catherine Wessinger.

6. Then canon III.9.1, now III.8.1, reads as follows: "Provisions of these Canons for the admission of Postulants and Candidates, and for the Ordination to the three Orders, Bishops, Priests and Deacons, shall be equally applicable to men and women."

7. Similar compromises have been made in England, following the decision of the church to ordain women. See "England's Bishops" (1993a). Their value, particularly as it applies to the ordination of women receives very different interpretations among Episcopalians. Walter D. Dennis, Suffragan Bishop of New York, writes, "The history of Anglicanism has ever been one of compromise and accommodation, of finding a working economy that is perhaps best described as being a form of theological *détente* rather than *entente*" (1981, 138). On the eve of the 1988 Lambeth debate over the consecration of women as bishops, Pamela Chinnis observed, "The bishops will probably make a statement in the tradition of the good old Anglican compromise, one that can be interpreted almost any way you want" (Pierce 1988, 16).

8. Mary Lou Steed notes: "The 'chief unit of church life' (Dawley 1961, 114), the 'working unit' (Simon 1961,101) of PECUSA [The Protestant Episcopal Church, USA], is the diocese, that 'area consisting of the parishes and people under the care of a bishop' (Dawley 1961,114). The relationship of the diocese to the rest of the church is one of autonomy due to the peculiar history of the Anglican Church in the American colonies. Any endeavor of the denomination is dependent upon each bishop's cooperation and participating. Each bishop has the responsibility of guarding the faith of the church, and the legitimate authority of apostolic succession to do so. Thus, he may interpret policy and cooperate in denominational ventures as he determines best for his diocese and the church. There is no archbishop or arbitrating court to determine if an individual bishop's efforts are proper (Satori 1978,24). It is evident that the proper unit of analysis in PECUSA is the diocese" (Steed 1986, 345–46).

9. In approving the ordination of women, the Church of England has made a similar series of compromises. For example, a year after voting to ordain women it moved to prevent defections to the Roman Catholic Church by providing suffragan, or "flying" bishops, who will minister to parishes opposed to the ordination of women. Not surprisingly, the move has elicited the same level of disenchantment that it helped to create in the United States. See "Traditionalists Get Our Bishops" (1994).

10. Since then, some of those dioceses have left the church completely. See Penn and Spohn 1993. The schism may be attributable, in part, to the leadership provided by the church. Drawing on the work of John Wilson, Mary Lou Steed notes that "there are three ways in which authority is exercised which result in secession: (1) the group in power fails to exercise control; (2) there is no clear definition of who has authority; and (3) the authorities fail to exercise their power with conviction and consistency. One must presume that if a schism has occurred, one or more of Wilson's conflict-exacerbating, authority-failure conditions is already present in the denomination. . . . Indeed, with regard to Wilson's first and third proposition, the PECUSA group in power had failed to exercise control

with conviction and consistency. The year after the 1976 General Convention approved the ordination of women, the House of Bishops instituted a conscience clause which stated this legislation could be conscientiously objected to by anyone, including bishops" (Steed 1986, 345–46).

11. The term, "permissive," was used by more than one interviewee to describe the nature of the changes made to canon law. "Yes, our canon law specifies now, after the General Convention of 1976, that gender is not a roadblock to being ordained. However, the bishops can still insist on not ordaining women, have said that this canon is a permissive canon and based on that they are still not ordaining women" (E7:21).

12. The reference is to seven so-called traditionalist dioceses that still refuse to ordain women or recognize their credentials.

13. Compare the comments made by Katie Sherrod, a confirmed Episcopalian, news commentator and contributor to *Ruach,* the journal of the Episcopal Women's Caucus: "Shakespeare said of conscience that it 'is but a word that cowards use, devised at first to keep the strong in awe.' Just so has the infamous 'conscience clause,' which allows priests to deny ordination to women perverted conscience. Conscience becomes a tool to silence people, to keep the strong in the church in power. You have not experienced the silence until you have lived in a diocese such as Fort Worth, Texas. Here, one learns that silence creates silence. Worse, one learns that silence has a suffocating, deadening effect. And the thing that dies first is hope. It is time to end the silence. Other consciences demand action, justice, respect and love. My conscience tells me that the inhuman, unequal and unfair practices sanctioned by the church through its so-called 'conscience clause' simply cannot be the will of a loving God. . . . As long as the current interpretation of the conscience clause is allowed to prevail, the church is a full partner in sexist repression. The least the leadership should do is acknowledge its complicity in that repression. The best it could do is change it" (Sherrod 1993, 23).

14. At its 1994 General Convention, the church's House of Bishops declined to pass a motion that would have revised canon law, explicitly affirming the access of women to every level of ordained ministry in every diocese. Instead, they voted to reaffirm the canon passed in 1976 and called for the formation of a committee that would discuss: "full access for women to the ordination process; opportunities for ordained women to carry out their ministries in every diocese in the church; opportunities for congregations that want ordained women to have access to them in every diocese; opportunities for those who oppose women's ordination to have access to ordination and to carry out their ministries." Much of the debate revolved around the issue of whether the church should implement the canon or discuss it. In the end, the bishops amended a resolution passed by the House of Deputies, which would have emphasized implementation. In spite of an impassioned plea, the Deputies voted to accept the amendment and adjourned until 1997 (Nunley 1994, 1).

15. There are two different interpretations of the conscience clause. A "narrow construction" holds that the decision applies "*only* to those Bishops who were then members of the House and, by extension, would not apply to those *later* elevated to the episcopate —thereby making mandatory the assent to women's ordination of all future candidates for consecration, in fact a *sine qua non.*" Others argue that the emphasis placed upon unity by the House of Bishops suggests that a narrow application of the decision is without justification. See Dennis 1981, 138–39.

16. For confirmation that this pattern is far larger than the modest sample interviewed here might suggest, see Nesbitt 1990; 1992; and 1993. Drawing on the first of Nesbitt's works and statistics provided by the Episcopal Church, Catherine Prelinger observes: "According to a report provided me by the Church Deployment Office of the Episcopal Church in 1988, 137—or 19 percent of all clergywomen—are either rectors or vicars in charge of individual parishes; vicars, who are restricted to missions and are not necessarily chosen by their parishioners but by the bishop alone, were not distinguished from rectors. Among the men, 893 hold these positions, about 46 percent of the total. Forty-six percent of the women and 36 percent of the men ordained since 1976 are assistants or associates. A total of 236, or 33 percent of the women are in various specialized ministries; they serve in hospitals, prisons, and colleges, or as interim ministers. The comparable figures for men are 348, or 18 percent. John Morgan, himself a priest and scholar writing in 1985, dealt with significantly fewer cases, but he also considered a wide range of factors, such as salary, housing provisions, and pension membership; he sent a questionnaire to 500 women priests, and on the basis of a response rate of 70 percent predicted that the Episcopal Church was creating a second-class priesthood. However rewarding the unconventional ministries may be—and many clergywomen we have talked with find them profoundly rewarding—they do not represent the commonly acknowledged route to authority in the church. Paula Nesbitt, writing in 1990, comments: 'Though Episcopal women priests have moved upward in their careers, their attainment has tended to fall short of positions enabling them to exercise a significant degree of denominational influence and authority, especially when compared with the attainment levels of men within their cohort' " (Prelinger 1992b, 292). On John Morgan's work, see below.

17. For a larger, statistical confirmation of this pattern, see Nesbitt 1990, and Morgan 1985. See also, however, Lehman 1993c. Lehman describes Morgan's findings as "unsurprising" (and, by that, I take it that Lehman has no doubt Morgan's observations are largely what one would expect); but he does identify serious flaws in Morgan's mode of reporting, if not his method.

18. The qualifications of the women matched against the professional frustration they have faced are stunning, and there is ample evidence to suggest that their level of preparation is hardly an exception. According to Catherine Prelinger, as of 1985, the mean educational level of ordained women in the Episcopal church was slightly above a master's degree (Prelinger 1992b, 292). She also notes that the majority of seminary administrators are forced to admit that their better students are women (p. 297). On the last point, see also Wilkes 1990, 61–62.

19. Again, for confirmation of larger patterns, see Prelinger 1992b, 294–97; and Nesbitt 1990.

20. The denomination's Committee on the Status of Women reported that "Data from the 1980s indicated that 92.6 percent of the male clergy, but only 75.4 percent of the women, found regular parish positions upon ordination. Of priests ordained to the diaconate in 1980, 40 percent of the men, but only 15 percent of the women were rectors of parishes by 1986" (Wortman 1992, 10). Another dynamic, which goes unmentioned here, because I have interviewed priests, is the effect "dual ordination tracks" have had on women. The Episcopal Church, among others, has a two-stage ordination process. One is ordained first to the transitional diaconate and then to the priesthood, but the church also

ordains people to a "permanent" diaconate, i.e., a "discrete, rather than sequential" office. Permanent deacons are allowed to "suit up on Sunday mornings . . . to help with the worship service," but they "cannot perform the priestly duties of celebrating the Eucharist, giving blessings or absolution" (Nesbitt 1993, 15). Paula D. Nesbitt has studied the careers of 1,158 men and women serving in the Episcopal church's permanent diaconate or in the Unitarian Universalist Association's equivalent, "the minister of religious education." Although it might be argued that the creation of a permanent diaconate may meet certain institutional needs (including budget constraints and clergy shortages), Nesbitt demonstrates that the creation of a discrete diaconate has also left "disproportionately" high numbers of males "in high-level positions" and could lead to enduring "marginalization, segregation, or discrimination in opportunities for women clergy" (Nesbitt 1993). If, as some have suggested, the Episcopal church dispensed with the "transitional diaconate" completely, the trend might accelerate.

21. Based upon my own research and the quantitative research done by others, I find it difficult to believe things have changed quite as much as Rima Lunin Schultz suggests, but she too attributes the changes in the Chicago diocese to the leadership of the bishop. See Schultz 1992, 60.

22. In fact, since the interviews, a majority of the diocesan standing committees and the House of Bishops confirmed the Reverend Jack Iker as bishop coadjutor (i.e., bishop-elect) of the Diocese of Fort Worth, and on April 24, 1993 he was consecrated. Iker succeeds a traditionalist bishop, Clarence Pope, and is himself an avowed opponent of women's ordination. Upon the ratification of his candidacy by the diocesan standing committees, Iker said, "The votes I received are not an affirmation of my views on women priests, but their [the standing committee's] commitment that I may hold the view" ("Traditionalist Clears Hurdle" 1993c). See also Hames 1993.

23. Admission of women to the House of Bishops has been slow and marked by the same kind of mixed bureaucratic messages that have bedeviled the ordination issue. Hesitant to complicate its ties with the larger Anglican communion and its ecumenical relations with the Roman Catholic Church, the General Convention did not affirm that it would set aside gender considerations in the consecration of bishops until 1985. Then in 1986, although the House of Bishops reaffirmed the decision made in the General Convention, it also passed a resolution acknowledging "the concern of the Primates for restraint in proceeding to the consecration of a woman as bishop before the 1988 Lambeth Conference" (Harris 1986, 17). See also Hiatt 1986; Evans 1989; Wilson-Kastner 1989; and Ruether 1989.

24. Barbara Harris was elected suffragan bishop of Massachusetts in September, 1988, and Jane Dixon was elected to the same office in the diocese of Washington, D.C. in May 1992.

25. Mary Adelia McLeod was elected bishop of Vermont. See "Woman Elected Bishop" (1993d).

26. One of the respondents noted that in cases of affirmative action, a woman of color is more likely to be chosen than is a white woman. This state may hint at a future arena of conflict among women themselves. Compare the comments by Catherine Wessinger in her 1993 address to the Parliament of the World's Religions: "Whereas there are tensions between women who do not want to change traditional gender roles and feminist

women who do, yet another very difficult issue to address will be the tensions between different types of feminist women. Women of color are increasingly pointing out that the feminist movement in the United States has been dominated by white women. African American, Asian American, Native American, and Latina American women feminists assert that white feminists' perspective falls short of addressing their realities and is blind to its own inherent racism. White feminists, on the other hand, who are genuinely concerned about the oppression of women in all ethnic communities are often shocked at being called racists. African American feminist women identify themselves as 'womanists' to indicate their solidarity with the African American community, and to indicate that their analysis and theologizing takes into account not only sexism, but also racism and classism. Native American feminist women particularly resent the appropriation of elements of Native American religions by white feminists for their own spirituality. Native American women regard this as yet another violation of their traditional culture by white imperialists. These conflicts and tensions will likely continue as religious feminist women in all these communities engage in the process of getting to know each other better" (Wessinger 1993, 13–14).

27. Lehman's sample (1978b, 276) included 1,414 lay members of four denominations: the Church of England (347), the Baptist Union (360), the Methodist Church (349), and the United Reformed Church (358).

28. The word "theology" is mine, not Lehman's, and is an attempt to describe in lay terms what Lehman describes as "ecclesiological localism," which—it seems to me—embraces a theological component. Compare Lehman 1987b, 278.

29. Sociologists prefer the term, "localism," which has broader utility in that it can describe a range of behaviors. Lehman explains: "According to 'local/cosmopolitan' theory ... persons differ in the extent to which they identify with their local community, view events in the world in terms of the limited perspective associated with that particular time and place, and thus respond to social and cultural changes introduced into their life space. At one extreme, persons classified as 'locals' are highly attached to their immediate social locale, define the world in highly restricted and sophisticated terms, are intolerant of out-groups, and tend to resist cultural and social change. 'Cosmopolitans,' on the other extreme, manifest few local attachments and instead identify with the broader society. They are well informed and relate to world events and other groups in broad universalistic terms. They correspondingly tend to favor social and cultural innovations" (Lehman 1987b, 275).

3

The United Methodist Church

Of Celebration and Behavior

"Organizations celebrate their own existence by manipulating environmental symbols of legitimacy." In action, behavior rarely matches the substance of this celebration.

—Thomas J. Sergiovanni, *Leadership and Organizational Culture*

In 1992 at its quadrennial conference, the United Methodist Church celebrated its contribution to the world.[1] Delivering the evening address, Bishop C. Dale White of New York declared, "The church has been a reforming and renewing presence in all our societies, precisely because it has courage to seek and to declare the new directions in which the Spirit is leading the people of God" (Ranck 1992, 6).

A Cause for Celebration?

As White's words might be applied to the experience of the church's female clergy, there is clearly reason for celebration. When asked, "Have you perceived changes in the impact your gender has had on your career during your tenure?" some of the interviewees' answers struck a clearly positive note. One of the most enthusiastic endorsements of the church's efforts to include women came at the expense of Southern Baptists. "Drastic changes. It really opens my mind and eyes to be a delegate to General Conference, and I was first alternate in '88. The United Methodist

Church . . . is a forerunner in women's rights and I'm very proud of our denomination for that, especially when I see so many fine Baptist women have to leave the Southern Baptist Church and come into our denomination to be ordained" (UM2:5).

Another responded at length, describing the efforts made by the leadership of her church to include women, sometimes at a rate that pressed both her and others to the limits of their preparation.

> [Because of my gender] I think I've gotten opportunities that might not have been there, if a male with the same abilities and . . . background had been considered. It's almost reverse discrimination in some respects . . . I've thought to myself, "Gee, I really don't deserve to be appointed to this board with my experience." . . . And I saw that happening all over our conference. That's why I think women here have tried to do a good job despite the fact that they were maybe moved to the head of the class when they really weren't ready. Not that they weren't ready, but that they hadn't been in as long as some of their male counterparts. . . . There were times when it was overwhelming and you just couldn't do all the things they wanted you to do and you had to make choices, whether it was on the conference level or the district level. But I really believe that they tried very, very hard in this area and in this conference and district to make sure that women were in every possible level of church government, as well as in the local church structure. (UM3:8–9)

Bureaucratic Linkages

As the comments of both interviewees suggest, the progress made toward including women in the Methodist church can be traced in part to the bureaucratic measures put in place by the church.

A Forerunner?

Depending upon how one traces the history of the United Methodist Church, the denomination has arguably provided for the full ordination of women since 1956.[2] The current discipline of the church explicitly includes women "in all provisions . . . which refer to the ordained ministry" (Book of Discipline 1992, III.412.2) and uses inclusive language throughout to describe the participants in that ministry.[3]

Given the fact that the language of the church's constitution is permissive, the changes made to the discipline in 1956 precluded the kind of debate about its official position that has bedeviled the Episcopal church. What debate there was revolved around the attempt of bishops opposed to the ordination of women to short-circuit the changes made to the discipline by simply exercising episcopal control. Today, United Methodist polity, in theory, safeguards against this eventuality by limiting the powers of the episcopacy. According to the discipline, bishops are required to ordain and appoint anyone approved by their annual conference.[4]

At one point the church also set inclusive quotas for its boards and agencies. Indeed, a number of the women I interviewed clearly based their confidence in the inclusivity of their denomination on such quotas. One minister observed, for example.

> It used to be in our church—and still is in a lot of local churches—that the board of trustees is the big board. Our church law says that the board of trustees has to be 50 percent women now. And on the conference level, and on the general conference, the national denominational level, this is very rigidly adhered to. . . . Some local churches still kind of thumb their noses at some of that, but on the denominational level, which is the large church, as well as the conference level, it's very intentional . . . I don't like "quota system," but it's very intentional that the boards and agencies of our denomination, of our conference, our districts, and hopefully the local churches, are going to be very inclusive of both gender and racially. (UM9:8)

Ironically, however, if such quotas continue to inform the assignments made in the church, the rigor with which they are applied must be credited to the church's leadership. Only one of the interviewees appeared to be aware that the church's Judicial Council declared such provisions unconstitutional in 1990.[5]

In addition to the formal bureaucratic provisions made by the church at large, some district superintendents have instituted a blind appointment process in which the profiles given to churches omit any reference to gender.

> They [the local churches] really don't have a choice. When they write up what we call a profile of what their needs are and meet with the

superintendent, when a pastor-parish committee meets with a superintendent, they discuss the qualities they are looking for and the skills
that are needed. And when a superintendent meets with them, they
don't know if it's a male or female, black or white, or what. They just
know—and this is my understanding anyway—that they are given the
profile of a person and they accept or reject that profile when they get
the name and meet the individual. I'm sure that doesn't happen in a lot
of the situations, but I've seen it happen. It happened with me. The
people here did not know when they were presented with a profile, they
had no idea it was male or female or what. (UM3:12)

Although most of these provisions are designed to engage women
in the ministry of the local church, Methodist ministers also gave their
denomination high marks for the extent to which women have been
involved at the national level. Aware of the contributions they make,
interviewees mentioned by name women serving on and leading a variety
of national boards.

Matching Behavior?

So far, then, the case for celebration. As Thomas Sergiovanni observes, however, "In action, behavior rarely matches the substance of this
celebration" (1984).

It is striking that having been asked to talk about stories, language,
symbols, icons, and rituals, when the interviewees were asked to talk
about "other dimensions of United Methodist culture," six out of ten
gravitated to the issues of structure and interpersonal dynamics. Comparing their responses with questions, I asked later about the impact of
gender on their career and the nature of in-groups within the denomination. Two patterns emerged.

One recurring pattern the respondents identified was that of a male-
dominated network, where most of the power in the denomination is still
concentrated. "The political tradition within the church is, of course,
one that is extremely male-dominated. . . . Even though there have been
women ordained in the Methodist church for the last thirty or forty years
and even though there have been women who have served . . . as lay
preachers for hundreds of years, the tradition is still . . . male-dominated"
(UM9:4). In a similar vein, another minister observed: "The one thing
that is especially evident is simply that men made all of the decisions,

men held all of the power, formal power.... I'm talking about in the past, moving into the present. I think that's still largely the case. In the local church that's not as much the case, but in the church hierarchy that seems to be just as much the case as five or ten years ago" (UM10:3–4).

"Moving South"

These observations are not as difficult to reconcile with a mood of celebration as it might appear. First of all, the reception women receive varies considerably from conference to conference and from region to region. Southern and midwestern states in particular are notoriously resistant to the ministry of women, even (ironically) Tennessee, where the church's international headquarters are located.[6] Asked whether the provisions of United Methodist polity were effectively administered on the local and conference levels, one interviewee responded:

> No, at least in our area, some wonderful leadership on the part of women has been relatively wasted. On the one hand, many of us simply were not assigned at the times when we were eligible. In fact, many of us were not under assignment at a time when every pastor was guaranteed an appointment; and it's interesting that the church law has basically been bent in order to avoid giving us the opportunities to serve as pastors.... I think what's happened is that many of the local churches that would have been open to having women, in fact ask for women by name as pastors, but they were denied that opportunity if that particular congregation was seen as being too lucrative or too prestigious to give to a woman. I really see in our area women have been systematically denied opportunities to serve churches any larger than the church I'm serving. I hope that's going to change, but I know there are many, many obstacles to that changing, mainly among men who do indeed control those resources and those assignments in our area. (UM10:9)[7]

Another interviewee who served as her conference's liaison and, as a result, had the opportunity to speak with a variety of ministers from other parts of the country, described the impact of gender on her career from a broader perspective. As elsewhere in the interviews, the southern states were mentioned explicitly:

In the larger church I've been the token. So I have this kind of notorious twelve years behind me where there are two female ministers in our conference, and we've kind of been their tokens. So I'm not going to have some of the same history as other women that you might speak to, because they obviously had to take one or two of the women and make sure that they were treated right and put them on the right committees and moved up, and that's been my story. So I have been treated at the conference level and at the national level with great respect, and I have been one of those who has been asked to do leadership. I was the liaison to some singles and some women things. I was the C-4 liaison from our conference, which had to do with women and with clergy couples, and so I've had some really wonderful opportunities to be on the ground level of making decisions and being a part of the structure as women came into that. So I don't have very many war stories. . . . What I do know is that I've had opportunity because of the opportunities to go to Chicago and to Nashville. I have certainly been able to hear the war stories from other women and I've just been overwhelmed. I do know some of the women in our conference have not been treated fairly. I do know that. . . . But I have never heard any war stories here that could compare with some of those who were in Louisiana, Texas, Florida, some of those southern states, and how they were just openly treated just really shabbily. (UM8:7–8)

Nor is this impression of the south purely anecdotal. The voting pattern for bishops in the Southeastern Jurisdiction of the United Methodist Church is, for example, stunningly exclusivistic. Analyzing election data in all five jurisdictions of the church, from 1944 to 1988, three United Methodists concluded:

The single most striking feature of that analysis is the difference between two jurisdictional groups that have emerged in the past 20 years. All five jurisdictions looked pretty similar before 1972. Since 1972, differences between the North Central, Northeastern and Western Jurisdictions on the one hand and the South Central and Southeastern Jurisdiction on the other hand are noticeable. Call the former three jurisdictions *Group A* and the latter two *Group B*. In the elections of 1976 through 1988, *Group A* has elected 13 White men, 6 Black men, 4 White women, 1 Black woman, 1 man of Asian background, and 1 man of Hispanic background, for a total of 26 bishops. The average ballot number for election of these 26 increased from 12 to 28 during the period. *Group B* has elected 28 White men and 3 Black men, for a total of 31 bishops. The average ballot number for election of these 31 decreased from 10 to 7 during the period.

While our purpose is not to assign causes to the differences, correlations are inescapable. The increasing diversification in ethnic identity and gender of the bishops elected in *Group A* accompanies an increasingly protracted balloting process, while the homogeneity of bishops elected in *Group B* accompanied a slight decrease in the length of the balloting process.

As might be surmised, not everyone is satisfied by present procedures for electing bishops. Concerns for *Group A* include time consumed and politicization in pre-vote events as well as the large number of ballots. A concern for *Group B* is the lack of diversity among elected bishops. (Fishburn and others 1992, 11)

Coupled with the fact that the church is "moving south" demographi-cally,[8] such voting patterns suggest that new struggles may lie ahead for a growing number of women seeking positions of service. The move southward may also mean the culture of the church will be sufficiently hostile to women's ministry in some areas such that the culture will simply fail to nurture the interest of girls and young women.[9]

Lyle Schaller, a United Methodist and parish consultant for the Yoke-fellow Institute based in Richmond, Indiana, notes that since the merger of the United Methodists and the Evangelical United Brethren twenty-five years ago, the membership of the church has been concentrated in the so-called rustbelt, a line of states running from Pennsylvania west through to Kansas. "Together," Schaller writes, "the North Central and Northeastern Jurisdictions accounted for *nearly one-half* of all worshipers on the average Sunday morning" (1992, 4).[10]

"Today, however, the South Central and Southeastern Jurisdictions account for *over one-half* of all worshipers in UM churches" (Schaller 1992, 4).[11] Differing with those who argued that this was a passing phenome-non, Schaller notes that all the other indices of future church attendance suggest that United Methodists are "moving south to the sunbelt." Fifty-six percent of church school attendance is now concentrated in the South Central and Southeastern jurisdictions. Even more "startling," argues Schaller, is the national distribution of large churches. In the last twenty-five years, "Three jurisdictions reported a 50 percent decrease in the number of large congregations" while, by comparison, the Southeastern jurisdiction stood alone in reported increases. "If we narrow the focus to those congregations averaging 1,000 or more at worship and shorten the time frame to only 15 years, the changes are even more startling," Schaller writes. "In 1974 the Southeastern jurisdiction included as many mega-churches as the three northern/western jurisdictions combined. By 1989 it was nearly three times as many as the combined total for those other three jurisdictions" (1992, 5–6).

Of the reasons Schaller identifies for this shift in church attendance, the last one may have the most direct bearing on our discussion.

> An overlapping explanation is suggested in James Davison Hunter's new book, *Culture Wars*. He contends that contemporary public policy debates cut across denominational boundaries and are in fact class wars. To a substantial degree UM leaders in the North and West have allied themselves with the faction that includes relatively few regular church-goers. By contrast, UM churches in the Southeast and Southwest tend to be attractive [to] those churchgoers who are more comfortable with traditional values. (1992, 6)[12]

It lies beyond the scope of this book to build the body of evidence necessary to argue with certainty that those traditional values include an all-male ministry or, at a minimum, an all-male leadership. But if Hunter is right, and the patterns of discrimination against women—in the parish and the episcopate—are closely allied with the factors attracting south-erners to an increasingly southern denomination, then there may be de-cidedly less reason for celebration in the future among United Methodist women. Furthermore, if Schaller is right, and the shifts in attendance signal future financial crises among the conferences in the Northeast, North Central and Western Jurisdictions, then the picture will prove worse yet (Schaller 1992, 6).[13]

Life in the Country (and Elsewhere)

None of this is meant to suggest that problems exist in the South alone. Interviewees from other jurisdictions reported patterns of discrimi-nation, and even women who were finally accepted by their congregations reported unsettling struggles at the outset of each new appointment. Asked how gender had affected her career, one woman in the North Central Jurisdiction responded:

> I only notice it at the beginning when they are suspect and standoffish and some say they are not going to come. And it always affects me because I'm hurt. I'm always so hurt to think that it would make any difference to know that I've been called by God, for goodness sake, that I had to give up my wonderful career and all I was doing and all the money I was making, and I had to go and do something like this, and go away and spend all my money and end up in debt. This isn't anything I wanted to do. I had never even seen a woman minister when I had my call to ministry. So I'm hurt and disillusioned and discouraged at the beginning of my ministries in different places. (UM8:7)

In addition, the denomination's own self-study program, launched during the second half of the eighties, is replete with descriptions of inequities in both the northern and western jurisdictions of the church. Referred to as the C-4 project, because it was designed to "assess the reception and experience of white clergywomen, racial/ethnic clergy women and clergy couples," the report describes patterns of discrimination that may go completely undetected because there is so much apparent attention given to involving women (Euzenas 1989, 4).

For example, consultation teams described conference level cabinets charged with finalizing appointments that resisted "moving women into solo appointments at higher salary and responsibility levels in second appointments." Yet, they readily did the same thing for men of "similar age and experience." In other conferences women actually reported " 'being deceived into taking a pay cut' " by the cabinet in their conferences. In still other cases women discovered that their salaries were $300 to $2,000 below that of their immediate, male predecessors. The pattern of discrimination was, in fact, sufficiently widespread to prompt the writers of the report to quote one clergyman who observed, "Even with the presumed closer attention to fairness and equity, the women have fallen to the bottom . . . the data suggests a pattern of discrimination, accidental, but nonetheless real." One might question the description of such inequities as "accidental," but the report leaves no doubt that the inequities exist (Euzenas 1989, 15).

Resistance in the South and elsewhere comes from a variety of
sources. Some resistance comes from the parishes themselves. Some
churches simply refuse to accept women as their pastors. Interviewees
often mentioned small, struggling, rural churches (of which there are
many in the United Methodist Church), but they are by no means alone
in their insistence on male leadership. "In this particular local church
things are great. Some of my friends speak from their local churches, and
some of them are doing well, and some of them are barely hanging on
because of the problems they have. Not all of our churches . . . are ready
for a woman to be minister or know they are ready. They may be more
ready than they think they are" (UM4:8–9).

Paying Dues

In other cases women have found that the implicit pyramid of appointments, which exists within many conferences, has slowed their acceptance at larger churches. Foreign as it might seem to idealized
understandings of ministry, many ministers in the United Methodist
Church climb a pyramid of appointments. In the early stages of one's
ministry, these appointments may vary in duration, but they are predict-
ably the assistant in large churches or (more often) the sole minister in a
much smaller church and, if not, a multiple point charge.[14] Only by
"paying dues" can one "move up," and that requires a considerable
amount of time. Because they are still relatively new to the church's
ministry, many women are excluded from the denomination's larger
churches. Furthermore, given the fact that women very often enter the
ministry later in life than do men, there is a good chance that they will
never serve in such churches.[15]

> *Interviewer:* Reverend _____, do you perceive there to be an in-
> group among United Methodists?
> *Interviewee:* Oh, hell, yes. We call them "the big boys."
> *Interviewer:* What does that mean, "the big boys?"
> *Interviewee:* That means those who have learned to work the system and
> have climbed the ladder. You can usually spot them. They all have
> the same haircut. They all go to the same barber. I call it the
> cookie-cutter look. You know, the gingerbread men. . . . They went
> through a spell of everybody wearing a green jacket. Now they're
> into the wide azalea, gladiolus ties, you know.

Interviewer: You called them "the big boys." Does that indicate that you
    don't see women as a part of that in-group?

Interviewee: Yes, we are, but we don't come through the big-boy system.
    We don't want to be a part of that system. This is all generally
    speaking, you understand. I think they are threatened by the
    women, and we quietly seek support in other places. My biggest
    support is the small membership church pastor who feels that he—
    and I say that on purpose—has very little support in the confer-
    ence, that he is out there in his little old country church. My support
    comes from there. Also the women have learned to band together
    with other groups—for example, the black pastors. (UM2:6–7)[16]

When an Appointment Isn't an Appointment

Not all of the resistance women encounter, however, can be attributed
to either individual parishes or (ostensibly) passive structures. For example, one of the respondents argues that both district superintendents and
bishops (for perhaps a variety of reasons) have compromised the appointment process, subverting the bureaucratic provisions intended to insure
that ordinands are fully involved in the ministry of the church.[17] When
asked if the level of acceptance she has experienced in her own conference
exists across the wider church, she responded:

No, not at all. Like I say, I had the opportunity to be the C-4 liaison
that had to do with clergy couples and clergywomen. . . . After we got
our training we were then to go into another conference and we were
to do a lot of research into what they did with women and clergy
couples and minorities. I was really appalled at what was going on there
. . . We did the process as we were taught to. We brought the Board of
Ordained Ministry together with the district superintendents and the
bishop to share with them what we saw was wrong with their system,
their conference, having to with women, minorities, and couples. And
they were saying things to us, like: "Well, but those towns would not
accept a woman." I just came out of my seat, "What do you mean those
towns won't accept women. There is no question about those towns
accepting women. This is an appointive system. You don't get to call
who you want. I would have never gotten into the towns I got into, if
it was a call system. We happen to be an appointive system. There's no
question about if you want a woman or not. The bishop will appoint a
woman and you take it or leave it." And they just looked at me like

they didn't know what I was talking about. So in this conference . . . they were not doing the appointment system at all. There were communities where blacks could not go, because they would not be accepted, and there were lots of communities where women could not go, because women would not be accepted. And I could not believe that was part of the United Methodist system. (UM8:14–15)

In some cases, interviewees have no doubt about the motives of their leaders. Two accounts are cited here at length:

When I was attempting to be ordained and going through the process of ordination, I had a real jerk for a district superintendent. . . . This was a man who didn't believe that women should be ordained, but this was a man who didn't believe liberals should be ordained either. . . . Anybody who was anywhere left of halfway to center was a flaming liberal, and those two things very much made it so that he did some terrible things toward me, in terms of the process toward ordination . . . which led to two years of extreme pain and kept me from serving churches. . . . For example, fifteen years ago, let's say twelve years ago, I was not given an assignment because I was a woman. A year or so later I was finally given an assignment, but in the process of that assignment I was told that I was being sent to the place I would be hurting the least. In the process of ten or twelve years, again kind of behind closed doors, it's time for an assignment change—which really confronts all of us with where we really are, not where we think we want to be or where we'd like to see ourselves—and when I go in and talk to the person who supervises this kind of assignment change, instead of talking about my assignment, I am asked during that time to sympathize with this superintendent over the other women in my district that he doesn't have a place for and doesn't want to have to assign. I'm given no opportunity to talk to him except over the phone, and even then I don't even have the opportunity to talk to him when assignments are being made. I find out that with my male colleagues, a number of folks had very frequent contact with the same superintendent. I don't know, it's pretty clear that a lot of things haven't changed at all. (UM9:6)

I know of two women in my district alone who were eligible to serve a local church, and our district superintendent simply never sent them anywhere, and if he treated them the way he treated me, he simply didn't answer their phone calls. He did let them come to make an appointment with him at his office. In fact, he took the liberty of complaining to me about them, and both of them were highly trained and respected in the work that they had done. One of them has served on the national level in our denomination and the other one has served in a university situation training other ministers. And I was very disturbed when I discovered that neither of them had been assigned a church. Then I could use one other illustration, which is a small congregation that does not have a full-time salary for a pastor near my own church, and I know that in two cases there were two men considered for that assignment, one of whom had not been to seminary and was not ordained, and had only recently been licensed; and another man who had been to seminary, who was not United Methodist and was not ordained. Both of them were given the opportunity to serve that church before and each of them turned it down. And then finally a woman who was ordained in our denomination, that had been open to serve, was finally called in at the last minute to become the pastor of that church. I think that's a perfect example of wasting the resources that are there and basically denying the opportunity that people are usually guaranteed in our system, to be assigned to a church. (UM10:9–10)

Bureaucrats, but not Bishops

The apparent contradiction in the accounts women give of their experience in the Methodist Church is more easily explained when one realizes that women frequently serve as leaders in the bureaucratic rank-and-file, but that relatively few of them are bishops and district superintendents with primary responsibility for parish life.[18] There are only five women serving as bishops, and nationally (as of 1991), there are only sixty-one women serving as district superintendents. There are no statistics available concerning the total number of districts in the Methodist Church, but there are 72 conferences, each of which consists of multiple districts.[19] Needless to say, there are a number of conferences that have never had either a female bishop or a female district superintendent.

Walking Dogs

Even the number of ordained women serving in the national headquarters may not be a sign of greater openness to the ministry of women.

At the national level for United Methodists, I think there have been a lot of opportunities open to women who are ordained in the church bureaucracy, and so that's where a lot of women have migrated when they were unable to serve in a local church as a pastor. So I'd say, by and large those bureaucracies have reaped the benefits of this wasted talent. . . . The sad part of that is often those women have been denied the experience in the local church that would make them even stronger leaders for the national church. (UM10:10)

Widespread stereotyping is also a problem. One minister, who identified this pattern, spoke both for herself and for others.

I'm not regarded in the same way as my male colleagues at all. In fact, I was with a group just recently in which we decided that maybe to speak of our male peers as colleagues was presumptuous. I think we're seen in large part—and I'm speaking of ordained women in my particular tradition—I think by an awful lot of folks and, in particular, by those who hold onto a lot of power as "dogs walking on hind legs," that it won't last. That if you ignore it, it will go away. I'm amazed that after ten or fifteen years of having what I would say [have been] really confirming experiences, I'm really astounded at how little has changed under the surface of tokenism. (UM10:4)

The same patterns had little affect on the interviewees' interactions with their immediate colleagues. Nonetheless, I detected the occasional intrusion of male networking and some outright caution around male colleagues. And some of the ministers I spoke with wondered out loud whether their success in relating to their immediate peers was the product of a process of selection in which they intuitively avoided contact with peers who would be less accepting.

The patterns reemerged, however, when I began talking about the impact of gender on the interviewees' careers. Stereotyping and male-dominated power structures were perceived as factors that had far-reaching affects: limiting the ability of women to "hear a call" to pastoral ministry; inhibiting the process of nurture one might expect from pastors; slowing the ordination process; extending the appointment process; and limiting upward mobility and, therefore, salaries (Euzenas 1989, 6, 17, and 18).[20] Asked if the attitude of her congregation or the attitude of others toward her gender had affected her career, one minister responded:

Oh, my goodness, yes. The major battle in my career has been over the fact that I'm female, of course. I am over qualified, I guess, or highly qualified for the position that I hold as far as education and background are concerned. My appointments are not what they would have been had I been a male in the same position. I understand that. As far as I know, I hold the highest paid position of any female pastor in my conference . . . and I am still not an upper-drawer kind of pastor, but I do have a church that some men would like to have. I'll put it that way. It is a loving church and a supportive church. But in previous churches I have served at places where I was not wanted, and it was bad—the church I served immediately before this one. I was sent there, and some people felt that they were being punished because they were getting a female pastor. They thought they had made the district superintendent mad and he was getting back at them—that sort of thing. Others just made up their mind before I got there that I wouldn't do, and that's the way it was. I stayed two years and fought and suffered intensively because of it. There were a few people, of course, in that congregation that made it tolerable. But by and large it was one miserable appointment. My first appointment was very hard because I couldn't tell which of my problems were problems because of the church, it being a troubled church; which were problems because I was new in the ministry; and which were problems because I was a woman. I had no way of sorting those out. I did not have much guidance. I guess I didn't ask for it. I didn't know I could. . . . At that time I recall having some very good times, but just being in the dark a lot of the time about what needed to be done. And, so, I served that church for two years, and it was time to move on. The people were not all happy. I guess they would have taken me back for another year, but they agreed, and I felt like we weren't getting anywhere, so I asked for another appointment. I was given another entry-level appointment, and I was under-employed. That was extremely frustrating, because I was pretty fresh out of seminary and just really ready go to work and do things; and in this church the people were old and ill and [there were] not very many of them. Other than being a handholder, I simply, well, I learned to crochet and I'm not a needlework person but, good grief, I had to do something. And so it was extremely frustrating. Though the people were loving to a certain extent, they wouldn't do anything. . . . In _____ . . . where I served, I was given a two-point charge and they were in a dying community, or two dying communities, really. Well, one was in the dying community and one was simply a dying church. And they were looking for a pastor who would come in and turn them around. Of course, that didn't happen with me and it didn't happen with my successors either. But all the same, we had some good times and I had some people in the community who did not like my being there, some of other denominations and, of course, the people in the churches had to deal with their neighbors all the time. And so they had to do some growing in the sense they either said, "well I don't like it either" or they came to my defense and said, "we've got a good pastor here." And so that plowed along and I stayed there four years and then I moved to the one I referred to previously. That's where I had such a bad time. . . . I do know that when it's time for me to have an appointment, the poor cabinet has to work very, very hard to get me an appointment. They have to be turned down a time or two about some places they would like to send me. (UM4:4–5)[21]

Pushing Through the Gates

It is not surprising, then, that although some ministers credited the church's leadership with the level of inclusion, far more attributed the changes that have taken place to women themselves—their own persistence and their growing (though still modest) numerical strength. As one minister observed, the church has moved from the "phone booth era" to the "van era" (UM7:6). Now she is one of the "elders" in a group of 150 ordained women of increasing diversity. Modeling ministry for women is easier. There are more models, and an ever-larger number of women are attending seminary.

No, I'm not really sure to what extent the conference or the local level would be working toward bringing women into ordained ministry. I'm really not—I really don't know. The women are choosing to come in, the women are pushing through the gates, the women are knocking on the doors, the women are breaking down the barriers. The women are being called and have probably been called throughout the ages, but couldn't even hear because of their being so subordinate, or being made to stay in their place, or reading the Bible stories and knowing that women just didn't exist, or shouldn't exist in that. So, the women—as I see it—it is the women pushing through, and I'm not convinced that the conference and the local church is doing all that much to provide opportunity for women to be helped to go into the ministry. (UM8:14)

Organizational Culture

The impression of Methodist culture one receives is also a mixture of institutional celebration and struggle.

Looking for Mentors

United Methodists cited far fewer stories than did interviewees from other denominations, and relative to the total number of stories they did tell, denominational history was marginally more important for them than it was for interviewees from other traditions. Furthermore, United Methodists were slightly more divided in their response to the traditional stories.

One interviewee, for example, found nothing of an alienating nature in the stories of her tradition. Without citing specific stories, she observed: "I've always been a Methodist. My father was a Methodist pastor. My grandparents were Methodist, my great-grandparents. Nothing has ever alienated me from the church because the church—and I speak of the Methodist Church—has always been family to me, extended family" (UM2:1). Another said: "There aren't any particular stories that have alienated me from the tradition." But then added: "A part of my journey has been reclaiming the stories" (UM9:1).

By contrast, the vast majority of women did struggle. One minister, for example, identified with a very traditional and male figure in Methodist history, John Wesley. But in so doing, she identified with him not as a "founding father" or establishment figure, but as someone willing to break with social conventions.

I would have to say the story that probably got my attention the most is one of our most traditional ones, and it's the story of Wesley himself. I call him my main-man, because I was so turned on by Wesleyan theology and by his willingness to speak in the language of the people to the people, wherever they were—not so much all of the intellectual training and so on he brought to that, but his willingness to forsake convention when necessary so that he could meet the needs of the people. I was working with high school kids at the time and even though I had been raised as a Methodist (it wasn't United Methodist then), I just was caught by that, and because I was working with high school kids, I was seeing the lack of our ability as a church, not just Methodist, but all churches, to communicate with kids. And I had taught on the college level and I saw the same thing there. And it was just so exciting to me that maybe I could be a part of a tradition, now that I understood it, where I could translate in everyday language something that was very profound, but yet keep it simple. And from day one, that's where I was and that story has never ceased to be a part of my everyday theological output. And people tease me because I have pictures of Wesley on his horse at Wesley Seminary in my office, and when I graduated, they let me sit up on the horse with him and it's not an exciting story or anything. It's not different than anybody else's. It's simply what turned me on despite the fact that I looked very, very hard for women mentors or women that I could look up to in our tradition. Wesley was the one. (UM3:1)

The vast majority of women interviewed, however, identified with women: Susanna Wesley,[22] Georgia Harkness,[23] and Anna Howard Shaw,[24] whose stories focused on empowerment and the willingness to break with social conventions. The stories chosen also allowed interviewees to find some measure of common experience.

Well, I remember even as a child hearing about Susanna Wesley, and even though she was held up to me because of her mother status, I always felt like she was a strong woman that was able to have kids and be more than just a housewife. So, yes, she would have been one. And then as I grew and went to seminary and learned about some of the early women preachers from Anna Howard Shaw on, I felt a lot of support of people, especially women who were strong in their time, even when they weren't always listened to or respected. (UM7:1–2)

The Bible as Put-Down

The same mixture of responses characterized Methodist reactions to the biblical text, which, as in the case of the other denominations, received far more attention than did the history of the church. One respondent, whose reading of the story of Mary, was without parallel in any of the comments made by the other interviewees, observed:

> I think the biblical stories of women have mostly affected me positively. Many of the stories of the women in the New Testament certainly portray women with a passive form of power, and that has been relatively easy to identify with and at the same time fruitful for me in some particular ways. Mary's openness to God, and a surprise, and a future that she could not see, her willingness to await and her willingness to be impregnated, that's a powerful image for me. Some of the other stories, Ruth somewhat, some of the others, of women who lived out of the center of themselves, were true to themselves and yet open to the unknown possibilities. Those are very positive and powerful images for me. I guess in my own call to ministry, and I don't know if this is jumping ahead for you, but the reasons that I came to ministry later in my life, I feel sure was that there was no expectation for me to be in ministry, or to be a person of active power. It is through a modeling of waiting for the activity of God—in some sense being impregnated or a sense of things coming to fruition and trusting—that this has led me to become a more actively powerful person. (UM6:1)

However, the response of most interviewees to the Bible's stories was marked by struggle and a process of sorting and sifting. Some of the stories that survived that process involved men. Jesus was mentioned twice and, in one case, he was described as a feminist. One respondent mentioned the Advent stories, including not only Mary, but Joseph. For the most part, however, the interviewees focused on the stories told about women, including the stories of Sarah, Esther, Ruth and Naomi, Mary, and Martha. Only one woman identified figures from the Bible that other denominations mentioned repeatedly (e.g., the woman at the well, the woman with the flow of blood, and the Syro-Phoenecian woman).

For most of the women who cited biblical stories, a process of "reclamation" was the key to discovering their affirming character. "I think that I identify through the stories that I've heard in my tradition. . . . Of course, the scriptural sources need to be sort of reinterpreted, but I have had a lot of fun with those, speculating about what were the positions of the women mentioned in the biblical stories. What really went on here? If a woman had been telling this story, how would it have been different?" (UM 4:1). Another of the respondents described her approach to the Pauline epistles as "maybe a bit of a rationalization."

As I was growing up, I realized—I maybe didn't realize—but I knew the stories were basically about men. Rarely was there a Bible story about a woman. It just seemed like that was the way it was. Then when I got older and I became more of a feminist, I guess probably in the sixties, and I began to understand what was going on and that so much of the Bible was male-oriented, I didn't accept that well. And as I went through those stories again it was hard for me to realize that all of those heroes were men and all of the people that I was thinking about out of my Christian culture were stories of men, and I didn't have, I just had hardly had any at all that I could lift up and say, "Biblically this is the person that I think so much about, or . . . this is one of my heroes and this is someone I fashion myself after." . . . So then I would say, perhaps after the sixties, and then when I went to seminary, I felt more alienated, even angry about that. But in growing up I just learned the stories and learned the lessons and read them, and I was in the church and they just were all about men, and God was a man, so that was just the way it was. . . . I think that was the beginning of my awareness about the "Paul stories" and the "Paul things" in the New Testament and the put-down, the actual put-down. Women shouldn't do this and women should be quiet. . . . I was really incensed that Paul needed to keep me in my place and Paul said to be quiet and keep my head covered and be subordinate. I don't know that those are actual stories. Those are his theories. But I think that's what angered me as I became aware, as I was coming into my awareness. . . . Well, I'm not of the theory anymore that Paul wrote all of that. I'm of the theory that Paul wrote only some of the epistles, and so right away I just discount a lot of that and say, you know, there were other scribes at that time and they probably wrote a lot of that. I pick up on Paul in Galatians: "Neither slave, nor free, nor Greek, nor male, nor female." I pick up on that and feel that may be more of where he was, and that may be a bit of a rationalization, but I do feel that I was harder on him than I needed to be in that probably some of it, a lot of it, wasn't even written by him. (UM8:1–2)

Like Everybody Else

As in the case of stories, the response of United Methodists is marked by seeming contradictions. A few are less disturbed by the gender orientation of the language used in their denomination, than are the respondents from other traditions. One interviewee, for example, suggested that she finds nothing of note of an either helpful or offensive character in the language used by her church.

> Nothing really jumps to mind. Methodists have adopted the Anglican language, the grammar, prayerbook English. Wesley was mostly a practical organizer and, so, the language—except for the older liturgy—in the years of my ministry as an ordained person, there's been a new liturgy in effect that I've used almost completely in the past decade. It's been intentionally inclusive or, at least, the parts of the liturgy that I'm most familiar with are much more inclusive. (UM10:1)

Another described the church she serves as a "transitional" church and, therefore, without language problems. "Language does not alienate me. I'm in a transitional church that has six different cultures. And we've got so many cultural differences going on that he/she just is minimal. That's not the issue here. Never really has been a big issue with me. I think God can be whoever God chooses to be and he cannot be limited. He/she *is* and that just never has been a big thing with me" (UM2:1).

A third interviewee conceded that her own congregation is conservative and that she regularly alters the gender orientation of the language used in her parish, but described her denomination as "on the cutting edge" in dealing with the challenges posed by language (UM3:4).

In addition, it is probably fair to say that both the tenor and the focus of the observations made by United Methodists differ from that of the comments made by their colleagues in other denominations. United Methodists, while sometimes expressing strong opinions about the language used in their church, were generally less expansive about the issue of language, and, when asked about the issue, tended to focus more on the changes they are making in the language their churches use.

Nonetheless, language remains a concern for Methodists, and eight out of ten women expressed some measure of concern about it. It is also certainly true that some of the ministers I interviewed expressed views as strong as any I have encountered: "Well, we would like to say in the United Methodist church that we've reached a consensus that inclusive language is best, but we cannot say that" (UM1:2).[25]

United Methodists also identify an array of language issues not unlike those identified by members of other denominations, including God-language, the language used for participants in the church's life, and (in one case) the issue of titles used to address clergy. Unlike Episcopalians, however, United Methodists talked about language with less direct reference to the ritual of the church—the only exception being the language used in public prayer (and even this concern received only a single mention).

Like their counterparts in other denominations, United Methodists also detected regional differences in the use of language and perceived some areas to be less sensitive than others to the presence of women. Again, as elsewhere, the South suffered in the comparison. "Well, I think that the church as I experience it is mostly open. I'm a west-coast minister and really feel the difference that knowing my friends in the South, for instance, have a very different perception. Here there's a lot of openness" (UM7:2).

The ministers I interviewed also distinguished between the progress made on issues of language at the official level, as against the progress made by the wider denomination. One interviewee noted, for example: "[Our use of language is] about like everybody else's. We've all grown up in a male-dominated culture. . . . The church politic is making a conscious effort, but in terms of the broadbased people in the church, that's a much more difficult thing" (UM9:3).

In many ways the tensions revolving around language are reflected in the debate over the church's new *Book of Worship,* approved at the 1992 General Conference. Mentioned by one of the interviewees, the book is an optional aid to worship. The vote to approve it, by a margin of 809 to 194, may belie the number of differences still at issue in the church. While introducing new, more neutral language for God, alongside more traditional terms of reference, the conference "stopped short" of approving direct addresses to God, such as "O Mother God" or "Bakerwoman, God." Those omissions, widely discussed in advance of the conference, prompted "several delegates" to launch an attempt to "resurrect" the language lost to the final proposal. Although the delegates were unsuccessful in their attempt, the conference's own reporters described the vote as less a whole-hearted endorsement of the new book, than the act of delegates desperate to deal with a backlog of other business.[26]

The Bottom Line

If for Episcopalians language and ritualistic actions are inseparable, for United Methodists ritual is almost entirely a problem of language.

Only one of the ministers I interviewed detected a gender orientation in the actions themselves. Interestingly, she discussed the "household life" mirrored in the Eucharist and baptism when I inquired about symbols, not when I discussed ritual. United Methodists also seemed to emphasize the conspicuous presence of male leadership in worship less often than others. Only one of the interviewees actually mentioned this factor. Even then, the respondent focused not on the roles played by ministers, but on the role of the laity in serving as ushers.

Instead, the women I interviewed focused on the language used in the church's ritual. Three of the interviewees believe that their denomination has made improvements in the area of liturgy. But all three identified different reasons for this impression, and all three clearly qualified the picture. One argued that she has found the church's liturgy less alienating over the last twelve years than it was at first. When describing the progress made, however, she did not focus on changes made by the denomination (although they did receive mention). Rather, she focused on the efforts of other women to create inclusive settings of their own for worship.

> Certainly I've been to services where I've really felt excluded, but those things—particularly in the last twelve years or so—have not alienated me. Rather, I think about some of the experiences I go to, where there are women's experiences. Most of the people present are women, they use more women's symbols, but they are also careful not to exclude the men that are present. It's not something that I get to participate in too often, but some more [of] the womanist type, feminist, more than anything else, feminist expressions. I can't say that I particularly have spent any time considering the non-Christian traditions, but once in a while somebody will share a little bit about that and I find it interesting and it's kind of exciting in its new look at things. (UM1:3)

Noting inconsistencies in her bishop's practice at annual conference, a second respondent emphasized that the process of change has been largely accomplished by supplementing the images used for God. She focused more specifically on the alternative approaches to worship approved by the 1992 General Conference.[27] She also noted, however, that the work was not without its opponents, particularly in the South.

> At our General Conference when they had a new book of worship that will be coming out, there were a lot of people—again, many from the

Southeast Jurisdiction—who objected to some of the newer images and some of those ended up being taken out, but there are still some references which are more inclusive. I know one of the ones that they took out, which I thought was strange was "God, you are like a grove of trees," or something, and they were upset about that. There was another one you may know, the prayer, "Bakerwoman God." Well, they ended up changing that [to] "Oh, God like a Bakerwoman," because that was less offensive to some people. So I think that's going to be an ongoing struggle still for awhile. But the new images are helpful to a lot of people, and I would think that there is a lot of generational division around that. There are still a lot of people who find their security in the old images and names. (UM7:3)

The third minister focused on her own church's efforts to supplement the language of liturgy. "In my practice as a pastor we've worked at making sure that in addition to the word, "Father," we use other terminology on a regular basis. So that the need to eliminate the term "Father" from our liturgical language has diminished. There's no need to leave it out when, in fact, it simply needs to be supplemented by additional understandings of God's relationship to us" (UM10:2).

On the other hand, four of the respondents emphasized what they perceived to be persistent problems with the language of United Methodist liturgy. They described themselves as engaged in a personal process of ongoing revision. They also expressed even stronger reservations about their church's ritual. Two of those responses helpfully summarize the views of all four:

When I can, I change some of that, in the liturgies, some of them they've changed. With the Lord's Prayer I will stay with the "Our Father," and other than that, I probably don't use any of the liturgies in the worship services as they are. I'm real likely to rewrite that or add "sister and brother," or I'm likely to add "Creator" as opposed to "Father and Son." . . . It's fairly male-dominated and still they've kept a lot of the male domination, but I read it in front of them differently as they might read it in the hymnal. The way it is, which is still male-dominated, exclusive. (UM8:4)

I think the part of ritual that is very difficult for me is the Trinitarian formula, "Father, Son, and Holy Spirit, or Holy Ghost." And the recent, sort of commandment that it will be used is very offensive to me. It really gets in the way. The Trinitarian formula is used extensively in the wedding ceremony, and to me, it doesn't even make sense, whether or not I have problems with it. You know those two places in ritual are difficult for me, in baptism and in the marriage ceremony and, to some degree, in the communion ritual. I have some trouble with the communion ritual in general. Mostly that is not, I don't know if it's a gender-related issue. I do not care much for ritual. It's too static. And, so, I prefer to write my own communion rituals. Sometimes they're pretty extemporaneous. What is firmly associated in my mind, interestingly enough, is an image that the persons who are demanding or insisting on the Trinitarian formula, Father, Son, and Holy Ghost, and who are promoting what is, to my mind, static and rigid, the picture in my mind is that those are males who are insisting on that. . . . I find that both limiting and offensive. (UM6:3–4)[28]

The other ministers I interviewed struggled less with the liturgy of their church. One reported experiencing no difficulties at all. Another acknowledged an isolated difficulty or two, citing the language of the church's "Korean Creed" as an example. A third acknowledged the presence of gender bias, but firmly insisted that it is not and need not be a problem.

My father's a pastor and he's very old-fashioned. When I went to seminary I remember one day we were talking on the phone and he kind of laughed and said, "Wouldn't it be funny, if you got ordained?" But I thought to myself, sort of like Sarah, "This is just ridiculous." You know, laughed to myself, because this is what I am going to do. One time I was visiting with him and he said, "Do you want to help with the baptism?" I said, "Sure" and he let me hold the water. These things could be put-offs to me, but I understand culture. I live in a very male-oriented culture in the South and I have learned to deal with it. I mean, this is my place to live too and I just walk around it. (UM2:2)

When asked what she meant by "walking around it," her response provided an intriguing window into the role of more than one person's will at work behind the organizational facade to which Thomas Greenfield refers:

What it means to me is, if you don't give people power, then they're powerless. . . . Well, an example: . . . They don't do this to me anymore because the hierarchy of the church here . . . has finally learned that I produce; and, bottom line, that's what they want. I mean we're running a business here. That's what the church is. I produce. This church grows, a church that they were trying to close down twelve years ago. We pay all of our conference askings. We're a thriving part of this community by, well, everything that happens in this community happens in our church. But I used to get called in about once a year, like getting chewed out about my dress. My grandfather made cowboy boots and I've worn cowboy boots for fifty-two years. I sit there and listen very politely, "Yes, sir. Yes, sir. Yes, sir," but I continue to wear boots. You know, I don't fight it. I just do it. (UM2:3)

Male Preachers Are an Oddity

United Methodists found questions about icons and symbols somewhat foreign to their experience. At times I was even asked to explain the question used in the protocol, which I attempted to do without leading the interviewees. Nonetheless, half of them expressed some measure of concern in this area. One minister observed:

> I like to visit churches and I like to be in churches. I went to . . . the Christian School of Mission . . . I got to see some wonderful stained glass, but as I wandered around and everyone says, "Ooh and Aah!", I'm so terribly aware that if there are ever people depicted there, they're never women, it is always men. And I must have seen in one church this summer, twenty. It was just filled. And everyone says, "Ooh and Aah!", but isn't it a shame that they're all men. There's always been something that I haven't liked about the raised pulpit, the pulpit that stands up and away from the people, and of course that it has always been occupied by a male. I mean there's always been a male. So, that always has taken on some additional authority for me, that the man was always over me and it was, you know, the God-person, not being on anywhere near an equal level with the people, but raised. And that's always been fairly offensive to me. (UM8:3)

Four of the five respondents had also obviously developed their own strategies for dealing with what they perceived to be the alienating gender orientation of the symbolic in their tradition. As they did with language, some engaged in a process of ongoing revision. These ministers clearly attributed the development of an inclusive symbolic tradition to the efforts of other women in the denomination and not to the denomination, as such.

Another minister noted that her very presence has helped to reshape the symbolic world of her parishioners, particularly that of the children.

> By my being in the church, I make drastic changes without even trying. By my being female, I've been in this church for twelve years. I've got children in this church who think that male preachers are an oddity. . . . To clarify: when I took the children to a Martin Luther King, Jr., memorial service last year and there was a male preacher there who was traditionally very loud, preached in the black tradition; and I happened to look down the row and all the children had their fingers stuck in their ears. I thought it was hysterical, because these are black children and they're use to a quieter voice, a woman's presence. (UM2:2)

Only Nuns

When asked to identify other dimensions of United Methodist culture they found had a gender orientation, the ministers I interviewed identified some of the features of life in the church that other interviewees mentioned. The United Methodist hymnal was cited as a dimension of church life that is more inclusive than it has been in the past. It was also described as an area where some ground had been lost. Two ministers observed that men still dominate the lectionary and church literature. Still others reported that they were self-consciously striving to be more inclusive in the language that they used in workshops and on bulletins.

What was more striking was that seven of the respondents used this juncture in the interview to argue that, not withstanding the progress made in their denomination, the United Methodist church remains male dominated. One minister, still in her thirties, and the newest to pastoral ministry of those interviewed, echoed the comments of others.

> The political tradition within the church . . . is extremely male dominated. . . . Even though there have been women ordained in the Methodist Church for the last 30 to 40 years, and even though there have been women who have served as lay preachers for hundreds of years, the tradition is still, as—I was growing up, was a very male-dominated clergy. In terms of that, I had never known a woman in the clergy role, period, until I decided to be one. I was probably in my early thirties

before I met a woman who was a clergywoman. And the only role model—and that is due to politics—that I ever had for women in ministry were Catholic nuns. And I knew early in my life that celibacy was not one of the things I was bowing to, and since I wasn't Catholic, those two things left me out of being a Catholic nun. So, the only role models, in terms of the church, for me, for women in ministry, were that; and so, a part of my journey into my call, into ordained ministry, was that in reality the call was there for years and years, because the first time I preached was in high school and did a lot of things even at that age. But because of the political system, where the only clergy were men that were visible to me, that was never even a—I didn't hear that call because the images of male clergy limited that, and so, the political realm has been limiting because of gender and alienating too, because as a woman getting into the process, one of the barriers I had to jump was working with men who were supposed to be making judgments about my qualifications on ordination, who made judgments on gender, because they didn't want women ordained. (UM9:4)

Of Celebration and Behavior

Being able to distinguish celebration from behavior is a key to seeing behind the facade of organizational life. A study of United Methodist culture brings us full circle in that effort. At first glance, United Methodist interviewees seem to be more at ease with their denomination than do others, and there are, no doubt, a number of reasons for a certain level of satisfaction. Their denomination has one of the longer histories of ordaining women, and there would appear to be occasion for celebrating recent advances.

Clearly, however, the denomination's "behavior" does not match the "substance of the celebration." Women report being "under employed," serving churches in "dying communities" (UM4:4–5). Even more inclusive conferences have "administrative strongholds" that are "male dominated" (UM3:6). And the careful, if basic, bureaucratic provisions made by the church are often subverted by informal dynamics: stereotyping; a leadership without the will to include women fully in the church's ministry; and a well-entrenched system of promotions protected by more than a little self-interest.

Of concern, too, is the strongly regional character of these patterns. Women are clearly at a greater disadvantage in the south central and southeastern United States. When combining the demographic shifts southward in the church's membership and the looming financial crises conferences elsewhere may face, one is tempted to suggest that even the days for modest celebration may be numbered.

Notes

1. Organized in 1968, the United Methodist Church is a union of the Evangelical United Brethren and the Methodist churches. The church is divided into five jurisdictions, each of which consists of annual conferences; each conference administered by a bishop. In turn, conferences are divided into districts with their own superintendents. For this and other information, see Bedell 1992, 128–32.

2. The history of women's ordination in the United Methodist Church is actually a good deal more complicated, and, for a time, the United Brethren branch made even better progress. See Keller 1984.

3. The part of the 1988 discipline, which governed the church's decisions for the last four years, includes paragraphs 4015; 412–25; and 429–35. The church has recently issued a new discipline, which is substantially the same. See *The Book of Discipline* (1992a).

4. For these insights into the history of this provision, I am indebted the Reverend Robert F. Kohler, Director, Division of Ordained Ministry, The United Methodist Church. The guarantee of an appointment also bolsters the optimism of United Methodists about the future—or, at least, it has. In a survey of nine Protestant denominations conducted in the early 1980s, United Methodists proved to be the most optimistic, with "just under two thirds of men and women believing an upward move will be relatively easy" (Carroll and others 1981, 117).

5. See decision no. 633 in the church's General Minutes.

6. The national headquarters are located in Nashville.

7. The positive attitude expressed here and elsewhere in the interviews, concerning the laity's openness to the ministry of women, is at odds with the findings of George Schreckengost. In a study of United Methodist laity and clergy in the East Ohio Annual Conference, Schreckengost found that "Clergy perceived the level of laity support to be much lower than the laity actually indicated" (Schreckengost 1987, 351).

8. The phrase is taken from the title of an article by Lyle Schaller (1992).

9. There are already differences in the way in which churches relate to girls. One interviewee observes: "Informally how men get encouraged and how women and how teenage girls and teenage boys [get encouraged], there's still probably some difference. . . . I think a person in the church or a Sunday school teacher would be still more likely to say to a young man in his teens, 'Have you ever thought about being an ordained minister?' I think probably boys would still hear that a little more than girls would. I have a teenager and I know people say that to him and I don't hear them talking to the girls in quite that same way" (UM 1:9–10).

10. Emphasis mine.

11. Emphasis mine.

12. Schaller refers to Hunter: 1991.

13. None of this is meant to suggest that problems exist in the South alone. Interviewees from other jurisdictions reported patterns of discrimination, and even women who

were finally accepted by their congregations reported unsettling struggles at the outset of each new appointment. In addition, the denomination's C-4 report is replete with reported failings in both northern and western jurisdictions. See, for example, Euzenas 1989, 15 and 17. It is true, however, that the South has proven far more resistant than have other parts of the country. C-4 was a denominational self-study initiated by the church's Division of Ordained Ministry in 1985. Designed to "assess the reception and experience of white clergywomen, racial/ethnic clergy women and clergy couples" (hence, C-4), the project summary was issued in 1989.

14. For example, they serve more than one church at a time, hence the language "two point charge" or "three point charge."

15. The church's C-4 study reported: "Salary and appointment issues run hand in hand; women who are generally at the low end of the salary scale are, for the most part, serving in predominantly small churches, rural charges, charges in declining areas of population, or as associate pastors. It is interesting to note that in many areas, student pastorates in small rural or low population charges are virtually not available to women who are student pastors; when ordained and ready for appointment, charges of this sort are available in plenty. An S[outh] C[entral] J[urisdiction] conference confirms this in stating 'that mostly rural, small churches [student pastorates] are not open to all C-4's, especially ethnic minorities and women.' An N[orth] E[astern] J[urisdiction] clergywoman notes that 'we have some of our best clergywomen hiding in small or struggling parishes with little chance of moving up to highly respected church positions. The emphasis seems to be on pushing up the bright young men and letting the women earn their own way' " (Euzenas 1989, 17).

16. Compare this comment from the church's C-4 study: "There is strong evidence of collegial mistrust between male and female clergy in many conference areas. A member of one of the consultant teams identified 'some real mistrust of "the women" who might usurp the places of eminence of those men who have "paid their dues" and "rightfully deserved to be elevated' " (Euzenas 1989, 11).

17. As is clear throughout this study, the role of ecclesiastical leaders in facilitating the involvement of women in the ordained ministry of the church cannot be underestimated. Quoting not only United Methodists, but Baptists, Lutherans, and Presbyterians as well, researchers Carroll Hargrove, and Lummis observe: "What these quite typical comments highlight is that for women to be placed it is necessary for judicatory officials of all denominations to be more than pleasant but inactive in support of women clergy; rather, they need to be active advocates if women are to find jobs. One large United Methodist annual conference was cited to the researchers as a case in point. The conference has very few women clergy, and several women have transferred out in recent years. Neighboring conferences, in contrast, have significant numbers of women. The difference is the attitude of the bishops" (1981, 122). See also the denomination's own C-4 self-study in Euzenas 1989, 6.

18. A similar conclusion was reached by the denomination in its own C-4 project. See Euzenas 1989, 6.

19. Statistics provided by the Division of Ordained Ministry of the United Methodist Church, Nashville, Tennessee.

20. The C-4 study concluded that the discrimination experienced by women had,

in some cases, led to a mass exodus of women who had completed the ordination process, leaving entire conferences without experienced women who could provide leadership.

21. This experience, echoed in the responses of other interviewees, is not unique to the clergy I interviewed. Researchers Carroll Hargrove, and Lummis observe: "Many seminary faculty and judicatory officials whom we interviewed expressed the opinion that entry level jobs are really not too problematic—if entering clergy are willing to accept what is available. Their fears, rather, are with second, third, and subsequent calls or placements. Not only does this fear reflect recognition of the present over-supplied job market, but also a suspicion regarding women that they may not be accepted as sole or senior pastors in larger, high-status churches as easily as men. One United Methodist official said, 'The jury is still out on second and third appointments. Will these appointments be horizontal or will [women] in fact be moving in their careers to more responsibility and more opportunity?' A faculty member at an interdenominational seminary echoes this apprehension: 'For a lot of women, it is time to move. They've been in parishes for three or four years. A lot of parishes that were initially open to women have sort of said, "Well, we've done that; we've had our woman," and so second level positions are becoming very difficult. And a lot of my friends are now looking for secular work. They never had any intention of doing that.... One of the things that needs to be raised with women who are in seminary now is to say, "Hey, look, it ain't all cake out there." It is really going to be difficult, and in terms of having a career that grows and develops within parish ministry.... women are going to have to be prepared. I think women going into the ministry today need to be prepared in two professions. That's tragic but I think it is true" (1981, 115–16). Describing the salutary affects of an initial contact with women in pastoral ministry, Edward Lehman cautions: "From the perspective of clergywomen trying to break into the system, these results of contact should be viewed as encouraging. However, there is a little cold water to be felt in relation to these patterns too. While the percent of congregations and individuals open to accepting female pastoral leadership is slowly increasing, there is also some evidence that church members experiencing the successful leadership of one ordained woman do not necessarily generalize to others.... 'Our Mary' may be viewed as a wonderfully competent woman, but Mary is also viewed as unique in her abilities to do 'a man's job.' While the next woman candidate won't be starting at 'scratch' when she applies for the position, she will still have to prove herself as another exception to the dominant pattern of assumptions that the ordained ministry is really a man's job" (Lehman 1987a, 325).

22. The mother of John Wesley. See Keller 1984, 100–101.

23. Georgia Harkness, "pioneered as a female seminary professor" and, among other causes, championed the ordination of women, arguing the case in print as early as 1924. See Keller 1986, 294–303.

24. "Probably the first woman to be ordained in the United Methodist family" (Keller 1984, 113–14).

25. The denomination's C-4 study confirms this finding: "The battle lines are still firmly drawn over the issue of inclusive language. A W[estern] J[urisdiction] C-4 notes, 'misunderstanding of inclusive language continues to be one of the most identifiable places of pain for many clergy ... one of the places where the tension between female and male

clergy is most easily felt.' ... C-4's from an S[outh] C[entral] J[urisdiction] conference report this maxim, which seems to hold true for many conferences in their usage of inclusive language and its success rate: 'Conference, good improvement ... district, so-so ... local church, terrible ... harassment, yes!' " (Euzenas 1989, 13).

26. But, beleaguered by a backlog of other business, General Conference delegates voted overwhelmingly to sidestep debate on language and to trust the work of both the revision panel and the legislative committee" (Burton and Motta 1992). See also "General Conference" (1992c).

27. Compare "General Conference" (1992c).

28. Two of the ministers I interviewed mentioned the affirmation of Trinitarian language made at the church's General Conference in 1988.

4

The Evangelical Lutheran Church in America

Hand in Hand to the Arena, Crucified Alone

A theory of organizations as will and imagination may be summed up in two statements: first, a statement that rejects group mind and rejects an overarching social reality thought to lie beyond human control and outside the will, intention, and action of the individual; second, a statement that acknowledges the tumult and irrationality of thought itself. Acting, willing, passionate, fearful, hoping, mortal, fallible individuals and the events that join them are always more complex, interesting, and real than the ideas we use, forever vainly, to explain them.... It is the individual that lives and acts, not the organization. It is therefore the experience of individuals that we must seek to understand. Huxley says it clearly: "We live together ..., but always in all circumstances we are by ourselves. The martyrs go hand in hand to the arena; they are crucified alone."

—Thomas B. Greenfield, "Leaders and Schools"

Bureaucratic Linkages

In June, 1967 the Church Council, the governing body of what was then the American Lutheran Church, requested that the Lutheran Council in the U.S.A., Division of Theologi-

77

cal Studies, examine the issue of women's ordination. Based upon the
council's work, a committee was formed with the mandate to make recommendations to the 1970 meeting of the Church Council. Rooted perhaps to some degree in the ambiguities of Luther's own claims to a
legitimate ordination, a resolution calling for the ordination of women
was submitted by the committee.

WHEREAS, A Statement of Findings Relating to the Requested Study on
the Subject of the Ordination of Women has been adopted and made
available by the Standing Committee of the Division of Theological
Studies, Lutheran Council U.S.A.; and

WHEREAS, The *ad hoc* Committee on the Ordination of Women concurs
in the Statement of Findings; and

WHEREAS, The American Lutheran Church accepted the following statement in 1964 with reference to ministry:

"Since the ministerial office is not precisely defined in the New Testament, and since the duties of early officers were varied and interchange-
able, and since the needs of the church down through the centuries are
subject to variation, we are led to Luther's conclusion, namely, that God
has left the details of the ministerial office to the discretion of the church,
to be developed according to its needs and according to the leading of
the Holy Spirit;" and

WHEREAS, Men and women are both resources for ministry in the church
and each other in the pastoral ministry; and

WHEREAS, Women are prepared to serve and have been certified for call
and ordination; therefore be it

RESOLVED, That the Church Council be requested to recommend to the
General Convention which will meet in San Antonio in October of
1970, that women be eligible for call and ordination in The American
Lutheran Church. ("Reports and Actions," 1970, 327)

The recommendation was accepted and, in the same year, the church
acted to change its constitution, introducing inclusive language where
male nouns and pronouns had dominated. Similar provisions were made

by the Lutheran Church in America, so, when the two churches merged in 1987, the most basic bureaucratic provisions for the ordination of women were clear, unambiguous, and already in place.[1]

The Quota System

An even more important factor in providing for the measure of security women experience, however, may be the ELCA's quota system.[2] Mentioned by nine of the participants, the quota system insures the placement of women on boards and committees at both the synodical and national levels. Significantly, the system itself is lodged in the church's "Constitutions, Bylaws, and Continuing Resolutions."

> Except as otherwise provided in this constitution and bylaws, the churchwide organization, through the Church Council shall establish processes that will ensure that at least 60% of the members of its assemblies, councils, committees, boards, and other organizational units shall be laypersons; that as nearly as possible, 50% of the lay members of their assemblies, councils, committees, boards, or other organizational units shall be female and 50% shall be male, and that where possible, the representation of ordained ministers shall be both female and male. . . . Processes shall be developed that will assure that in selecting staff there will be a balance of women and men, persons of color, and persons whose primary language is other than English, laypersons, and persons on the roster of ordained ministers. This balance is to be evident in terms of both executive staff and support staff consistent with the inclusive policy of this church. (1989, 21–22)[3]

For the ministers with whom I spoke this system demonstrates a willingness on the part of their denomination to enforce what they claim to believe about the participation of women in the ministry of the church. The system also appears to ameliorate the sense of exclusion that women might otherwise feel. There is comfort in knowing that there are women represented on the church's committees and boards, whether they themselves are actually there, or not. Indeed, when asked if women are included at the national level in the church's decision-making process, interviewees who were clearly not involved answered, in an off-handed manner, "Yes, because we have a quota system" (ELCA5:7).

The Trickle-Down Theory

The quota system, however, has serious limitations, and Lutheran ministers are aware of them. For one, quotas apply only to the national level. Neither synods nor local churches are required to apply the same principles of inclusion to their work. "The quotas really only affect who serves on national committees and who is a delegate to a synod assembly. How a particular synod is organized in terms of who is serving in the various capacities, that is not covered by quotas. That really just depends on the individual synod and that's where the conservatism and liberals will come in" (ELCA5:8).

Furthermore, even at the national level, quotas extend only to membership in the church's bureaucratic machinery (i.e., its commissions and administrative offices). They do not guarantee that women will be given leadership roles, even on the national level. "I think in terms of staffing of committees and commissions and some offices, there is certainly the groundwork or the polity-work laid for that. . . . There are, of course, no women presidents of seminaries, there are very few women deans. . . . There are very few women heads of commissions. There is a woman who is the lay vice president, the vice president of the church, but she is a lay person and not an ordained person" (ELCA1:13).

One could, of course, hope that such quotas would model an approach readily adopted on other levels and in other arenas, and, in some cases, interviewees reported that their bishops provided leadership to that end. Whether for lack of numbers, legislative legitimacy or commitment, however, the policy has not found the measure of matter-of-fact expression on the synodical level that it has found on the national level. Interviewees argue they often represent only a token presence on the committees to which they are assigned and that even that level of inclusion is contested by "traditionalists" or "black shirts," who argue that other standards should be used in determining the composition of councils and committees.

On the synod council and on any political decision-making body, women have to be included. We do have a very strong policy about that. For example, for our synod conventions and stuff, they have to be sixty percent lay and forty percent clergy. Of the sixty percent, it has to be always 50/50 male/female in the lay population. Among the clergy on our synod council and all those kinds of things there are provisions made for inclusion of women. Now the women do complain on occasion that they feel like tokens, because they are the one or the two only, and there are some moves underfoot amongst our conservative "black shirts" who say let's use spiritual gifts, rather than gender. (ELCA4:11)

Indeed, in the judgment of some, the principles applied at the national level have simply failed to find widespread expression elsewhere. "I think that at the national level they are a bit more intentional about involving women. Again, there is a smaller pool of women clergy to choose from, but it seems to me that at the national level there are women in some pretty influential spots and they are pretty intentional about gender, language, all that kind of stuff and placing them. It just hasn't trickled down very well" (ELCA3:3).

Woman and the Episcopacy

Still more troubling is the all but complete exclusion of women from the episcopacy. Although women were eligible to serve as bishops for sixteen years, the Reverend April Urling Larson, Bishop of the La Crosse Area Synod in Wisconsin, was the first woman ever elected to the office ("It Took Just," 1992e). The church has sixty-five synods. It is not surprising that, while her election is a cause for celebration in some quarters, it also elicits a certain amount of cynicism as well.

I don't know, I just see a lot of selling out. You sell out if you want to survive. Somebody asked me the other day, "Now that the ELCA has a woman bishop, do you think things will change?" No, I don't. I don't. She's going to have to conform, or she's going to be out. She can do a few liberal things, because they'll expect her to do them, because she's a woman, but she's going to have to be very, very careful. So, I don't see changes coming. (ELCA10:7)

Certainly it is the bishops who shape the church now. Ostensibly, they are bound by the church's constitution, and when seminarians (male or female) first enter the ministry, the ELCA uses a bureaucratic mechanism designed to work in favor of inclusion, a process one interviewee aptly likened to a pro-football "draft."

When we come out of seminary it is like the football drafts for Lutheran seminarians. All our names are submitted to Chicago and we get divided up dependent on the need of the synod, rather than the preference of the bishop or whatever. So, for example, come November the bishop of _____ says, "I need seven pastors, or eight pastors because I have eight vacancies." And the bishop from _____ says, "I only need three." There is a whole board that will make the decisions as to how the seminarians are divided up. (ELCA4:12)

Notwithstanding this system, however, the experience and careers of most ministers is strongly shaped by the commitments of individual bishops.

You know, a lot of it [i.e., the effective administration of the provisions for women's ordination and deployment] depends on the local bishop. The standards are there and the paperwork is all there, but some bishops are more aggressive at placing women than others. For instance, I know some bishops who will have a candidate and the church will say, "We don't want a female candidate" and they say, "Okay, we will find you someone else." Other bishops will say, "No, I'm sorry, this is the candidate and you must interview her" and so then we will go from there. So a lot of it depends on how committed the bishop is to making that happen. (ELCA3:3)

Some bishops have obviously distinguished themselves in their attempts to include women in the ministry of the church. Some have applied the quotas used on the national level to the work done in their synods. An isolated few, in fact, could arguably be described as having a better record in this regard than does the national church. One minister, in particular described the work of two successive bishops in her synod:

I will always be grateful for the way things happened when I was looking to change denominations. I was really welcomed quite warmly into, well, at the time it was LCA before the church merger; and the bishop at that time ordained more women pastors than any other bishop in the ELCA during his tenure.... He was extremely supportive of women candidates [and] would not meet with call committees seeking a new pastor if they would not consider women. He's been a real advocate.... And right now we have a new bishop who is entering his second year. He's much younger but has four assistants working with him and [he] has two women assistants. . . . That's been another helpful thing. (ELCA1:12–13)

Others, at a minimum, have distinguished themselves in their attempts to place women in parishes, even when the churches themselves have been resistant.

Our synod, our bishop, has set up some rules about inclusion of women. If a name is submitted or if the bishop submits a name to the congregation and it's a woman and the congregation says, "We don't hire women" or "We don't call women," the bishop has this rule to say that "I'm not going to give you another name until you reconsider—next year or whenever you change your mind. So, at least on the bishop's level, as far as the call of women is concerned, he's very firm about that. He will not take any flack in that respect. He will not allow a congregation to say, "We don't call women." (ELCA4:10–11)

A rare bishop has also placed a woman in charge of overseeing the actual call process.

Fear, Resistance, Sexism, and "the Call"

In the estimate of one of the women I interviewed, the vast majority of synods do not possess the kind of episcopal leadership that fosters inclusion. The interviewees offer several explanations. One is fear. Bishops may be granted apparently sweeping power, but they also clearly attempt to "win" the continued good will of people, whose participation and cooperation are to some degree voluntary in nature. In one sense pastors may not serve voluntarily, but they can claim with varying degrees of legitimacy to represent the views of people voluntarily involved in the life of the church.

Closely related is a second explanation—the resistance of the congregations themselves. Although, in the view of the women I spoke to, bishops need not and should not be deterred from providing women with interviews, it is equally clear that in some synods congregations regularly resist interviewing and calling women. To some extent this dynamic will continue to shape the experience of Lutherans, because the emphasis upon "call" leaves the initiative in the hiring process with the individual congregation. Reflecting on a conversation with her bishop, one interviewee observed:

> I think they try to involve women at the synod level in committee and that type of leadership, but . . . I don't think they do a very effective job at getting women into pulpits in a lot of the congregations in this area. . . . The way our system is, when a congregation asks for candidates, they usually receive three biographies, and many of the congregations choose which of those three they will choose to interview. Many will choose simply not to interview a woman. . . . The bishop told us recently at a meeting that there's never a call that he does not offer a woman's name, but, that congregations choose, for whatever reason, not to interview. (ELCA6:8–9)

A third explanation offered is the bishops' own sexism. Reflecting on her experience and that of a colleague in a previous synod, one minister observed:

> Not every bishop is the same. The synod where I came from is very sexist and not very helpful to women. A friend of mine. . . . who was already a pastor in the synod, heard about a pastoral vacancy and felt that she was absolutely the right person for this particular call. She called the bishop's assistant and said she wanted to have her name submitted to this congregation for consideration. The bishop's assistant said he wasn't going to do that, so Marsha camped in front of his door until he did. And she got the call. The call was, indeed, right for her. So down there, you have to kind of take some radical steps to be heard every once in a while. (ELCA4:10)

Organizational Culture

Together, factors such as these may help to explain the snail's pace at which women are finding their way into the ministry of the ELCA. A 1990 report on the participation of ordained women in the denomination reveals that at the time there were 1,198 ordained women in the church's ministry. That figure represents 6.3 percent of the total clergy. However, while the number of ordained women within the church has increased, there has been no significant increase in the proportion of the total clergy represented by women (Pellauer 1990).[4]

Hand in Hand into the Arena

Statistics of this kind, in a denomination with a number of bureaucratic provisions for the ordination of women in place, suggest that the church's culture may somehow mitigate against the full inclusion of women. In this regard, the interviewees were not so much polarized, as they were seemingly unaware of the experience of one another. There were those who were positive about their church and its degree of inclusivity; one compared her previous experience in the United Methodist church, concluding that the change had been a good one. Another noted that, fortunately, younger women do not need to experience the stereotypes of the past. And a third conceded that her experience may have been colored by the people she has met, but she had found the Lutheran church consistently affirming. A fourth interviewee sidestepped the issue noting that she read and heard the gospel as a message that unites.

The remaining six were not as uniformly positive as their colleagues, and, although there was no single complaint, there were criticisms voiced by more than one participant. The most frequent criticism was that, in the final analysis, Lutheran culture is male dominated. The exact expression it was given varied, however. As had women in other denominations, one minister argued that "an old boys' network" shaped the "call system."[5] Another reported that she had encountered a typically male approach to leadership:

> I am a consensus builder. In the past . . . the experiences I've had of [a] negative nature . . . have been with male leaders being very dictatorial, the "Herr Pastor" types, not that all males are, but I have known some that are, and have felt that for me that was not commensurate with being a leader, a person whom God had called into the ministry. So. . . . I strive to be democratic in leadership and to get input from many places, many people, to have people feel that this is their congregation, and they have input wherever they want it. You can't have four hundred people making major decisions, although we do try to vote on most things, but at least to have input and give and take. I think that's very important, so that people can really identify with being a part of the people of God. If everything is dictated to them "from above," what stake do they have in what the church is? (ELCA2:3–4)

Perhaps the observation that most clearly underlines the analysis of Lutheran culture as male dominated was a broader assessment made by still another interviewee:

> One thing that I have seen in the Lutheran church and probably other denominations also, is that even though the ELCA is called liberal I think that it isn't. I think that on social issues that deal with Central America or South Africa, I think the ELCA is liberal. But, when it comes to what is going on at home, it's not; even though the words are there, the actions aren't. The church is still covering up for what is going on. What scares me is that it's not in the open. That it's something that's covered up and we are not as honest as we used to be. At least the Catholics are saying, "Well, you know you can't be ordained and women are this and that. Jesus is a male and all of those things." They might be silly arguments but at least they are saying something. The Lutherans are ordaining women, but when you look at how many women are in the congregations after five years, there aren't very many, and you wonder what happened to them. It just seems to me that the Lutheran church isn't being very honest about what's going on. (ELCA10:6)

The same woman's comments may also provide one key to the conflicted picture interviewees gave me of their church.

> I did my internship in a very liberal congregation. It was wonderful! We had an inclusive ministry committee, and I got to take charge of that and do what I wanted. I had lots of freedom. They did a lot of social action sorts of things, and it was just a wonderful place to intern. Then I interviewed for this position at St. _____, and the guy knew where I had interned and this internship congregation has a reputation. Everyone knows that it's like that, and he was telling me that, yes, St. _____ is like that and I would have all the freedom. Well, it wasn't true . . . In a congregation like St. _____, which is much more conservative (and it's more like the normal Lutheran congregations) the person either (a woman especially) has to fall into line and do what's expected or you just don't last. It's really sad. What I have seen over the years is that most women conform. . . . I have seen a lot of women sell out. They stay in the system and they think that they can make a change from within the system. I used to think that too, that I could do something that would make women feel

comfortable in the system and make it work for women and for men who are uncomfortable with the patriarchal system. . . . But, I have come to believe that that's not true. (ELCA10:7)

Crucified Alone

The culture of the Lutheran church has had an impact on the careers of women I interviewed—which is a mirror image of the conflicted picture I saw elsewhere. Three ministers reported having had trouble-free experiences in the churches they serve. Of those three, one described her experience as "very positive." Another did not deny that there is sexism in the church, but she defined her ministry in a manner that made sexism an irrelevancy. Responding to the way in which the question was phrased, she observed: "The first thing that came to me was the word "career," which bothers me, because I am not in a career. I'm in a call. By looking at it as a call rather than a career, I think it makes a difference. I'm not in this to try to 'get ahead' as I would be in a career. I'm in the ministry because I feel called to it. Although there might be some resistance here and there, it's not going to make a difference to what I'm called to do" (ELCA5:3).[6]

Another of the interviewees acknowledged that sexism is prevalent and she confronts it whenever possible. Indeed her estimate of the ELCA's culture is all the more telling because she "grew up" in Germany.

I have to tell you that my first pastor, when I grew up in Germany, was a woman. It never occurred to me that women couldn't do this. The first pastor I ever remember seeing or identifying as a pastor was female, and that was in Germany. And so, for me, that was always a career option that was just like any other. And I also have to say that I think my father was one of the first feminists in his day and age. He was born in 1905, and at the same time when I was growing up, the one thing that I remember him saying over and over again was "I don't care what you do with your life, just whatever it is, do it well." He always encouraged and celebrated with his daughters anything they tried. And so, for me, coming into a culture that was a lot more sexist, at first I think, shocked me, but it didn't overwhelm me. It really didn't, because I think I had a really strong foundation, given my religious upbringing at home and my father's unconditional grace toward me. I think I had

that always to fall back on if things weren't going very well, or if I ran
into some attitudes or something like that. (ELCA5:5)

On another level, however, her strategy for dealing with sexism was
broadly similar to that of the interviewee described above.

I know it's out there, I mean, it's even in my own congregation. I know
that sexism is out there, but I don't want to become a one-agenda
person. If I let that rule my life, then it's like the bastards have won. I
can't make that my number-one issue and my number-one agenda. I
simply refuse to let anger about that build up or any of those kinds of
things. That's not what the kingdom of God is about as far as I'm
concerned. I will call them to justice. I will do the best that I can to
speak about how sexism and discrimination and all of those kinds of
things are not in keeping with the kingdom of God, but I won't make
that my number-one priority. (ELCA5:5–6)

The majority of the women I interviewed, however, had a very different experience. Some of them confronted considerable resistance initially,
much of it revolving around sex-role stereotypes. In some cases those
stereotypes narrowed the number of positions actually open to women,
and, as a result, the search process was often longer for women than for
men. One minister's story hints at the dynamics involved:

I'm pretty positive that I would not have been called to this church had
they not been in very, very desperate straits, which they were. They
had three pastorates within the previous seven years to my being called.
Initially, the concerns [were] about having woman pastors. They were
mortified that I would have a baby; also, that my husband's job would
change; and that I would leave to follow him, wherever that might take
him. My husband is also ordained, and there were some expectations
for us to work, that they would be getting more than one person's work
within our parish. (ELCA1:3)

More than one woman indicated that gender had an affect on the
kind of salaries they had been given by their churches. One interviewee
observed:

My sneaking suspicion is that because it was assumed that my husband
was the breadwinner and was making lots of money, that my salary

could, therefore, be less than what it should be. I . . . you may guess from my voice, that I did not agree with that. And for the first, I would say, five years of this call, I literally felt I was fighting an uphill battle for equity in pay. That has changed, I'm happy to say. This congregation merged . . . so now I do feel that my pay is where it should be in terms of my years of experience, etc. But early on—I have been ordained almost 11 years—I did not feel fairly compensated and I definitely felt my gender and my marital status were negative factors in that regard. (ELCA2:9)

Not surprisingly the differences in salaries may be related to the nature of the calls women have received. In a rare moment of awareness of what women elsewhere in the church have experienced, one interviewee observed:

I think I'm probably one of the luckier ones. Part of that is because I have been called to larger congregations in areas where the people have been aware of women in professional positions for a long time. I think other women in smaller, rural congregations in the ELCA might not have been so blessed. The communities don't receive them with the same positive outlook. I don't know that from personal experience, but in hearing some of their stories, I hear them in quite a bit more pain in the process than I've experienced. (ELCA6:2)

Similarly, another interviewee observed:

I have to say that women in the Lutheran church, . . . are still in smaller congregations, . . . that the big cushy jobs in large churches, big senior pastor things, are still primarily male. That sometimes bishops, if they are consistent in their inclusion of women have a hard time trying to get women to be called. But I think it depends on the area, the geographical area; it depends upon the size of the congregation and age of the congregation; it depends on all kinds of factors. Our congregation, for example, is a very young congregation. The majority of our members are under forty-five. I'd say like eighty-five percent are forty-five. They are much more receptive to a woman pastor than, let's say, a congregation of 100 people out in the country whose age range is over sixty, because they are much more close knit and can be much more resistant to having a woman pastor. (ELCA4:11)

Statistics gathered by the denomination confirm these impressions. Although there has been a 26.9 percent increase in the number of ordained women, that represents only a .5 percent increase in their proportions to the total number of ELCA ministers. Of note too, are the numbers of women "on leave from call." Out of all male clergy, 6.8 percent are "on leave from call." By contrast, 12.4 percent of all women are on leave. Women are also 4.5 times more likely to be serving part-time, accounting for "fully one-third of all clergy" serving in that capacity (Pellauer 1990).

On the "Mommy Track"

The effect, then, of informal dynamics on the careers of Lutheran ministers has been considerable. Beyond issues of job availability and salary, however, one of the most striking affects has been on the style of ministry interviewees have adopted. Reflecting on the expectations of her church, one minister said:

> I remember a couple of years into my pastorate, the council vice-president at that time confided to me that at the call meeting she had really spoken up for me, saying that they should vote for me because I would be different. All the men who had come before me had been ambitious, and, as a woman, I—the center of my life would be my home and my church—I would stay there for them. I was really angry when I heard that, even though it might have brought me the votes I needed to clinch the job. (ELCA1:3)

Nor were all of the women I spoke with simply expected to be less ambitious. More than one had apparently conformed to this expectation, shunning all but the responsibilities in her "call."

> I think being a woman means that, for me, my family has a large place in my life. So, there's this constant tension between how much time I put into my family and how much I put into my career. So, I'm the one that says to the guys, "I'm not going to work four nights a week doing meetings. I need to be home with my family." What I've discovered is that the congregation has honored that. Whereas, the other pastors they kind of say, "Well, of course you have meetings every night of the week." They'll say to me, "Don't you think you should take some time off and be with your husband?" I think that's—again, because I'm a

woman, they've been very affirming of not only my ministry but also my personal life.... I discovered that most of the men that I work around or work with don't ask for personal time. In fact, they are quite proud of the fact that they've taken fewer vacation days than anybody else and they've never had a sick day. I guess, I don't feel that same pride in being a workaholic. Even though I am a workaholic, I don't tell people about it because I'm kind of embarrassed by it. That doesn't seem to be what a woman should be doing in the ministry. (ELCA6:2)

Inevitably, women are less often a force in denominational in-groups, and where they are involved, they tend to be women without young children. Focusing on their efforts in the local church, they have developed what many of them describe as a distinctively feminine style of ministry, which provides a much-needed "mother image," "openness," and the kind of "patience" necessary in small, "troublesome" parishes. Other areas of involvement and leadership are postponed for later in life.

With women, I think it's mostly what I call the "senior women pastors," people who preceded me into the church ... by probably five to ten years, who either have grown family or no family, women who are single or do not have children, and then, also some very young, new women pastors who also do not have family—are either single or do not have children. Within the men, it's a much more mixed group. Mostly people who are, you know, more vocal, and some who are very good leaders.... I think there's very decidedly a "Mommy track" within the church, and I'm on it, if not the head of the pack. Part of it's practicality. Like I've mentioned before, who has time to focus their attention in a really meaningful way on so many things? The parish is a very demanding animal, at least it is in my experience. My family is a very demanding—taking care of my family is a very demanding role for me, and I don't want to do a bad job of that. There just isn't time enough or energy enough or focus enough for me, and I think it's also true for other women who are having families, to get involved in synodical things to a great degree.... Of course the men are not the primary providers, you know, care-providers for their children, and so it doesn't matter how old they are, they always have somebody else at home who is helping to cover family needs. And, I don't think that they choose their involvements nearly so much based upon family commitments, as women are forced to.... I was on the Candidacy Committee for two or three years. They of course work with seminary students who are in

various stages of preparation for the ministry. . . . My church is very
into this inclusivity, and all of the committees and boards and everything
are staffed with attention to a balance in gender and a balance in race
and ethnicity. So, I was chosen to be "one of the females" on this group.
That was really supposed to be a good thing. I quit before the end of
my term because of my frustration of being on the committee. When it
came to interviewing candidates we used to take turns leading the interviews, I found men, even men I knew and liked, talking over me, kind
of dismissing my comments. I remember at one point asking a woman
who had just had a baby how her experience of motherhood had perhaps affected her understanding of her ministry, and they called that
question and said we could talk about those things later; we could talk
about those mother things later, after the interview. And I was very,
very angry at that because I thought it was a very legitimate question,
certainly one that I could have elaborated on at length had I been in
that person's shoes. . . . I think I certainly have the capacity to serve
well in any of those positions, and I do believe that given another fifteen
years, I will probably be there, if not in this synod, someplace else.
(ELCA1:9–10)

"Black Shirts"

Given the patterns of discrimination and the choice made by some
women to opt out of leadership roles (even temporarily), it is not surprising to find that the in-groups of the denomination are often male dominated. "Climbers," "workaholics," and the "pastors of large churches,"
the members of such groups are described as theologically conservative,
defending (in particular) a kind of liturgical purity.

> I can tell you that for our synod there is a definite in-group. . . . We
> have what I and a whole bunch of other folks would call the "black
> shirts." The black shirts are those clergy who are extremely conserva-
> tive and think that the only thing that keeps the Lutheran tradition
> whole and together is our liturgical tradition, and all they want to do is
> perform "the rightness of the rite," is what I would call it. They are
> extremely conservative, extremely law-oriented, and they have, at least
> in our synod, some powerful voices in the synod council, and they,
> at least, have the bishop's ear partially. He's afraid of them.
> (ELCA4:9)

Wielding very real power in some synods, the in-group influences the bishop. In others, the bishop actually plays a role in selecting members. One interviewee described the in-group in her synod as a hand-picked circle of people whose responsibility was to bail out the bishop.

Doing What She's Supposed To

As with the ministers in other denominations, the majority of the Lutherans interviewed began with the Bible, and nine women mentioned it at some point in the interview. Out of those nine, seven described the text entirely in positive terms—some because they simply found nothing there having a striking gender orientation and one because she had originally belonged to the considerably more conservative Missouri Synod.

Respondents identified many of the same stories cited by women in other traditions and, as in other traditions, they focused primarily on stories involving women: Mary Magdalen, Mary the mother of Jesus, Martha, and the woman at the well (among others). Lutheran ministers also tended to tell stories that validated their ministry or modeled struggle and persistence—sometimes in silence. In addition they contributed to the body of stories I heard, citing the description in Isaiah of God as a woman comforting her child and the inclusivity of the message found in the Gospel of Luke.

But not all mentioned stories or images centering on women. One of the participants observed: "The gospel story speaks to me in a kind of holistic way. And I don't feel that stories of particular women in the Bible, or stories of men, are that influential, other than contributing to a whole picture of people whose lives have been built up and guided by God in many different ways" (ELCA1:1).

In contrast to respondents from other denominations, there were far fewer women who reported having been adversely affected by the biblical text. One described it only in a negative light, and another found the Bible problematic, as well as affirming. The stories that figured prominently in the interviews included the rape of Lot's daughter, the description of qualifications for ministry in First Timothy, and the portrayal of the woman at the well.

It is this near complete absence of struggle that may help to explain the near complete absence of strategies for reading biblical text, which I found so often in other traditions. Only one of the interviewees hinted that she experimented with such an approach. "Part of what I wanted to do was to reinterpret some of the stories. . . . The Mary and Martha story has been a problem for me, because Martha's always the one getting the short end of the stick. That's the way women are brought up. I think, 'Fine, here she is doing what she's supposed to be doing and she gets ragged on for it.' And I think, 'Hardly fair' " (ELCA10:1).

Neither Katie nor Martin

The Lutheran tradition figured far less prominently in the thinking of the interviewees than did the Bible and, relatively speaking, it fared less well. Two of the ministers began with the Bible, and a total of four eventually mentioned the church's heritage. Without exception, conversations focused on Luther, and discussion was evenly divided in its evaluation of Luther's impact on them. Far from finding Luther's story merely accessible, one interviewee felt that the reformer's story actually provided authorization for her own insistence that women be included in the church's ministry. "Luther's story is one of being exceedingly radical for his time and place and being willing to speak out from his own point of view. I think that carries over into the gender issue, giving courage and permission to be radical" (ELCA7:1).

By contrast, however, others felt that Luther's story and that of his family was one of a "troubled" man whose experience is hardly "normative." Indeed, two of the respondents felt that neither his example, nor that of his wife, Katie, possesses a point of contact with which women can identify.

> One of those that was a negative, that is commonly used, is Martin Luther's wife, Katie, who was this sort of support for him and raised all these children for him. . . . That was not a particularly helpful one for me, because she was the "sidekick," the one who fed all his friends and kept food on the table and managed the household and raised all these children . . . that didn't help at all, in where I wanted to go. And I suppose the strong emphasis on just Martin Luther, as a male who did all these things and no strong female stories was a negative. (ELCA3:1)

Unlike ministers of other denominations, Lutherans mentioned no other figures from their tradition.

Strongly into Male Language

A similar picture emerged in the discussions of language, but in this case the respondents were more evenly and more deeply divided. Five women reported that the language of their tradition contained nothing of a gender orientation that they found "personally troublesome." According to three of them, their level of satisfaction was due to the fact that the denomination had been open to "healthy debate" and an ongoing process of liturgical revision. Together, these provisions had resolved most if not all of the difficulties the women experienced. Others in the same group identified themselves as people who (for a variety of reasons) were already comfortable with the traditional formulations used by the church. One observed, for example:

> In the Lutheran church at the present—well, I'm sure it's not just within the Lutheran church—there is a healthy debate going on the Trinitarian formula and language used for God. The Lutheran church being rather traditional in that way—use of Father, Son, and Holy Spirit within the liturgy of our church—it's just such a part of it that I think it's going to be hard to extricate that. And, that's not been something that's been a particularly problematic issue with me. That terminology has positive meaning for me, and I have no roadblocks through my life experience that make it difficult. Of course, otherwise in the liturgy, we are encouraged to make our language more inclusive, both in preaching and in worship. But, I would probably be more of a traditionalist along those lines. (ELCA1:3)

An equal number of women found the language of the church clearly alienating. This half of the interviewees cited language used to describe God, traditional Trinitarian formulations, the maleness of Jesus, and a lack of sensitivity to the presence of women in the church. These same women also argued that it is the national church, the seminaries, and women's groups, not the local congregations, which are making progress in their use of language.

> As far as language, most of it has been negative. We're very strongly into male language in the Lutheran church. There are breakthroughs in that. Mostly when it's done is in women's groups that have gotten together, whether it's a study group or a worship group, or something

like that. We've talked a lot about language and use inclusive language. And, at seminary, inclusive language was stressed very much. But for the most part in growing up, and for the most part in my church experience, it's been all male language. And that has been real frustrating to me. . . . God language is bothersome a little but not as much as the people language (mankind, all men should be brothers, councilmen) it's a church hierarchy . . . that's changing some. At the national level, I feel good about that. As you get down closer to the local level, it gets worse. I find that the argument there is that most people just don't think about it. They are so used to that language that it seems normal to them, and attempts to change it sound very odd to them. There's also a real strong Lutheran witness toward Father, Son, and Holy Spirit, and that's it. It can't be any other words and, that's bothersome. (ELCA3:3)

A Feminine Sacrament

Attitudes toward the ritual of the church were also divided. On the whole, a greater number of the women I interviewed were positive about the ritual of the church. This perspective, however, appears to have more to do with a view of Christian ritual as intrinsically feminine in character.

I think the richness of the liturgical tradition and the richness of the Lutheran tradition in and of itself is something that is very good for women, because I think we are, as a gender, more symbol-rich and we live there more easily than males do. I think for women, particularly, all the different kinds of symbols in the Lutheran tradition—anything from the robes and the colors to all those kinds of things—are helpful because I think for us that's something as a gender, that we've always lived with—we've been the "keepers" of family traditions and family symbols. So, for me as a woman, it's been very easy to live in a symbol-rich and liturgically rich tradition. (ELCA4:2–3)

One of the few who objected to ritual argued that the church insists on doing what women have already done.

Baptism was something that I really enjoyed and it was something that I thought was meaningful . . . I had heard . . . the complaints from other feminists that it's just a way of taking away from what a woman does and it's redoing a birth or something, but I thought there were ways of explaining and reinterpreting and making it useful for myself and for

other people.... Now I'm to a point where, if I had small children, I
don't know what I would do about getting a child baptized, because it
does seem to me that it has become a way of taking something away
that was already there. And it concerns me when people talk about
becoming a child of God at baptism and I think about the children who
aren't baptized. Are they not children of God? I don't believe that. So,
that's been a question for me, and then I think of the place of communion and feeding of people and something that has traditionally been a
woman's thing, but now it's ... been taken over by ordained clergy and
put into this ritualistic mode. (ELCA1:3–4)

Unique to the interviews was one argument that the "sameness" of
ritual is, itself, characteristically male. Clarifying her view by comparing
men with women, the interviewee observed:

I do think that one of the gifts women offer is a willingness to be
innovative and to take risks and to be more interpersonal in leading
worship, to be more informal. I see that as among my gifts, and I have
seen that in others of my gender. I'm not saying that men cannot or do
not do that, but there is a process, I think, that women, being seen
sometimes to be more relational, find these kinds of gifts and approaches
easier than some of my male counterparts do. (ELCA2:2)

A Cross of Oppression

All but two of the ministers found something to say about icons and
symbols. However, it was clear that the women lacked a strong orientation to both the iconographic and the symbolic. Few symbols and icons
were cited, and four of the respondents were unable to identify icons of
either an affirming or an alienating kind.

As far as gender orientation is concerned, six participants responded
positively to the symbolic in their tradition. One of the six acknowledged
that there are those, however, who find the tradition's symbols difficult.
Another, though positive about the tradition's symbols, was selective in
her response, noting that she found three intertwined circles a more
positive image than others her traditions uses for the Trinity.

Nor were all of the respondents positive about the symbols used in
their church. Two found the symbols of the tradition either completely
alienating or mixed in character. One, reflecting on the symbolism of the

cross, observed: "That verse that says, "Take up your cross and follow me," indicates that not only must I give up my identity to a man, but now I must give up even more—my whole self" (ECLA10:20). The other interviewee seemed to share these sentiments, but had ultimately come to a somewhat different conclusion:

> For me, personally, I looked at the word "icon," and of course in my tradition as a Lutheran, the theology of the cross and the cross itself is the one icon that we hold to. For me, that has always been both extremely attractive and also repellent. Let me begin with the repellent part: As a woman the one verse in the Scripture that has always been an outrage to me was "pick up your cross and follow me." The reason it was always repellent to me was because as a woman I had been raised to give up all identity that I already had. So, to "pick up my cross" was a preface, rather than the word of freedom directed towards me. Women are very quick to give up the identity that they do have. They are already picking up their crosses too much and giving away too much, and, I think that's their sin. It wasn't until I started recognizing this [that] it became a symbol of freedom rather than oppression. The attraction of the cross is indeed that at the foot of the cross with Jesus any kind of notions—cultural notions of who we are, our whole identity of male and female, power, all those kinds of things—die with Jesus on that cross. It becomes the ultimate symbol of freedom that there are no pretensions left that I can bring forward or anybody else over against me in the symbol of the cross, but, it took me a while to get to that point. Originally, the cross was very oppressive because I thought women were indeed oppressed by that symbol. I don't feel that way anymore. (ELCA4:2)

We Are by Ourselves

In the course of interviewing, I spoke first with a number of Roman Catholics and then with Lutherans. The order was determined entirely by chance. During the interview process, against the backdrop of the Roman Catholic experience described in Chapter 6, I jokingly referred to ministers in the ELCA as the "happy Lutherans." Relatively speaking, they appeared to work in a more supportive atmosphere, in which a far greater number of provisions had been made for their involvement in the church's ministry; and, certainly, measured against the experience of Roman Catholic women, that is undoubtedly true.

In reexamining the interview material at length, however, I discovered that the interviewees were neither as positive as I first thought, nor as widely impressed with their denomination as I thought. Just beneath the surface of the scattered affirmations of Lutheran life lies a heavy undercurrent of protest against the ELCA's male orientation. "Polarized" is probably too strong a word for the seemingly contradictory points of view I discovered, since the tensions are not widely felt, nor is dissent given strong public expression. Indeed, at times I sensed that those who were comfortable with the church's orientation were scarcely aware of those who were not. But it is a deeply "conflicted" culture, as the discussion of stories illustrates.

How one accounts for this silent contradiction is difficult to say. A partial explanation probably lies with the considerable diversity of the ELCA, which is marked by perhaps as much or more ethnic diversity than is found in any other denomination.[7] One interviewee, however, offered another explanation:

> I think that some of what happens to Lutheran women is that they latch onto the words and blindly hope against hope and believe—sometimes contrary to the reality with which they are faced—that the words are true. It reminds me of children from dysfunctional families who are confused by all of the mixed messages that they receive. They believe in order to survive. It would not surprise me to find out that this is why Lutheran women are less discouraged than those in other denominations. . . . Lutherans have been thrown just enough crumbs to keep them loyal and relatively quiet. If a woman dares to speak up, she's not grateful for all she's been given. She's one of *those* who wants it all. (ECLA10:21)

Fleshing out his theory of organizational life, Thomas Greenfield embraces this conflict in his assessment:

> A theory of organizations as will and imagination may be summed up in two statements: first, a statement that rejects group mind and rejects an overarching social reality thought to lie beyond human control and outside the will, intention, and action of the individual; second, a statement that acknowledges the tumult and irrationality of thought itself. Acting, willing, passionate, fearful, hoping, mortal, fallible individuals and the events that join them are always more complex, interesting, and

real than the ideas we use, forever vainly, to explain them. . . . It is the individual that lives and acts, not the organization. It is therefore the experience of individuals that we must seek to understand. Huxley says it clearly: "We live together . . . , but always in all circumstances we are by ourselves. The martyrs go hand in hand to the arena; they are crucified alone." (Greenfield 1984, 152–53)

Notes

1. Organized in 1987, the Evangelical Lutheran Church in America is a union of the American Lutheran Church and the Lutheran Church in America. The church has 65 geographical areas or synods, each of which has its own bishop. In turn, the synods are grouped together into nine regional centers that coordinate a variety of missions and service projects. For this and other information, see Bedell 1992, 73–75.

2. On the history of the considerable debate and dissent, which led to the establishment of quotas, see Grindal, forthcoming.

3. The paragraph quoted above appears in Chapter 5.01. "Principles of Organization."

4. Whether this will continue to be the case remains to be seen. Several of the participants mentioned the large number of women within Lutheran seminaries, and, indeed, the report cited here supports their observation. However, see the comments below on the growing number of women in seminaries.

5. For example, the process by which ministers are chosen for churches.

6. She is referring to the use of the word "career" in the interview protocol.

7. Compare Grindal, forthcoming.

5

The Southern Baptist Convention

The Priesthood of Some Believers

> The alternative to action and probable evil is disengagement.
> Orwell . . . uses the metaphor of Jonah inside the whale to
> express the individual's best approach to forces that are totally
> beyond [her or] his control. The image here is of security
> attained by personal detachment from the maelstrom that
> swirls around the individual. But detachment from events does
> not mean nonawareness of them. As Orwell says, we should
> think of the whale as transparent. In this circumstance, Jonah
> becomes an observer who can see what others locked in the
> struggle are oblivious to.
>
> —Thomas B. Greenfield, "Leaders and Schools"

Isolated dimensions of Southern
Baptist culture and bureaucracy could foster the full involvement of
women in the church's ordained ministry; and if they did not, the same
dimensions might at least insure considerable variation in practice within
the church. One such cultural dimension is the doctrine called "the priesthood of all believers." Mentioned by some of the interviewees and often
mentioned in Baptist literature, this doctrine asserts that all people are
competent to know God and God's will for themselves (Ammerman 1990,
21; Cothen 1993, 47). If that is true of the believer in general, then why
not women?

Similarly, the loosely structured character of the Southern Baptist
Convention makes it one of the country's self-consciously "decoupled"

denominations.[1] Everyday life in all denominations carries on in only occasional contact with the national organizations they represent, but historically each church in the Southern Baptist Convention enjoys a far greater measure of autonomy. There are no bishops, nor does the church have district superintendents. Furthermore, affiliation with the state and national conventions is on a voluntary basis. One could conclude that (at a minimum) individual congregations might "go their own way" and that under the best of circumstances a significant number of churches might choose to ordain women.

Organizational Culture

Women in the Baptist church, however, are part of an organizational culture that increasingly values a brand of theological conservatism. This conservatism plainly labels the ordination of women as heterodox and, at the same time, fosters a bureaucratic structure increasingly directive and hierarchical in character.

Put in Their Place

Of the Southern Baptist ministers I interviewed, five began with biblical stories. Three began with stories from the denomination's history. One recounted an experience from her own life. Another had no stories to tell at all.

Of the stories drawn from biblical text, broadly speaking, there were three kinds: stories in which women provided a positive role model; stories in which men dominated; and stories in which the plight of women was somehow underlined or illustrated. There were one or two stories of the first kind, some of which included men. Most, however, focused on women: Esther, Sarah, Ruth, Mary, Martha, and Mary Magdalen.

The vast majority of the stories told, however, were considerably more negative in tenor, suggesting that the Bible had been consciously used to exclude women. More than one minister, for example, noted that the Southern Baptist Convention had used the text of Genesis in order to deny women access to ordination.

> The Genesis account of the creation of male and female has been thrown in our faces quite a bit. If you are familiar with the Southern Baptist Convention you will know in 1983, or '84, I guess it was, a resolution

was passed at the National Convention level which—actually said that women were responsible for the origin of sin. So, this has, of course, helped to alienate women and women ministers. . . . When this resolution went through . . . it still had a way of "putting women in their place." (SBC1:1)

Others indicated that the biblical text had been used in a way that had excluded them more systematically, though perhaps less consciously. One respondent noted, for example, that there were stories other than the handful she cited that might have been helpful to her as a woman, but she had been unaware of them growing up, because "the men that told the stories mainly lifted up other men" (SBC8:2). Another observed that the biblical text focuses on men and that the church's use of the stories in worship emphasizes their male orientation, with the sole exception of Mother's Day. Still another described the way in which the church's use of the Bible had shaped her thinking from an early age:

When I was a little girl in Sunday School, all the stories were really what I was weaned on, all the Bible stories. I do remember that growing up all of the real heroes of the Bible seemed to be the men, and the women, while they were good folks and great Bible figures, always seemed to be in a supportive role to the men who were really doing the important things. I think that certainly over time in some subtle ways really helped me to clarify perhaps what my role would be in the church, and that's changed since then, but I think as a little girl I really was pretty much steered in a different direction. (SBC6:1)

By contrast with their counterparts in other denominations, Southern Baptists all but omitted any reference to strategies for reclaiming women's stories in the biblical text. Instead, they appeared to rely almost entirely on a process of sifting and sorting. The closest that any of the respondents came to taking another approach, said:

Men have definitely been focused on in our tradition, and women have always been in a more supportive and sidelined role in the stories that I've heard. . . . The stories are pretty much the same, and I can't get around the fact that it was written from a patriarchal point of view. I can't go back and rewrite Scripture, and there may have been many more women who made a significant contribution to our religious history, but—because of the times that they were living in and because of the writers—they were sidelined. . . . I've pretty much have come to terms with that, but it hasn't made me feel that the women of the Bible were only sidelined figures. I have a feeling that the women from the Bible and from early church history made very significant contributions, like they do today. . . . Do I draw on those same stories or others or just differently? I probably draw on them differently. Whenever I am preaching about women in the Bible or the contributions that they made or just the theological story that comes from that particular story in the Bible, I think I try to reflect on it maybe a little differently than when I was in Sunday School. (SBC6:1–2)

Exactly what accounts for this difference in approach to the biblical text, one can only guess. If seminary proved to be a significant force in prompting women in other denominations to actually reread the stories, then the absence of such strategies in the interviews of Southern Baptists may suggest that the reverse is true of the seminaries attended by the women I interviewed. Be that as it may, the Baptist ministers I spoke with clearly lacked the sophisticated strategies used by others.

Hell-Raising Women and Significant Men

Postponing any mention of the biblical text, three of the respondents began with stories from their denominational history. Of those who began with this kind of story, one focused on Addie Davis, the first woman to be ordained in the Southern Baptist church.

The first person I though of was Addie Davis, who was the first woman ordained Southern Baptist, and she was ordained, if I'm remembering correctly, in the 50s[2] at Watt Street Church in Durham. She was, I think, middle-aged when she was ordained. There were two other men going through the ordination process at Watt Street when she was . . . so, the three of them went through the process together, two like seminary-aged men in their twenties and Addie Davis. The two men, or one of the men, had a problem affirming completely the virgin birth. . . . The people, however, were all up in arms about ordaining Ms. Davis. . . . The pastor said, "Well, if you don't have any problem ordaining two men who aren't quite sure of the virgin birth, I don't see how you can't ordain the virgin!" So, they did it. . . . That's a story that's real helpful to me. (SBC5:1)

Ironically, however, having said that women in their church have been largely confined to work in the church's missionary efforts, the majority of those who told stories from their tradition began with those of female missionaries. Indeed, the stories of Baptist missionaries Annie Armstrong and Lottie Moon dominated.[3]

For the most part, these stories included elements that are frequently recounted—self-sacrifice and care for others. One respondent departed from the norm, however, seeking to recover the "real" Lottie Moon.

> There was a Southern Baptist missionary to China named Lottie Moon that we now have the Lottie Moon Christmas offering named after. She has sort of been sanctified and become two-dimensional to most people. They view her mostly as a saint, but the real Lottie moon was a "hell-raiser." She went to China, and the women missionaries in China were supposed to live with married families, and she refused to do that. They were supposed to only sit in the mission meetings and not participate, just listen; and she refused to do that. She wrote back to the mission board and said "If I'm going to be here, I'm going to have a full voting voice." This was in the 1860s or 70s. She ended up dying in China; she apparently had a lot of psychological problems; and she ended up starving to death. But anyway, the whole time she was there, she absolutely refused to do anything that would not put her on equal footing with the male missionaries who were there. It's real funny now, because everyone views her as a little haloed saint, but the truth is she drove everybody crazy the whole time she was there. The establishment just really couldn't stand her. I really relate to her very well. (SBC10:2)

Another felt that even the stories of missionary endeavor had been co-opted by men.

> The lives of missionaries, which make up a lot of the rich stories in Southern Baptist life, have been about some significant women, like Lottie Moon and Annie Armstrong. But it seems to me in thinking about it, whenever they are mentioned, it's always in the kind of tone like "the women, God bless them, the sweet women." And the real stories about all the great, significant contributions have been about the William Carrie, Bill Wallace of China, lots of men who've been out there doing the work on the mission field. So, I don't know. I think in a general way, the men have definitely been focused on in our tradition

and women have always been in a more supportive and side-lined role in the stories I've heard. (SBC6:2)

Personal anecdotes also figured prominently in the stories told by Southern Baptists. Some of the messages focused on the subtle forms of socialization that had shaped their self-understanding, even as children.

My father was a Southern Baptist pastor, and I remember when I was five or six years old just saying to myself, "If I were a boy I would be a preacher when I grow up." All the preachers I'd ever seen were men, so I just sort of talked myself out of it.... Nobody told me that, I just drew that conclusion for myself.... Most of the stories I heard about people and how they served God and lived out their faith that had to do with women were missionary kinds of stories. (SBC4:1–2)

When I was young, we had a pastor and we would tip-toe by his office. I mean it was like we were on sacred ground and, this is how we were taught.... And it was, I guess too, it was the way male ministers came across to me as a child or to me as a young person. They were just people that you really could not approach or you were not worthy to approach. (SBC1:1)

Others focused on the more recent struggles encountered by their colleagues, including those teaching in now embattled Southern Baptist seminaries.

I also have a lot of friends who have been through difficult times that have caused me to have a lot of ambivalence toward my tradition. There's a woman that I knew in Boston, when I was doing summer missions, that was hoping to be a chaplain at Yale Divinity School, and there was a big stink about funding, whether the home mission board would fund those positions, because it was a new convention area and there wasn't a lot of money. So she went through a real rough battle, these committee meetings that would vote on whether she was qualified. One vote went for her, one vote went against her and both of them were real close votes. So, you know, she was like on a trial.... Then, ... [there's] _____ and what had gone on with her ever since she's been ... [at the seminary].... She's kind of been on trial down there ever since she came. And that's a difficult thing to watch. My niece is now in her class, or was in her class this year. It's difficult to teach when you feel like you're under fire all the time. It's really been difficult to see my tradition really hurt people who are trying to serve God the way they feel called. (SBC5:2)

Notorious

The nature of Southern Baptist responses to questions about language may be traceable to the largely nonliturgical character of Baptist worship, but the ministers I interviewed reacted even more strongly to the gender orientation of the language used in the church than they did to the stories told in their tradition. Given its impromptu character, the male-dominated nature of church language gives the impression that Southern Baptist males are repeatedly and willfully exclusivistic in its use. Whereas in other traditions, at least some of the language appears in fixed liturgies for which the denomination as a whole shares some measure of apparent (if not real) responsibility. It may be too that exclusivistic language in a fixed liturgy appears to constitute a single offense, while in less structured contexts, the offenses multiply as yet more statements are made.[4] Whatever the cause, reaction to the language used in the denomination was uniformly negative.

Male-oriented language for the community of faith was mentioned more often than any other kind of language, including that used to refer to God, although the latter ran a close second. Respondents did not simply describe ministers as insensitive, or uninformed, but spoke instead of men and women who were "unwilling" to speak inclusively (SBC9:2).

> Well, I think the male language has been in more recent years a very alienating part of what I have experienced in the Baptist tradition. A lack of willingness to begin to use inclusive language by both genders, the women and the men are equally resistant to changing their way of expressing themselves, and you get—you hear preachers always talked about in the masculine. You know, the term "man" is supposed to be generic and it doesn't do that for me. And it's just the unwillingness as I perceive it for the Baptists to begin to move toward an inclusive kind of language. That, in my opinion, would be helpful to women and young girls. (SBC9:2)

Another described her denomination's male-dominated vocabulary as both "notorious" and "deliberate" (SBC6:3).

Well, as you may know, if you've had a lot of dealings with Southern Baptists, we're notoriously exclusive gender-wise with our language, and sometimes in other ways. When I was growing up, because of the very, very conservative tradition that I came out of, language was never an issue. It was not something that I was really aware of. I sang the hymns and read the Scriptures with the very male-oriented language in it and it never really occurred to me that there was anything wrong with that. When I went to seminary and began parish work here, I did become aware of it, and over the last seven or eight years, my tolerance for exclusive language has really dwindled down to just about zero. And I think that in a lot of ways, because language is so fundamental, that has been a big reason why right now I feel very alienated from the Southern Baptist mainstream, because it's still deliberately male-oriented language that they use and that is exclusive of women. So that plays a very big part right now for me. (SBC6:3)

As the comment suggests, women also feel that the use of language in their denomination has helped to marginalize them. The descriptions of language's impact took a variety of forms. One spoke of being made to feel "less important" (SBC8:3). Unlike women from other Protestant denominations, Southern Baptists argue that exclusive language is particularly common on the national level and when leadership or pastoral roles are the topic of conversation. Indeed, it is probably fair to say that the National Convention evinces considerable hostility to the use of inclusive language.[5]

Well, it goes back to the same thing. It's just a male-oriented language. Throughout history, the history of Southern Baptists, throughout Scripture, everything that refers to instruction, etc., refers to males—male church leadership, male instruction. . . . When you go to a national level convention, you very seldom hear "she." It's always "he this" and "he that," especially when you're relating to the pastor or relating to leadership positions. It's always male-oriented. (SBC1:2)

Even the denomination's literature deals in sexist stereotypes:

All the way coming up, only male language was used to refer to, particularly, pastoral roles—male pronouns, male language, 'man of God.' I remember hearing that a lot as it related to pastors and minister-types.

I don't remember feeling excluded by them until seminary, and I didn't even acknowledge exclusive language until late in seminary . . . I should also say that in the denominational liturgy . . . the language is very gender specific. . . . I remember, not long ago, seeing a deacon magazine, they call it *The Deacon,* and it had—almost all the way through—there is male. . . . The picture on the front was a woman playing tennis with her husband, a deacon male. So that's kind of the role the woman has. (SBC2:2–3)

Not at Home, Even Here

None of this is meant to suggest that language used to refer to God was unimportant for the respondents. Four of the women I interviewed mentioned struggles they had with the kind of language used by their church when referring to God, and such cases may have been implicit in many of the more general comments made. Those who did mention it found that such language made it difficult to fit their own experiences into the language of their faith. One woman observed, for example, that she found it difficult to imagine what the phrase "made in the image of God" could possibly mean as applied to her, given the language of her church.

There are several vehicles for this kind of language in the Southern Baptist church. The pulpit, hymnals, the ever-present King James Version of the Bible, and even church by-laws provide forums in which this kind of language is heard. The women I interviewed make allowances for linguistic conventions and even the age of those whose language is male dominated. Indeed, one might rightly argue that even women in the Southern Baptist church are surprisingly conservative in their orientation to gender issues.

I've been using inclusive language when I talk about God, and when I preach I don't say "he" or "she" I usually just say God. Any setting I go to anymore in Southern Baptist life, it seems no one does that, even if they are inclusive regarding humankind, they still talk about God as he. . . . I don't know if alienating is the word—but I find that it always catches me. Even in our church when someone says "he" and they're talking about God, it catches me for a minute and I have to—it kind of gets me off track. Not everyone in our church uses inclusive language. We have a lot of low-income people, uneducated people, who will probably never use inclusive language for God, and for people too.

That's okay with me, but it's more when educated people in our church that are seminary folks, who, I think, "ought to know better," that's when it catches me off guard. In terms of alienation, I went to a Southern Baptist Women in Ministry Convention a couple of years ago in New Orleans, and I thought: "Oh good, this is where I fit in. This is Women in Ministry." And, the language that they used in the songs, and in the call to worship [was male in orientation]—I was just sitting there—I felt so alienated. I felt like "I'm not at home even here. They're not even using inclusive language even here." I just felt so alone, because I felt like, you know, even the Women in Ministry aren't doing this. (SBC7:4–5)

A Male Process

By contrast with the women in the other denominations, Baptist women saw ritual as less intimately tied to questions of language. They detected nothing in the rituals themselves of a problematic nature. What caused them to struggle was that only men perform them.

One of the rituals most often mentioned was the ordination service itself. The objection the women lodged against it was simple; it is for men and done by men.

The ordination process in the Southern Baptist Convention usually excludes women or women's call, and is very, I don't want to say demeaning. It just does not . . . recognize a woman's call to ministry. That was the first thing, then also the ordination process, in the past, has excluded women when it came to time for the ordination service and the laying on of hands. The way that women were excluded was usually only the ordained people were to [do laying] on hands, and that would be ordained deacons and ministers. (SBC1:3)

Of course, the impact of such practices goes beyond the exclusion of women from the rituals themselves. One minister, for example, compared the church's cool reception her "call" to pastoral ministry with that of her seventeen-year-old brother.

I think of my brother who what they called, "surrendered to preach"; he was very young, maybe seventeen, and how the church rallied around him, just applauded him and they were so thrilled, and literally,

I remember, crowded around him that day and hugged him. Nothing of that sort was done for me and it was, well, not the opposite, but very little acknowledgment whatsoever. And then on into the ordination process, which was the setting in which I was raised, was a totally male process. Council, the laying on of hands, the whole thing was a male process. (SBC7:4)

The other objections raised by the interviewees touched on other rituals, but the objection was of a similar nature.

I know that growing up as a young girl, one of the rituals was the Lord's Supper. . . . Every quarter when we'd get to the Lord's Supper, it was always the preacher and the deacons, which were always men. And even when I was in college and still wasn't really thinking in terms of women participating in all levels of worship, there still just struck a chord in me that only one-half of the segment of the congregation was really having a chance to participate either in the prayers for communion, the distribution of the elements. It was always the men, and ordination was the same way. It was always the ordained men who were able to come forward to lay hands, even the wives and very close family, significant people to the candidates, were not able to voice a prayer over them. (SBC6:7)

A Preacher with a Big Hairdo

Given Southern Baptist theology, which interprets the Old Testament proscription of "graven images" in the broadest fashion possible, the women I interviewed had little or nothing to say about the use of icons and symbols. As one interviewee observed, "Southern Baptists don't use them" (SBC7:7). But three women identified uniquely Baptist symbols that did have a gender orientation, and the orientation involved the same concern raised in discussions of ritual: the all-dominating presence of men. In this connection, the women cited three all but synonymous symbols: the presiding role of men, men in three piece suits, and men in pulpits. "One of the biggest symbols that I think about . . . is a [male] preacher with a big hairdo standing up at a huge pulpit. That's sort of a symbol about where Baptists have their power and stuff. It's the preacher and the Bible—there's always kind of a—you know, some big man preacher with his big fancy hairdo, almost like a cartoon character" (SBC5:6).

The Priesthood of Some Believers

When asked if there were any other dimensions of their church's culture with a gender orientation of either an attractive or alienating character, the interviewees' responses were telling. Eight of the ten returned to the dynamic reflected in stories, language, and ritual: male domination and female subordination.

> In the years before I became a pastor . . . I felt that the old tradition of "women had their place and they were to stay in their place," and I think that has held into the church and in many grass roots churches and many denominations, and that has spread out into our culture, or our culture has spread into the church—I think that's inter-related. You know, you keep your place. Now, it's not so where I am now, not in the local church . . . women in my community of faith have a very active role, needless to say, in fact, almost more so than the men now. . . . [What was that place like when you were being put in your place?] You felt like your ideas were not valued to the point that you would not even want to express them. Many times, you felt intimidated. Even if you did think that you had an idea on something, you would keep quiet because women weren't suppose to share ideas or speak out. It wasn't your place. Even if you disagreed with what was going on, you still kept quiet. That's not the way it should be, but that's the way it was. (SBC1:4)

According to the women I interviewed, the vehicles of that culture exist throughout the denomination and follow women from childhood into their adult lives. Sunday school and youth groups are replaced by the Woman's Missionary Union, but the message is the same. Interviewees spoke of being socialized and of being a part of an organization that conditioned them to accept a well-defined and subservient role in the church. Ironically, however, they argued that the church in which they were socialized also taught them to expect more responsibility than it was prepared to give them.

> I certainly internalized what the church taught me. Women had very specific roles to play in the church. Those roles were important, but . . . they were gender-defined and you didn't go outside of those, even though what the teaching in Southern Baptist life, was very much "the

priesthood of the believer." I caught that teaching, even though it was rarely practiced. I caught the teaching that we are all ministers of the gospel, that you are ordained when you are baptized. I also caught that each of us is called to a specific ministry in our lives and that will be unique to who we are. So, I caught both of those. And yet, what I found was resistance, culturally. The church was teaching one thing and practicing another. So, my dilemma with the congregations has been breaking that barrier. That's been a culturally defined barrier, rather than a theologically defined barrier. (SBC8:6)

This Is It for Me

The response of the interviewees to the overtly male culture of the church varies greatly. Some have mounted their own effort to effect changes from within the denomination. These ministers appear to be prepared to stay, even though that effort requires them to overcome both the resistance of others and the way they themselves have been socialized.

What that has meant is it's very difficult to get a job. It was real hard for me to get a job. So, on the day-to-day stuff, it was just trying to break through the major barrier of not being able to find a position in pastoral ministry. If I wanted to live within very well-defined arenas like education ministry or children's ministry or youth ministry, I could find a job in loads of Southern Baptist churches, but to step outside of that has been very difficult . . . especially in Southern Baptist life. The pulpit is where the power is. So, preaching has become the major place to break down the barrier for women, because that's where the power and authority has been assumed. So in my own ministry, I had to overcome some of my own internal resistance to preaching, because I felt I was not worthy, that men had a much more powerful and authoritative voice and who was I to be in that role. So much of my own pilgrimage has been overcoming my internal barriers. (SBC8:6–7)

Others remain within the church, but the local congregation functions as a surrogate for the larger church, providing a refuge from a larger denominational climate that is opposed to their ordination.

Well, I do [think that the attitude of my church has had an affect on my career] as far as the local congregation in which I am serving now [is

concerned]. . . . Eight-and one-half years ago they welcomed me without any reservation about my gender and actually never made it an
issue. They had a job they expected me to do. They saw gifts in me that
they affirmed, that really had not so much to do with gender as just
gifts that would serve the church. It was really the first opportunity that
I had ever had to be in a community that functioned in that way. You
never know what might have happened, but I think that because I am
still a minister today and am very optimistic about continuing in this
vein, I think it had a lot to do with them opening a door then. I don't
know where I would be today if they hadn't. . . . Along the way, I know
in seminary, to the reverse, some of the professors in seminary had
some other very definite ideas about women in ministry. I think had I
not been in this church that was so affirming of my gifts, I think I really
could have listened to the voices of others who were very definitely
opposed to women in ministry. I remember in my preaching class in
seminary, this preaching professor on the first day of class—there were
four women in my preaching class. His comment was that he always
found that hearing a woman preach in the pulpit was kind of like
watching a dog walk on its hind legs, that he never does it very well,
but you're surprised he can do it at all. That was the comment on my
first day of preaching, and I think that I could have listened to those
voices and it could have had an impact on my career, but thank God
there were other voices too. (SBC6:7–8)

The presence of those voices is not enough in some cases. Among
the interviewees were ministers who have distanced themselves from the
larger denomination. "I have withdrawn from the denomination. I don't
feel accepted by the leadership. Therefore, I do not involve myself extensively in the denominational processes. I don't read much of the literature.
I resist a lot of the programs. I guess, I'm a little bit cynical" (SBC2:6).
And there are still others for whom the breach is all but an accomplished
fact for them and, in some cases, their congregations.

Well, I'm choosing not to relate to the Southern Baptist Church. I'm
hoping that our church will become something else. To be honest, we're
looking at our denominational identity. I don't want to be a Southern
Baptist anymore. . . . Now, the church may decide to stay linked to the
Southern Baptist Convention and I can live with that, but after I leave
this church, I will not. I don't know when that would be, but I don't
plan to be Southern Baptist anymore, because I've had it. Let me say,
the only reason I'm Southern Baptist now is that this church is Southern

Baptist and I love this church. Two years ago [at the] convention in New Orleans, that's when I walked away from the Southern Baptists and said, "This is it for me." (SBC7:10–11)

Where's She Going?

The strength of the interviewees' reactions are undoubtedly rooted in a variety of informal dynamics that shape the church and women's roles within it. One of those dynamics is the stereotyping that characterizes so much of Southern Baptist life. "When I first came, I was the second woman minister in the state. . . . There again, it was male clergy who had the hardest time. I remember walking into my first associational meeting and the women were gathered to go into a pastors' wives' conference, and one of the male pastors looked to another one and said, 'Where's she going to go?' " (SBC1:7).

Commenting on the power of the church's culture, one interviewee observed: "I think that [local congregations] are sensitive to where the national leanings happen to be, but I don't find that in our state that is the sort of controlling factor. I think that has a whole lot greater effect on why they do or mainly do not call women pastors" (SBC9:14).

Bureaucratic Linkages

Such dynamics are of perennial significance in the Southern Baptist Convention. However, it is all but impossible to understand the experience of women serving in its ministry unless one is aware of the extent to which fundamentalism has made inroads into the Southern Baptist Convention.[6] The theological and political controversy that has fragmented the Convention emerged publicly in the 1979 election of the Convention's president. The election of Adrian Rogers, pastor of the Bellevue Baptist Church in Memphis, was the result of efforts spearheaded by Paul Pressler, Appeals Court Judge, and Paige Patterson, who at the time was president of the Criswell Center for Biblical Studies based in Dallas.[7]

"A Hostile Takeover"

Committed to theological conservatism and to the reshaping of Southern Baptist Institutions in accord with their own social, political, and theological views, Pressler and Patterson succeeded in gaining control of the denomination's bureaucratic structure through unprecedented manipulation of the church's political process.[8] Most Baptists considered the presidency of the Convention an honorary position, but Pressler realized that bureaucratic provisions existed, which would allow the president of the Convention to wield considerable power over the denomination. With the power to choose his own nominating committee, the president could, in turn, control the nominations of trustees and, through the trustees, the denomination's agencies and seminaries. (Cothen 1993, 6–7; Ammerman 1990, 168–71, 174).

Although loath to describe his efforts as political in nature, Pressler (with Patterson's help) guaranteed the election of Adrian Rogers.[9] Highly skilled in publicizing his position, Pressler devoted considerable time and energy to orchestrating what sociologist Nancy Ammerman describes as "a hostile takeover" (Ammerman 1990, 14).[10] Their message, as Baptist historian Bill Leonard observes:

> was authoritative and orthodox, easily preached and understood. Their rhetoric was suitably populist, able to touch the hearts and rally the support of the masses. They were articulate opponents of modernity, warning that only through the affirmation of biblical inerrancy and other fundamentalist dogmas could the convention retain its evangelical zeal and fulfill its divine mandate.... [They] fostered a sense of ideological conviction that created a new coalition of true believers with a crusading mentality directed against the destructive forces of pluralism, modernity, and liberalism.... In short, the fundamentalists set themselves to the task of remythologizing the SBC. (Leonard 1990, 176–177)

By contrast, the church's moderates were slow to respond and ill-equipped to counter the efforts made by Pressler and others. At first, they underestimated the significance of the elections won by fundamentalists. They considered the success an anomaly that would have little impact on the conservative, but hardly fundamentalist, mainstream of the church (Ammerman 1990, 73–80).[11] When, at last, they recognized the significance of what was happening, there was little they could do.

They had lost the initiative. Fundamentalists had successfully defined the issues by arguing that theirs was a crusade for biblical truth, and this message had widespread appeal in what is, by all accounts, a conservative denomination. And they had captured the minds and hearts of suburban "super-churches" and rural southerners. Moderates were unable to extend their influence beyond the suburban and urban enclaves of the church. Leadership, too, was a problem. Younger moderates considered themselves out of step with the church's conservative theology and felt, probably rightly, that there was little chance of persuading the larger church to embrace their vision. More prominent moderates, who had the wherewithal to travel the country, were the leaders of church agencies, who ran the risk of appearing to abuse their office in the interests of self-preservation and the protection of heretics.[12]

As a result, fundamentalists were able to elect presidents who shared their views throughout the eighties and into the nineties. By 1988 their control over the church's boards was complete. With the help of those boards, fundamentalists restructured the mission statements of many of the church's agencies and its seminaries, as they saw fit (Cothen 1993, 273–360; Ammerman 1990, 11, 168–252). Moderates were forced to the boundaries of the church and left many of its institutions in droves. Where contractual agreements or the structures for recruitment made it possible, fundamentalists installed likeminded leaders.[13]

An Emerging Hierarchy

For those unfamiliar with the Southern Baptist Convention, such changes might seem unexceptional from a legislative point of view. But, in fact, they represent a dramatic transformation of Southern Baptist polity.

The Southern Baptist Convention is, by design, "decoupled," and it is not by accident that its membership is described as consisting of "cooperating churches." Indeed some, if not most Baptists would argue that there is no such thing as The Southern Baptist Church.[14] The denomination's constitution makes that clear: "While independent and sovereign in its own sphere, the Convention does not claim and will never attempt to exercise any authority over any other Baptist body, whether church, auxiliary organization, association, or convention."[15] Accordingly, in the past, resolutions approved by the Convention functioned as forums for public expression, but not as legislative mandates, and the officers of the Convention took their cues from the programming to which the already diverse Convention could agree.[16]

Now a new polity is emerging, one that is hierarchical in character and in which the Convention is playing an ever greater and more directive role.[17] The church has become self-consciously doctrinaire, stipulating the positions that member churches and " 'good Southern Baptists' " should take on the nature of Scripture; the historicity of Adam and Eve; the authorship of biblical literature; the nature of biblical miracle stories; the historicity and accuracy of biblical narratives; abortion; divorce; the ordination of women; and school prayer.[18] In turn fundamentalists have made some, if not all, of these positions a prerequisite for selection and employment in the church's agencies, committees, and seminaries.[19] On the national, state, and local level associations have refused with greater frequency to seat the delegates of member churches who fail to hold orthodox views on these issues —a practice rather akin to excommunication.[20] And prominent leaders, including the former president of the Convention, the Reverend W. A. Criswell of Dallas, have advocated an authoritarian style of leadership at odds with the church's democratic and theological tradition.[21]

A Symbol of Division

The ordination of women has been at or near the center of the dispute from the beginning, though not always of first concern. Even in 1979, when Pressler and Patterson began to push for control of the Convention's presidency, opposition to the ordination of women appeared as part of a larger legislative agenda, which functioned as something of a trial balloon. Although defeated, a resolution was brought to the floor of the Convention mandating that "all appointments of the [church's] mission boards refuse to 'recognize the ordination of women as being scriptural truth held by Baptists' " (Cothen 1993, 8).

Undeterred, fundamentalists eventually succeeded in 1984. Carl F. H. Henry, former editor of the magazine *Christianity Today,* presented a resolution declaring that " 'Scriptures teach that women are not in public worship to assume a role of authority over men lest confusion reign in the local church' and that Paul 'excludes women from pastoral leadership to preserve a submission God requires because man was first in creation and woman was first in the Edenic fall.' " The resolution went on to say that, although the church holds women "in 'high honor for their unique contribution to the advancement of Christ's kingdom and the building of godly homes,' " they should be encouraged to serve " 'in all aspects of church life and work other than pastoral functions and leadership entailing ordination' " (Groves 1984; Cothen 1993, 145). Some delegates protested from the floor that the resolution violated the autonomy of individual churches and, for that reason, the constitution of the Convention. Nonetheless, the resolution was passed in a scant eight minutes, in part through parliamentary maneuvering. Then in 1986 a subcommittee of the Convention's Home Mission Board successfully recommended that "future requests for church pastoral aid categorically be denied to any church with a woman pastor" (Wright 1986).

Nor has the opposition of fundamentalists to the ordination of women been restricted to the legislative forum of the church or even ordination to the pastoral ministry. The Capital Baptist Association refused to "seat the messengers [i.e., delegates]" of First Baptist Church in Oklahoma City because it had ordained three women to the diaconate (i.e., a lay ministry).[22] The Oklahoma State Convention withdrew its invitation to a minister from Nashville when his church ordained a woman as deacon. The Home Mission Board hired a pastor and then recommended he resign, when the Board discovered that his church had more than one female deacon. There was little surprise, then, when (in a now well-known case) the Shelby County Baptist Association refused to "seat the messengers" of Prescott Memorial Baptist Church in Memphis, when it ordained the Reverend Nancy Sehested.[23] The ordination of women "had become symbolic of the division facing the Convention."[24]

A Matter of Risk

Under the best of circumstances, Southern Baptist women face considerable obstacles to their full involvement in the ministry of the church. The Convention lacks both the structures and the regional or episcopal leadership that would expedite their deployment. Both have proven a valuable means of speeding the acceptance of female clergy and of raising overall optimism about the future.[25] Now, however, women in the church's ministry find themselves facing new obstacles.

In some senses, Southern Baptist women find themselves in a position analogous to that of the denomination's moderates.[26] They are part of a tradition, which, historically, acknowledges no other form of authority than that of the local church. One interviewee observed, for example: "There is no church law that prohibits women from being part of the ordained ministry of the church, because, in our church polity, each church is autonomous in the decision-making process. So each church can decide who it is that they will ordain." Indeed, when asked about the implication of recent resolutions passed by the Convention, she insisted that such decisions had no bearing on the possibility of ordination. "In the annual conventions they have already passed resolutions that have discouraged women from being in leadership positions in the church. But, that cannot be binding on a local congregation. So, our church's polity would say that you can ordain women" (SBC8:15–16).

In spite of the Convention's congregational tradition, however, the resolutions passed over the last decade have proven that it is not only prepared to legislate against the ordination of women, but is, in fact, capable of exercising some measure of real control over this issue as well. Faced with the prospect of being "disfellowshipped," even local churches are now forced to consider the possible implications of hiring a woman. As one interviewee observed:

> In the Southern Baptist church it's supposed to be the [congregation], the association, the state, and the convention. . . . The church is supposed to be the ruling factor, the local church, not vice versa. This is what's happened in our Convention though. We've established this hierarchy of National Convention tells state what to do, state tells— you know, down that way. When resolutions are passed on the national level that say, "No, we do not support ordained women or women in ministry and so forth," a lot of local churches are buying into those resolutions thinking they are law, when they are not. The majority of local Baptist churches are affected by what the National Convention says. (SBC1:11)

Obviously, observations such as these are hardly grounded in widespread ignorance of denominational polity. Instead, they reflect the fact that an organization's structure can be altered by members engaged in "displacing goals, subverting roles, and amplifying rules." Structures are, in other words, both "constituted and constitutive" (Ranson and others 1980, 2–3).

To make matters worse, the denomination is disintegrating around ordained women. The Convention as a whole is becoming increasingly factious[27] and the part of the denomination that was the most likely to receive them has now been decisively sidelined, left with considerably fewer resources to train and support them. The triumphant pronouncement made by the former chair of the board of trustees at Southeastern Baptist Theological Seminary, when the fundamentalist takeover there was all but complete, could just as easily apply to the denomination as a whole: "The question now is not who's leaving, but who's staying."[28]

So deeply rooted is the notion that the leadership of the church is rightly male, that nine of the ten women I interviewed said that there were few churches, if any, that would hire them in the future. Furthermore, only two state associations mentioned in the interviews appear to foster a climate in which women are welcomed, and, according to an interviewee, one of those has been "targeted" by conservative leaders (SBC2:22). Indeed there is a sense that things are getting worse. "At this particular point I think that in the denomination itself it's more difficult to find a position for women in ministry than it was ten years ago, because our denomination is falling apart and so women are finding even the churches that might have been willing to risk hiring a woman on their pastoral staff are playing it safe and being more cautious. So, it's much more difficult for women to find positions" (SBC8:10).[29]

Statistics would appear to justify this concern. By 1991, 810 women had been ordained (three were retired). Thirty-eight, or 4.7 percent, were serving as pastors. Fifty-six (or 6.9 percent) were serving as associate pastors. Apart from those without a paid position of any kind in the church (320, or 39.5 percent!) the vast majority were serving either as chaplains (182, or 22.5 percent) or as support staff working with, for example, music, children, or youth (166, or 20.5 percent). Nine (or 1.1 percent) were serving as missionaries; twenty-one (or 2.6 percent) were serving as social workers or counselors; and fifteen (or 1.8 percent) were serving as college or seminary professors (Anders and Metcalf-Whittake 1993, 213). In other words, the most "visible" roles remain largely closed to women.[30]

In addition, 46 percent of the churches ordaining women and 47 percent of the churches and church-related institutions that employ them are located in four states: Kentucky, North Carolina, Texas, and Virginia. This pattern is due in large part to the presence of two seminaries that have been supportive of ordained women in the past—Southeastern Baptist Theological Seminary in Wake Forest, North Carolina and Southern Baptist Theological Seminary in Louisville, Kentucky (Anders and Metcalf-Whittake 1993, 212). However, now both are controlled by fundamentalists.[31]

I Don't Fit

It would be wrong, however, to assume that the women who have been ordained consider themselves theological moderates, let alone liberals, with a natural home elsewhere in the denomination's spectrum of beliefs. Indeed, some ministers' sense of isolation is deepened because they consider themselves conservatives.

> I am moderate, if I have to put myself in a camp, but I'm not liberal in my theology. I am moderate and I'm probably moderately conservative in my theology. I am Southern Baptist to the core. I was raised Southern Baptist. . . . But, what I'm finding is churches who would even consider me are liberal churches, because I am a woman. [They would] pull my résumé, but once they get to know me, then my problem is that they're not in agreement with my theology. The churches who I would be in line with on a theological stance would never even look at me because I am a female. . . . Because you wear a skirt, then you are supposed to be, you've got to be, theologically liberal. That's not so. That's just not so. My stand is my stand and I am very conservative on some issues. I am liberal on some issues, such as women in ministry. But the churches who would even look at me are usually the very liberal churches, where I do not, or would not ever fit. . . . It's like I don't fit into anybody's mold. . . . Sometimes it's very disheartening. (SBC1:13–14)

Even women who do describe themselves as "liberals" or "moderates" have difficulty in identifying a segment of the church prepared to endorse their ministry. In fact, while nine of the interviewees identified the in-groups within the denomination as male and theologically conservative, the few who identified in-groups of moderates were also quick to note that such groups were male-dominated.

To make matters worse, what one might describe as a "fatigue factor" has begun to set in. Many women fear that moderates struggling to find a place in the Convention, or driven to apathy by the tensions at work in the denomination, may be willing to trade their cause in exchange for peace with the fundamentalists (Wright 1986, 998–99).

It is perhaps surprising, then, that the ministers I interviewed speak positively about their careers. However, they focus all but completely on the congregations that have called them and the changes in perception taking place there. Noting how completely the son of a parishioner had accepted her, one interviewee recalled:

Stan, my husband, went up visiting this home-bound man and his wife, and one of their sons . . . their youngest, who is about four, lived in a trailer beside them. Stan drove up and walked into the house, and Alan's little boy looked out the window and saw the car and said, "The preacher's here! The preacher's here!" He ran up to the house and looked in the door and saw Stan and then came back home real slow and told his mama, "Oh, it ain't the preacher; it's just that old man she's married to." (SBC5:10)

Like Greenfield's Jonah, Southern Baptist women have chosen the security of detachment, but they are not oblivious to the storm that surrounds them.

Notes

1. The Southern Baptist Convention was organized in 1845. In turn, the Convention is composed of 1,208 local congregations, which affiliate with the Convention as "cooperating churches" but retain their autonomy. The structure of the Convention consists of 1,208 district associations and thirty-nine state conventions (or fellowships).

2. Actually, Davis was not ordained until 1964. Unable to find a church that would call her, she moved north to take a position in an American Baptist church. See Anders and Metcalf-Whittake 1993, 211.

3. As Nancy Ammerman notes, "it was in the WMU [i.e., Woman's Missionary Union] that women made and kept their own history" (1990, 92).

4. None of this is meant to suggest that Southern Baptist worship is not fixed by the unspoken conventions of the tradition. As Nancy Ammerman observes: "The Southern Baptist family was one in which a strong sense of ritual prevailed. The worship styles of SBC churches were in fact so routine that only the hymn numbers might change from Sunday to Sunday or place to place. Services varied mostly in the degree of polish and formality given to them in churches of varying sizes and resources. An organ (Hammonds and Wurlitzers were popular) played familiar hymn tunes as the congregation gathered and again later as they dispersed. A period of congregational singing and prayers opened the service, followed by an offering (usually taken up by deacons). There was a special number from the choir or a soloist, a sermon of about thirty minutes, and an invitation hymn—often 'Just As I Am' or 'Softly and Tenderly'—when sinners were exhorted to be saved and new members were encouraged to join. Both sermon and invitation focused the attention of listeners on the importance of making a personal decision to accept Christ. The service closed with a spontaneous prayer from someone in the congregation. Then everyone would file past the preacher at the door, heading home for a special meal, or perhaps just in time to beat the Methodists whose liturgy often took a bit longer. Although Southern Baptists vigorously claimed to be a 'nonliturgical' denomination, there was a liturgy as predictable as in any church with a prayer book. Like the Latin Mass, it provided a universalizing experience for those who participated in it" (1990, 59–60).

5. Nancy Ammerman, a firsthand observer at the Southern Baptist Convention re-calls: "At annual meetings, motions and resolutions against women in ministry were often on the agenda. In addition to this overt opposition, women had to face routine exclusion and invisibility, along with occasional jokes and hostile remarks: There were often jokes about inclusiveness (One trustee laughed that a 'balanced' committee would have to include a 'Jew, a woman, and a cripple'); and there were sarcastic references at the Pastors Confer-ence to the 'other' meetings and 'other' people who let women preach. At the 1988 annual convention meeting several routine proposals came to the floor containing all male pronouns. Moves were made to amend them, altering the language to include 'he or she.' Those moves, however, were met with boo's and cat calls, and the votes were so close and rancorous that the chair finally suggested making such editorial changes by the common consent of those bringing the motion. . . . More commonly, women were simply invisible in this official world. The language used was so uniformly male in gender that even moderate women sometimes did not notice that they were referred to as 'gentlemen' all day" (1990, 94–95).

6. In choosing to use the terms "fundamentalist" and "moderate" I follow those used by Nancy Ammerman (1990, 16–17, 72–125). See also Cothen 1993, x–xi, 85–94.

7. Patterson is now president of Southeastern Baptist Theological Seminary. See Cothen 1993, 370. It is no accident that Southeastern was, along with Southern Seminary in Louisville, one of the first Baptist seminaries to prepare women for pastoral ministry (Ammerman 1990, 92). This, combined with its supposed reputation for "liberalism," made it an early target for fundamentalists (Cothen 1993, 279–95, especially 281–83). By 1987, fundamentalists controlled the Board of Trustees at Southeastern (p. 282) and immediately made plans to seize control of the Board's chair, reshape the process by which faculty are selected, and even dictate procedures shaping the day-to-day life of the seminary, including the selection of adjunct faculty (p. 284). Faced with a *fait accompli,* the seminary's president, Randall Lolley, resigned, and the board, having at first agreed on a transition process, forced a new president on the seminary, giving Lolley two weeks notice (pp. 285–87). Lolley's successor, Lewis A. Drummond, was handpicked by the Board and served until 1992, when Patterson was elected president. By that time, thirteen administrators and seventeen of twenty-seven faculty members had resigned, and the seminary was placed on probation by the Association of Theological Schools (pp. 284–95).

8. On the intimate connections between the fundamentalists and the political right, see Rosenberg 1989, 180–214.

9. Pressler denies this is the case, preferring to describe his efforts as simply an attempt "to inform other Baptists about the problems of parking and transportation [at the Convention]" (Cothen 1993, 16). Ammerman writes: "Even as fundamentalists organized to fight for the change they wanted, they sought to resist the label 'political.' Many of the rank and file seemed to believe quite sincerely that encouraging people to attend a conven-tion and vote for a president who would protect the integrity of the Bible was a normal activity, not out of the ordinary, and certainly not political. One group of messengers at the Dallas convention recalled that they had attended a meeting in their state where Paul Pressler had spoken about his concerns. There they had been 'encouraged to attend' the Dallas convention; but one of them said, 'there was certainly no organized effort to get out

the vote.' Even one of the leaders of the fundamentalist movement told us that he 'hadn't really been active' that year. He had only made four or five trips a month before the convention—as he promised he would. Whether consciously or unconsciously, fundamentalists seemed not to perceive their activities as any departure from the usual ways of doing things" (1990, 168–69).

10. See also Leonard 1990, 183–84. Leonard observes: "In a sense, the denomination has experienced something akin to the hostile takeover of a corporation. A new management has taken control and is intent upon placing its people in leadership positions. With the new leadership comes the elevation of a new subgroup from within the old coalition, thus one possibility for the future is that the fundamentalists will simply replace one constituency with another, transforming the SBC into an identifiable fundamentalist denomination (p. 183).

11. Ammerman provides a helpful "theological definition of the parties" in the Southern Baptist Convention, dividing them into "self-identified fundamentalists," "fundamentalist conservatives," "conservatives," "moderate conservatives," and "self-identified moderates" (1990).

12. I am indebted to Nancy Ammerman's insightful analysis at this point and throughout in describing the fundamentalist takeover of the Convention. For a fuller discussion of these and other obstacles encountered by the denomination's moderates, see Ammerman 1990, 174–78. See also Leonard 1990, 180–82.

13. Compare Ammerman 1990, 253–58.

14. See, for example, Cothen, 1993, 45.

15. The quotation is from Article IV. See Plepkorn 1978, 409.

16. How much real agreement ever really existed is a matter of debate, and I do not want to overstate the point made here. As Bill Leonard observes: "The genius of the SBC was its ability to shape a center—and identity a mythology—around which a diverse regional, theological and popular constituency could cooperate. The center did not eliminate diversity and conflict—far from it—but it created an environment in which numerous factions could join together (unite would be too strong a term) in common endeavor" (1993, 905).

17. Grady Cothen describes it as a "rapidly developing ecclesiastical authoritarianism . . . it is not the orderly, carefully articulated, slowly developed gradually implemented ecclesiological authority of some of the older denominations. The lines of communication that process decision-making are often private. The agenda is worked out in unofficial caucuses." But the results are tangible: "a developing order of 'high priests;' " a " 'shadow cabinet' " with substantial power; and "a system of reward and punishment" (Cothen 1993, 364). Bill Leonard describes it as "a growing 'presbygational' polity" (1993, 905). This is not to suggest that the Convention did not already wield considerable influence over the church, in spite of its congregational structure. As Nancy Ammerman observes, "[Moderate] Denominational leaders were caught in a fatal dilemma. . . . Denominations whose official polity is congregational have no basis for acknowledging the very real power wielded by their bureaucrats. They refuse to grant legitimacy to a group that, under normal circumstances, has enormous influence over the local churches. They continue to assert that it is the local congregation that is the only legitimate source of authority, while

allowing a de facto oligarchy to prevail" (1990, 177). The change, then, was in some senses one of degree, not kind.

18. The stunning mixture of inerrantist and right-wing political commitments is " 'no accident,' " according to George Marsden. Indeed, according to Marsden, it was only when Southern Baptist fundamentalists allied their theological cause with the cause of the political right that they won control of the Convention. See Leonard 1990, 164.

19. See Cothen 1993, 157–63, who describes the development as one of "Creeping Creedalism." Elsewhere Cothen observes, "Each of the presidents since 1979 has emphasized that he would not appoint anyone to a committee who was not an inerrantist or a believer in a 'perfect Bible.' Thus, it is easy to see how this effort would, within a decade, result in agencies and seminaries controlled by fundamentalists. It has come to pass" (p. 83).

20. See below.

21. Criswell's views on pastoral leadership are illustrative. Speaking to what was the Criswell Bible College, he declared: " 'The pastor is the ruler of the church' . . . Lay leadership of the church is unbiblical when it weakens the pastor's authority as ruler of the church. . . . A laity-led, deacon-led church will be a weak church anywhere on God's earth. The pastor is the ruler of the church. There is no other thing than that in the Bible" (Cothen 1993, 245).

22. Deacons assist with communion and often serve as members of a church's executive council. See Ammerman 1990, 94.

23. See Ammerman 1990, 94; Anders and Metcalf-Whittake 1993, 214; and Cothen 1993, 142–44. On more recent demonstrations of opposition to the ordination of women, see Wingfield 1993, 7.

24. Ammerman goes on to note: "When fundamentalists claimed that moderates did not really believe the Bible, they were likely to point to women pastors as the perfect example of defying God's Word. And when moderates wanted to contrast their tolerance and open-mindedness with fundamentalist oppressiveness, they pointed to their acceptance of women as proof. When a fundamentalist seminary student wanted to peg the stance of a professor, he might ask (as one Midwestern student often did), 'Do you believe in the ordination of women and homosexuals?' (They were apparently equally abhorrent to him.) And on the other side of the theological fence, when moderates talked about how they might visibly identify their churches, they joked that perhaps their church signs should read, 'Women ordained here.' Every time the convention passed a resolution or a Board adopted a policy against women, a defiant surge of new ordinations took place in moderate churches. Positions on women became a litmus test on both sides" (1990, 93–94).

25. On the value of a structured deployment process, see Carroll and others 1981 118–24. On the significance of contact with female clergy as a key to changing attitudes, see Lehman 1985, 139–92.

26. Compare the comments of Nancy Ammerman cited in the notes above.

27. It is doubtful that even the fundamentalists will be able to sustain the kind of unity they enjoyed during the early days of their crusade. See Cothen 1993, 368; and Leonard 1993, 905. The latter observes: "Desperate to create a new center for the SBC, fundamentalists find themselves increasingly factionalized between subgroups that I call

militant and moderate fundamentalists, the former intent on rapid purification of the SBC, the latter a more pragmatic group willing to move more slowly and deliberately in accomplishing its goals. Many agencies are on the edge of another takeover by various types of fundamentalists anxious to impose their own agendas on the denomination or its institutions."

28. See Cothen 1993, 294. Evidence of the complete and irreversible changes in the denomination is to be found everywhere. In a recent article Nancy Ammerman describes the moderate Cooperative Baptist Fellowship as the model for a new, "postmodern denomination," which might even avoid leaving the Convention. See Ammerman 1993. In the same issue Bill Leonard suggests that the Convention might make room for a "society method" in which churches are provided with a number of cooperative efforts they can opt to support. This is, after all, what is slowly happening anyway, and, Leonard argues, this would provide time for "new centers" to emerge. Leonard also acknowledges, however: "The divisions are so deep and the stakes so high . . . that society-based denominationalism may not be possible" (1993).

29. The hopeful words of Leon McBeth penned over a decade ago have an ironic ring to them: "The ordination of Southern Baptist women to various forms of ministry may signal fundamental changes in our attitudes and interpretation of the ministry. The growing number of women ministers, their effectiveness in the work as acknowledged by opponents and proponents alike, and their growing acceptability among Southern Baptists apparently represent a new day for Southern Baptist ministry" (1981, 529).

30. Compare Anders and Metcalf-Whittake 1993, 206.

31. On Southeastern, see above. Southern's new president (Al Mohler) was introduced in April of 1993 at an open forum convened by his predecessor, Roy Honeycutt. Melanie Childers, a staff reporter for the Convention's *Western Recorder,* described the encounter: "Inquiries directed toward Mohler at times escalated into dialogue and even lectures. However, the president-elect maintained a calm demeanor throughout the session. Such issues as his vision for the school, his age and his involvement in a secret society on campus while a doctoral student were broached, but the conversation continually returned to the ordination and ministry of women. Of 14 questions asked, five directly related to women in ministry, and others touched on the subject. Mohler responded by saying the seminary deserves to know both his stance and the denomination's trends. He emphasized that the seminary's guiding document, the Abstract of Principles does not address the issue, and that the school's focus is to train ministers, not call them. 'I believe in women in ministry,' he said. 'It's a question of what kind of ministry. It is impossible for me to square the ordination of women to the pastoral ministry with what I see in the New Testament' " (Childers 1993, 2). On the fortunes of Southern Seminary, see also Cothen 1993, 295–306.

6

The Roman Catholic Church
A Defining and Excluding Bureaucracy

The question is whose will is to predominate. Or, as Hodgkinson says, "We are all either administered or administering" ... while William Blake says, "I must Create a System, or be enslav'd by another Man's." And G. B. Shaw's Don Juan argues that it is better "to be able to choose the line of greatest advantage instead of yielding in the direction of the least resistance. ... To be in Hell is to drift; to be in Heaven is to steer." This leads us to think that it is better to run organizations than to be run by them.

—Thomas B. Greenfield, "Leaders and Schools"

If Southern Baptist polity allows for the unintended possibility that women might be ordained, Roman Catholic polity clearly does not. Canon 1024 of the laws governing the church clearly specifies that "Only a baptized male validly receives sacred ordination." Commentaries on canon law offer no hope the sentence may be interpreted in any way that allows another possibility.[1] As a result, the bureaucratic character of the church has a defining and excluding role missing from the other denominations that I studied, including those with an episcopacy (i.e., bishops).[2]

Bureaucratic Linkages

Reflecting on the significance of the canon and the way in which its 1917 precursor was modified, one interviewee observed:

> Women have no decision-making power in the church. Decision making is tied to jurisdiction. Jurisdiction is tied to ordination all away along the line. We are locked out. Absolutely locked out. . . . Canon 1024 says, very simply, ordination can be validly received only by baptized males. And when you read the commentary on that . . . when the canons were revised in 1983, the commentary says that the pope at that time pushed for that, that there was absolutely no discussion. . . . We are just frozen out. (RC6:32)

"Frozen Out"

The sense of being "frozen out" at the administrative level evolves in large part from the way in which decisions are made on the parish level. Here, the clergy alone possesses veto power. Accordingly, with only rare and "illegal" exception, parish councils are viewed as purely advisory.[3] Not only are women excluded from decision making, so are men. Nonetheless, the interviewees clearly feel that gender ultimately deprives them of involvement in a way that goes beyond the church's "clericalism."[4]

This is not to suggest that women are without significant roles in the life of the church. By their own admission, they are, in fact, widely influential and they often make decisions about issues one would at first think are clerical prerogatives. Deprived of ordination, however, women feel powerless to shape the larger life of the church, and because they are so capable, their sense of powerlessness is all the more striking.

> Women who are employed by the church, either by the diocese or by the parish, are involved in decision making in certain areas only, the area of their expertise, for instance. There are some women who hold a degree in canon law and they are hired by the diocese and they might work, say, in the marriage tribunal office, which determines whether an application for annulments of marriages is going to be advanced or how they are going to be dealt with. There are other women who are specialists in family-life issues and they're hired and they make decisions

about the programming. But nowhere do women make decisions about universal church discipline or even the discipline in the diocese and nowhere do they make decisions about the theology of the church. (RC7:29–30).

This sense of exclusion extends to every level of the church's bureaucracy. Nine of the ten interviewees insisted that, whatever their own role elsewhere, it was clerics who wielded "overriding authority" in the church and therefore shaped both its life and its theology.[5] One hinted that even a certain measure of manipulation is necessary if a woman is to hope for any degree of influence.

At the local level—well, at any level of the church—lay people are nothing more than advisory. So when you talk about real decision making the only real decisions that are made are through the clergy. . . . You have to get into these local parishes. You have to be able to fit into any of these local parishes. You have to buy into the party line and kind of work your way up as a good girl . . . then maybe the bishop will see that you get on one of those committees so then you can bend it there a little bit. . . . that's never been my style, and it's most certainly not decision making. (RC63:31–32)

All the Skirts Are Worn by Men

Nor is administrative power the only bureaucratic issue. Controlled by canon law, as are all aspects of Catholic life, involvement in the church's liturgy is also at issue, as is the opportunity to minister to church membership. Practically speaking, the responsibilities assigned to women and men appear to be determined in large part by sex-role stereotypes, assigning nurture to the former and effective sacramental power to the latter. The result is more than a little ironic.

Yes, I'm asked to preach a great deal, but never, of course, to preside at the sacrament.[6] I just prepare people for this, and this is an especially problematic thing because I am the one who is responsible for preparing people for the sacrament of confirmation, yet, when it comes to the celebration of the sacrament, I am excluded from the sanctuary while the rectory's cook's cousin, who is a retired priest, is included and the deacons who don't know one name of one candidate for the sacrament of confirmation are also included. (RC1:32)

Even on the diocesan and national level, where (with the exception of Southern Baptists) so many of the women I interviewed found their churches more inclusive, Roman Catholics felt excluded on the basis of gender. "There are women who work at the United States Catholic Conference. . . . They might run an office there, the office of the laity, or something like that. But actually very few women do those things at the national level. I mean, it's really the Old Boy's Club that makes the decisions there in the Vatican. . . . Virtually all the skirts are worn by men" (RC9:31–32).

Over-Qualified

Not surprisingly, Roman Catholic women feel equally powerless in shaping their own futures. This sense of powerlessness takes a number of different forms. Career goals, for example, are sharply circumscribed. "My gender has truly limited my career. I have two masters, one in counseling and a Masters of Divinity. So I have 150 graduate credits, but because I am a woman I am very underemployed. I cannot be ordained, which means . . . there are a very few jobs that I can apply for that are stimulating and for most of the jobs I am over-qualified" (RC8:15). And, having found a job, many find that the range of responsibilities with which they are entrusted is similarly limited. "Even in my job as a campus minister, because it's a small school they would ask the priest who I work with to bless the college fans, although it doesn't take an ordained [priest] to do that or to pray at faculty dinners. . . . They won't ask me to do it, so those are real negatives" (RC8:15).

Silent Observers

In turn, this despair extends to the issue of ordination itself. The failed attempt of the National Conference of Catholic Bishops to produce a pastoral letter on women's role after nine years of work is a case in point.[7] Having begun in 1988 with a document that featured the testimony of women interviewed in hearings conducted by the bishops, the fourth draft (issued in 1993) featured instead Pope John Paul II's contention that equality between the sexes cannot be achieved at the expense of minimizing the differences (Steinfels 1992). Other changes to the fourth draft included:

1. A new emphasis on the argument that women's equality with men is tied to "a respectful appreciation of sexual differences"

2. A warning "against oversimplification in discussions of sexism"

3. A "shift to treating sexism as just one of the several societal evils harming women"

4. The introduction of "more material on sexual morality"

5. The omission of "most criticisms of alleged clerical insensitivity to women"

6. The omission of "a statement that 'an incapacity to treat women as equals ought to be considered a negative indicator for fitness for ordination' " ("Once in Christ", 1992d, 221, 223).

One interviewee reflected on the bishops' work, and when asked if women are involved in the church's decision-making process on the national level, she responded: "Barely.... For instance, the bishops have been writing for eight or nine years a pastoral letter on women that received a wonderful consultative process where ... many women were listened to very well. The first draft spoke to those ... sessions and quoted many of the women; it was, in many ways, a better document than the one just released" (RC1:30).[8]

Another interviewee was not convinced that women were taken seriously, even in the process of preparing the first draft. "Those women who were on those committees when the pastoral that was being written on women, they were advisory. Some of them got mad and quit. They were silent observers and advisors at best" (RC6:32).

According to Their Own Particular Nature

It would be wrong to assume, however, that the failure of the bishops to produce a pastoral letter more sensitive to the voice of women in the church is the sole catalyst for the sense of frustration felt by the interviewees. Since 1975, when, during the UN International Women's Year, Pope Paul VI called on the church to study the role of women,[9] the bureaucracy of the church has repeatedly made it clear that ordination is closed to them.[10] In the process the church has also defined what it means to be a woman.

Early in 1976, Pope Paul VI himself led the way in comments addressed to the National Congress of the Italian Women's Center:

> Like the Church of the origins, so also the Church of today cannot but be on the side of women, especially where the latter, from being an active and responsible subject is put in the humiliating position of a passive and insignificant object: as in certain environments of work and in certain of the worse instrumentalizations of the mass media in social relations and in the family. We are of the opinion, however, in accordance with what the Second Vatican Council said, that women must "play their part fully according to their own particular nature" (*Gaudium et spes,* no. 60). And it is her "own particular nature" that women must not renounce. In fact the same "image and likeness" of God which she has in common with man and which makes her fully his equal (cf. Gen. 1:26–27) is realized in her in a particular way, which differentiates woman from man, no more, however, than man is differentiated from woman: not in dignity of nature but in diversity of functions. It is necessary to beware of a subtle form of belittlement of women's status, in which it is possible to fall today, by refusing to recognize those diversifying features stamped by nature on both human beings. It belongs on the contrary to the order of creation that woman should fulfill herself as a woman, certainly not in a competition of mutual oppression with man, but in harmonious and fruitful integration based on respectful recognition of the roles peculiar to each. It is therefore highly desirable that in the various fields of social life in which she has her place, woman should bring that unmistakably human stamp of sensitiveness and solicitude, which is characteristic of her. (Luyckx 1980, 6) [11]

It was already clear from correspondence with Donald Coggan, Archbishop of Canterbury and Primate of the Anglican Church, exactly how the Pope's thinking applied to the question of ordination. In a letter to the Archbishop, dated 30 November 1975, the Pope wrote:

> Your Grace is of course well aware of the Catholic Church's position on this question. She holds that it is not admissible to ordain women to the priesthood for very fundamental reasons. These reasons include: the example recorded in the sacred scriptures of Christ choosing his apostles only from among men; the constant practice of the Church, which has imitated Christ in choosing only men; and her living teaching authority

which has consistently held that the exclusion of women from the priesthood is in accordance with God's plan for his Church. (Luyckx 1980, 7)

Later in the same year, the Sacred Congregation for the Doctrine of
the Faith, an organization charged with the responsibility "to safeguard
the Church's teaching on faith and morals" (Doyle 1984, 29), followed
suit. Drawing on the work of the Pontifical Biblical Commission and
the International Theological Commission, the Congregation issued its
Declaration on the Question of the Admission of Women to the Ministerial Priesthood *(Inter Insigniores)*. The declaration lacked the claim to infal-
libility that some of the Pope's own statements are assigned, and on this
basis some have contended that the issue of women's ordination not only
remains open, but its continued discussion remains "imperative" (Doyle
1984, 29–30). Nonetheless, the Pope did approve, confirm, and order the
Declaration to be printed and distributed (Doyle 1984, 29); and the language of the Declaration leaves its readers in no doubt about the will of
God: "The Sacred Congregation for the Doctrine of the Faith judges it
necessary to recall that the Church, in fidelity to the example of the
Lord, does not consider herself authorized to admit women to priestly
ordination."[12]

In 1988, Pope John Paul II reaffirmed the views of Paul VI, making
it clear that God, never mind the church, had substantive reasons for
refusing women the sacrament of ordination. Addressing himself to the
subject of "the dignity and vocation of women" (a phrase and the title of
a document that would figure prominently in the aborted pastoral letter
of 1993), the Pope observed:

> Since Christ, in instituting the Eucharist, linked it in such an explicit
> way to the priestly service of the Apostles, it is legitimate to conclude
> that he thereby wished to express the relationship between man and
> woman, between what is "feminine" and what is "masculine." It is a
> relationship willed by God both in the mystery of creation and in the
> mystery of Redemption. It is *the Eucharist* above all that expresses *the
> redemptive act of Christ the Bridegroom towards the Church the Bride.* This is
> clear and unambiguous . . . when the sacramental ministry of the Eucha-
> rist, in which the priest performs acts *"in persona Christi,"* is performed
> by a man. This explanation confirms the teaching of the Declaration
> *Inter Insigniores,* published at the behest of Paul VI in response to the

question concerning the admission of women to the ministerial priest-hood. (Field-Bibb 1991, 193–94)[13]

These statements represent only a fraction of the official pronouncements that have been issued on the subject. For the outsider, bureaucratic control in the Roman Catholic church is expressed in a bewildering number of ways by an equally bewildering number of agencies.[14] And to make mat-ters more confusing, pronouncements made by those agencies have very different levels of significance and are binding on Roman Catholics in a variety of ways. The message, however, remains clear. Women cannot be ordained; God will not permit it, and that prohibition is bound up in what it means to be a woman.

The control exerted by the church, however, is not always applied in the form of polite theological discourse. One interviewee, who readily admits that she has publicly expressed her interest in being ordained, has, in fact, been sanctioned by her bishop. As a result she has been asked to desist from calling for the ordination of women; she has been denied the opportunity to serve on diocesan and interfaith committees; and, in correspondence from her archdiocese, she has been described as an "embarrassment" to the bishop (RC8:22ff.). Still others struggle in a less public fashion: "Being called to ordination in a tradition that does not even necessarily want to admit you exist becomes a question of survival and then one of staying healthy. . . . Since seminary this has been my task" (RC2:22).

Organizational Culture

None of what I have said about the bureaucratic character of the Roman Catholic experience means that its culture is a matter of indiffer-ence to the women within its walls. For women, at an early age, it is a potent force for socialization, shaping vocations and religious self-under-standing.

As a child in grade school, seventh grade specifically, the sister who was teaching class had provided vocation material and there was a book, *Boyhood's Highest Ideal* and *Girlhood's Highest Ideal;* I couldn't go with the boy's so I ended up being a sister because I couldn't be a priest (RC5:2)

Well, the religious tradition, you see, has always been male-dominated in our religion and the only way you find out who God was, was through males. For example, I always thought that men were closer to God than women were because it was the men, the priests, who got all dressed up in their fancy vestments which were satin, and they touched the gold dishes, and they always presided. So I always thought that men were closer to God, more Godlike and the only way that I could get closer to God was to obey what all the men, especially the priests, had to say. So it's been real hard for me to realize that God also mediates through me, since it's always been men. (RC8:4–5)

Notwithstanding the thorough-going exclusion they have experienced, the Roman Catholics I interviewed also identify with their church's culture more strongly than does any other group of interviewees. One interviewee felt so strongly about this issue that she began her interview with a disclaimer of sorts: "I want to make a little preparatory note, which is that whatever I say, obviously I have been very strongly linked to my tradition rather than alienated from it. The indication being that I'm still here and practicing it and still an active member in my church. So . . . even though . . . there have been alienating things, my behavior belies that because I behave as linked to the institutional church" (RC7:1). Another felt strongly enough to end her interview in a similar fashion:

I realize I'm talking about a lot of negatives, but, you see, I find a great amount of—I hate to say—hope, because sometimes I'm not in a very hopeful state. But if all good women and men leave the Roman Catholic Church, how are things going to change? . . . All we can do, all I can do is respond to God's call to holiness, and what that means to me is continuing to speak up prophetically and saying this needs to be done, but am I still a Catholic? I sure am, because I am not going to let the official church define me. Where do I pray, how do I—I feel so sacramentally starved, I don't know what I'm going to do yet. (RC8:30–31)

As strongly attracted as they are to the church's culture, it is at the same time the one area left to women in which experimentation is possible. As a result it is here, that, ironically, Roman Catholic women are also moving away from their church in a decisive fashion.

A Namby-Pamby Virgin

In discussing stories, Roman Catholic women related as rich a variety of stories as I encountered. But as had the other interviewees, the majority began with stories from the Bible. No one figured more prominently in our conversations about the Bible or the saints than did Mary, the mother of Jesus.[15]

For many, Mary represents the church's attempt to shape the behavior and self-understanding of women, beginning at even the earliest stages of their lives. However well intended, the stories are often used in a coercive fashion and often without regard to the personality of the child.

> As I grew up in Catholic grade school Mary was personified as a person who was the handmaid of the Lord, who was a passive figure, not an active figure. She was silent. I grew up in the forties and fifties. And she was held up to me in specific instances of a person who was very good and was chosen by God for this specific role as the mother of the Savior. Yet, she was not an outspoken person. I had some tendency to want to be assertive and . . . I can think of a couple of instances where she was cited as a model for me, for a submissive figure. (RC6:1–2)[16]

Mary is also portrayed by the church in a way that is largely foreign to the experience of most Catholic women and, which, by definition, robs them of a model for leadership. Deeply committed to the image of "the Virgin" on one level, interviewees' disdain for the church's use of the image is unmistakable.

> I've had my ups and downs with Mary, and I feel that the Roman Catholic tradition has done a great deal of disservice to Mary, the Mother of Jesus, which leaves most Roman Catholic women presented with a virgin as their primary model. Well that's not most women's experience, and it invalidates most women's experience and it robs most Roman Catholic women of someone who I really believe not only could be, but is a really strong model for discipleship, for commitment, for perseverance. . . . But what we are presented is some sicky-sweet little namby-pamby virgin, isolated, separated from the experience of most women. (RC4:2–3)

Broadening the Tradition

The same tension colored the stories respondents told of the church's saints.

> I taught a graduate course called "Women's Spirituality in Story," where we have a look at women saints through the ages . . . which ones give us heroic role models and, on the other hand, . . . what stories do we question. For instance, there is a medieval St. Rita who was abused by her husband . . . the traditional books . . . said she was so wonderful and so holy because she patiently endured her husband's abuse for years and years . . . and prayed for him. . . . Within our own century when I was a child people emphasized the story of St. Maria Goretti. She was a twelve-year-old in Italy. A man wanted to rape her. She refused to be raped and he stabbed her about fifteen times or something like that and we have glorified her as being so wonderful. . . . Yet, you know, at this very time many women are the victims of rape and I don't think that it is a better thing to be dead than to be alive and raped. . . . I think that is a sort of patriarchal emphasis. (RC10:2–3)

In response to these tensions, the women I spoke with have pursued two very different strategies. One might be described as a process of reclamation. In both the biblical text and in the history of their tradition, Roman Catholics have identified stories of a completely different tenor than that of the stories told during their childhood. Mary is described as one who had experienced "oppression" and who, in response, announced revolutionary changes to come. Miriam is seen as one who led the people in a prayer of thanksgiving for deliverance. Mary Magdalen is described as "apostle to the apostles," and St. Catherine of Sienna is valued as one who possessed the courage to challenge the Pope.

For others it is not enough to reclaim the stories of their own tradition, or even those of the larger Christian tradition. For these respondents, the search for an adequate narrative tradition has moved them to draw on the stories of women in other religious traditions as well. The key to the process of selection appears to be a shared experience of oppression, the example of perseverance and, of course, gender itself.

> I have to broaden my religious tradition. I can recall about 16, 17, 18 years ago meeting with a women's interfaith coalition and meeting two

women that had survived the holocaust. One was in a very conservative temple. . . . She would go every day to pray and would not be counted. . . . Finally after years of this they began to include her, count her . . . Rosemary Moser was the first woman president of Temple Sinai, which was a Reform Congregation. I guess I want to broaden my religious tradition. Those were instances where persevering women were able to make changes. . . . They helped me confirm my spirituality, which would include a spirituality of endurance and perseverance and liberation. (RC1:2–3)

A number of factors have changed the way in which the interviewees understand the narrative traditions of their faith. For some, graduate school was the key. Others had been prompted to explore new approaches by feminist writers. For still another, the catalyst was Vatican II. However, it was not simply the changes set in motion by Vatican II that prompted this interviewee to reexamine the church's traditions. It was also the perception that, notwithstanding the emphasis of Vatican II on social justice, she remained marginalized by her fellow Catholics.[17] Whatever the cause, I had the impression that Roman Catholic women are engaged in a process of discovering their own narrative tradition, a new tradition often far removed from the one in which they were raised.

Women are Invisible

Despite the leadership provided by Roman Catholic women in challenging the nature of the language that dominates the conversation and liturgy of the church, the Roman Catholic Church remains one of the least progressive.[18] Unlike I had in some of the other denominations, I detected no broad-based sensitivity to language issues.[19]

One respondent said that she "read women" into the language used by the church in worship. For her, "actions are more important." This, however, was an exceptional view. I found that the remaining nine spoke in strong terms concerning vertical language (having to do with God) and horizontal language (having to do with the community of faith). The male-dominated nature of both appears to have had a number of affects.

One affect has been to undermine the self-esteem of some women. Interviewees spoke, for example, of having been left with the impression that they were "second class citizens" (RC8:6). More than one woman argued that such language made worship difficult if not intolerable in the parish churches they attended.

> I find extremely offensive sexist or noninclusive language in the liturgy or the worship of the church. In fact, it's so bad that I find it impossible to go to regular liturgies in parishes because almost none of them [make] any attempt to clean it up, by that I mean both the language referring to humanity, men and women, and the language that is referring to God . . . it has literally driven me away from church. . . . That is not to say that I don't worship. I do, but I worship with a couple of feminist communities where we're very careful about that language and around which the worship can be a real joy and a faith experience. (RC9:3–4)

"The Eucharist became a painful experience for me," commented one interviewee, "contrary to the meaning of the word [to give thanks]" (RC2:2). And still another intimated that male-dominated language had made it difficult for her to "understand how God can understand women" (RC8:5). One particularly perceptive interviewee identified the source of the problem in concrete terms:

> I went through the standard text that we use in the Roman Catholic lectionary. I also went through the standard text that we use for Sunday Eucharist in the Catholic Church. On an average Sunday we . . . use over sixty male metaphors for God, and there are not any female metaphors written in the standard texts. . . . If you typically go to Roman Catholic worship, sixty times you're going to hear male metaphors: Father, Lord, Him, He. . . . Women are invisible, so to speak, in the linguistic structure of the services. (RC10:5–6)

Perhaps even more striking are the initiatives women have taken in response to the male-dominated language of their church. Notwithstanding the tradition of a shared liturgy, the women I spoke with have begun to experiment with new ways of referring to God, incorporating feminine and spirit language. Still others are experimenting with alternatives to speaking at all, relying instead on mime and dance. There are also changes in worship patterns. Two of the women with whom I spoke have abandoned the parish setting altogether and worship instead in feminist communities or house churches where there is a greater measure of inclusion. The experience, however, is not without its price. One seminary graduate shared this observation about her experience: "To me it's a representation of how it must have been in the early house churches in the first century. . . . It's difficult, because then you have to ask yourself, 'Is this Catholic, or is this Christian? And does it make any difference?' But for me it does make a difference, because I'm Roman Catholic. . . . Where am I? I'm alienated. . . . I don't have a church that's Roman Catholic. . . . I don't fit" (RC8:14).[20]

The Myth of Eating the God

The rituals of the church pose even greater challenges. Rarely, however, is activity itself problematic. In the cases where it is, respondents mentioned the practice of confessing one's sins to a male and the practice in marriage ceremonies of giving the bride away. Another mentioned the now abandoned practice of "churching" in which women are "purified" after childbirth. The central problem for the interviewees, however, lies with the dominant role males play in nearly every ritualistic act of the church. Reflecting on the act of confession, one woman observed: "Well, one of the difficulties is that because all of the sacraments come from males, I feel sacramentally starved. . . . For example, even during confession it's always to a male if you want to have it official. That's very difficult to do. So what are my options? My options are to—it's just very difficult because we have no options" (RC8:12–13).

The male-dominated character of Roman Catholic worship has, in fact, become such a painful dynamic that the Eucharist itself has become an "alienating" experience. Only when one appreciates how central this sacrament is to Roman Catholic theology can the significance of this complaint be fully understood.

I have been attending Protestant churches for the past sixty days. My sense of alienation has increased to the point that I am looking elsewhere . . . I am at the point where I can no longer go into a Catholic Church and participate in the worship and partake of the Eucharist. . . . It has been a process of increasing awareness, and along with that increasing alienation . . . I have heard more Catholic women say that they cannot leave because they feel so drawn to the Eucharist. That is where their pain is at that level, and that need is so strong, and their tie is so strong to that understanding of the Eucharist and communion with God, that they will go through all other kinds of shit in order to get it. It's like you're hooked. It's like you're caught. . . . We were discussing that at one of our meetings in June, and there was a women who was very powerful in the church, she was a sister. She died about five or six years ago, and she said something about "the myth of eating the God is so strong." And that's what's got us! That's why those who cannot leave because they believe this so strongly, and they don't know where else to go to get it, that they keep going. So, it's a peculiar set up, because the belief at that other level is so strong that whatever else the institution does to them, they are satisfied at that level. . . . It almost sounds like the woman who keeps being beaten by the husband and yet she says I love him. But it is almost like there are two layers in the church: there's this layer of when you have the experience, the real experience of God, and then you have all this other stuff. (RC6:17–18)

Another said,

I love the celebration of the Eucharist. It's always been a centerpoint in my life and it's very important. It's very interesting to me now when I go to feminist liturgies that are sometimes Eucharist, and very often are not, that I miss the Eucharist not being there because I believe very deeply in it, but the problem is when you go to [a] typical Catholic church it is celebrated only by men. And you find as many as half a dozen or even [more] males, you know, with nary a female in sight, celebrating the Eucharist. That's another reason I don't go to regular parishes. I stay away from them like the plague. They're a danger to my faith. I mean that quite literally. And then, of course, in a lot of places, altar servers are strictly male. There are some parishes that have girls do that function, but, you know, the bishop sort of looks the other way, but there are other places that enforce the rules, which say no females. And then there are parishes where although you could have women reading or distributing the Eucharist, they don't do it because the pastor is a stick in the mud on it, or something. And so, I guess, any time there are all male casts or predominantly male casts in the rituals then, yeah, I really have a problem and that really affects me, 'cause the Eucharist is so central to my faith. (RC9:7)

Different Pictures

Of the five theological traditions I have considered, the Roman Catholic tradition is the one most often associated with iconography. The interviews held some surprises for me, although none of the observations made were at odds with ones I have already made. One surprise was the number of interviewees who were relatively unaffected by the icons of their tradition. Seven of the ten women reported that the gender orientation of the icons in their tradition had little impact on their relationship with the Roman Catholic tradition.

The reasons for this assessment varied. Some simply did not deal with icons on the gender level. Another suggested that there were very nearly as many female images as there were male icons. By contrast, some of the women I talked to had focused on the feminine images, where they found either comfort or attractive images of courage. Hinting that the reason might be that icons were no longer central to their faith (if they ever had been), the majority described them as "friendly," "Byzantine," or as "part of a scrapbook" (RC7:7–8).

This is not to say that all of the interviewees felt the same way about the church's icons and symbols. Three expressed strongly negative feelings about the icons used by their church. For example, one woman observed:

> I'm having to redefine . . . religious icons. For example, I really am struggling with the cross. I don't know what to do with that. I'm finding, for me, when I image God, I'm imaging interlocking circles, a wreath. Sometimes I can see it looks like a spider web, that concentric thing, with God not only in the middle, but God throughout. I see interweaving, sometimes I have weavings on a loom of some cloth or some yarn. Those are really important because of some interwovenness of what God is. . . . In my office I have a wonderful picture of God and she is holding a baby, and she is rocking this baby. It's particularly important to me, because I just became a grandmother in January and I can imagine God, the mother God—grandmother God, rocking this baby and, you see, what is so wonderful is that God, in order to love this baby, needs to be engaged. And when I rock my grandson I can really identify, because I need my grandson and God needs me as well as I need God —so the interconnectedness. So, yes, the different pictures are becoming more and more important to me. (RC8:10–11)

In the Shadow of Men

In addition to mentioning these features of Roman Catholic culture, more than one of the women interviewed mentioned the lectionary. Deeply rooted in the life of the church, some Catholics found it to be male dominated.[21]

> The daily routine of the church and the liturgical calendar is central to Catholic worship . . . almost every day, there is a saint that is commemorated and the readings are picked that in some way exemplify that person's life or that person is mentioned in the liturgy of the day. And, there is such an overabundance of males in comparison to females that is very noticeable and very disturbing. (RC6:5)

> I did a very extensive analysis finding out that less than ten percent of the time in our worship do we read about women. . . . When we do read about women, we tend to focus on women who are healed or helped or rescued or saved and we also focus very much on Mary as the mother of Christ. (RC10:1)

What was both striking and unique, however, was the complaint that the Roman Catholic Church controls women, not within its walls alone, but beyond. One interviewee observed, "The church has instigated and has been successful at social control . . . and has kept women from being whole human beings, not only in the church, but in society as a whole." In this connection, four of the respondents focused on the "categorical prohibition" of abortion and contraception, arguing that women live "in the shadow of men," without control over their own bodies.[22]

> I see that the institutional church, by the way it presented its understanding of who women are and what women are to be, that they have instigated—and I think it has been rather successful—social control of women into passive roles really not being able to, without great effort, to assert themselves and be full human beings, not only within the church, but within society. It's only those of us who, maybe, by our own inflation or by our personalities, by our education, have really been able to work ourselves out from under that. Now I, you know, I'm talking I suppose, more accurately of my own generation. I was born in 1940, so it's really hard for me to say exactly how that works. I have a

nineteen-year-old daughter and I know that it's different. The grip isn't as strong, but I see an awful lot of kids coming out of those Catholic high schools that are awfully traditional and I think a lot of what they're being taught in terms of morality is just really obviously doing a disservice to women, you know, at the official level not being able to use birth control. I'm not a person who believes in abortion, but I sometimes think people find themselves in situations where there is no good alternative, and just to be told categorically that this is something that you cannot even think about—that does something to a woman's psyche without somebody telling them beforehand what they can and cannot do. (RC6:14–15)

No other denomination I studied evinced such widespread influence over the lives of its members.

Authority as Effective Power

The Roman Catholic Church exercises what students of organizational theory describe as "authority as effective power." In other words, authority is exercised over both resources and subordinates by people in designated positions, holding the appropriate titles. In such settings "the authority symbols are built in, and the messages transmitted are specific, literal, and relatively 'hard' " (Hirsch and Andrews 1984, 176).

Hierarchical and Clericalized

The complete and formal exclusion of women from access to ordination has had a number of discernible results. For example, the kind of informal dynamics that interpenetrate and overlap closely with bureaucratic structures in other churches are, in a sense, missing in the Roman Catholic Church. In-groups are perceived to be bureaucratic givens which are, by definition, male dominated, "hierarchical" and "clericalized."

Although many of the fifty respondents feel that membership in such a group is important, more often than not Roman Catholics believe that membership in an in-group is indispensable. The reason is clear:

I don't think it should be important, but it is. . . . That is where the structural power lies. And there is no way that I, as a female, can be part of that 'in-group.' Just by gender I am excluded. . . . I think it should

be a church of equality, of the people of God working together under
the power of the Spirit. I think that's where, in a sense, the real spiritual
power is. But we are talking about spiritual power and then the power
of the church as institution in the world, and if you are going to talk
about that kind of power, then . . . in a certain sense it is important and
it would be nice to be a part of that, and I'm never going to be.
(RC6:29–30)

Oh, absolutely, because you have to have that involvement, because
that's where the decisions are made and if you're not involved, how can
you affect the system? You see in our own Catholic Church there's a
great amount of systematic change needed and how can I do that if I'm
not a member of it? (RC8:20)

Forbidden ordination and, in some cases, the right to even address
the issue, Roman Catholic women have only one other mandated option
open to them: silence and submission. In fact, given the nature of their
church's bureaucratic structure, Roman Catholics lack even the ability to
insulate themselves from the denomination in the same way that Southern
Baptists do. With largely autonomous congregations, Southern Baptists
can treat the local church as a surrogate for the larger denomination.
Roman Catholics lack that "luxury." This is not to suggest that there are
no informal structures inhabited by women. It is to suggest, however,
that the informal structures open to them are, necessarily, "clandestine."[23]

For instance, when asked if canon law prohibiting the ordination of
women was effectively administered on the local level, six of the respondents gave me precisely the answer I anticipated—yes. Indeed, even
those who did not confine themselves to this rather direct answer acknowledged that no one in their acquaintance had been ordained. However, three of the four mentioned another kind of story: stories of ongoing irregularities in the administration of the church's affairs and in
worship. Still others at various points in the interview told stories of
women presiding over baptisms, hearing confessions, and giving absolution—all of which they are not allowed to do, but which are accomplished
by observing a number of technicalities.

One of the things about this particular parish is that [if] its written
constitution . . . was sent to the diocese, it wouldn't be acceptable. But it
has operated with that constitution for a number of years, and the

decision making in this particular parish is made by the parish council and by the constitutional directives of the parish. The priest is a member of the council and cannot veto what decisions the council makes. Now that's not in accord with canon law. (RC4:19–20)

The celebration of the Eucharistic liturgy, which is the central ritual for Catholic worship, has become increasingly painful for me because there it is only the male who can act in the role of presider. This has been mitigated somewhat by the fact that in the church that I was attending women were brought in as lectors and acolytes. In other words, they were brought in [to] supporting roles so that there would be something other than men at the altar. And that was helpful, however, it . . . was not ultimately satisfying because the male was still playing the central role. In some of the more progressive congregations they're just doing it; and they're defying the law of the world and even the law of the local . . . bishop who has to enforce that, and the bishop, if he's progressive, knows that's going on. He just pretends like he doesn't. See, there's a lot of equivocation that's happening. It's happening at the grassroots. In selective areas these changes are taking place and the rules are just being bent and stretched as far as they can be, but the top—it's still got the lid on this thing. There's a tremendous amount of pain and torment that's going on within the Roman church. (RC6:7–8)

I have frequently preached at . . . ceremonies and rituals and special liturgies just for our community. However, there are some around the country who are preaching at parishes. In addition, I and other women have presided at services, and I would call that more than private, I would call that clandestine. All that lends a sort of pseudo scandalous note to it, or sensational note to it. There are many of us who preside at worship in small groups, very small, very private groups. (RC7:32)

Refuge or Revolutionaries?

A special case of informal activity involves women who are members of religious orders. Within the religious orders, women can and have attained some distance from the sense of alienation that they feel and a greater measure of freedom than they experience in the larger denomination. There they are able to use a vocabulary that is rejected by the larger church; they have cultivated an alternative spirituality that is better suited to them; and they have even been able to practice a certain measure of the priesthood denied to them by the church's bureaucracy.[24]

> What has helped me greatly to identify with my religious tradition and, even today, keeps me identified with it, is my religious community. I said the other night to a friend of mine, "My religious community is my church" meaning they are church to me in a much more meaningful way than say the parish community is or where I happened to be linked for worship. . . . I have very little recourse to the clergy for spiritual growth experiences or input. I have a lot of trust in my religious community for that. . . . That's where I get spiritual challenge and spiritual input and the kind of demand to stretch and to grow. I guess I've never said this before—I think I only participate in church for Sunday worship. I certainly don't tap into it for any spiritual growth experiences. I use it, I guess, for a reinforcer for my identification with the tradition once a week. (RC7:11–13)

On one level, membership in an order appears to provide some measure of compensation for the women who serve in orders, tempering their reaction to the state of affairs in their church. They, like their counterparts outside the orders, are prohibited from seeking ordination, but as members of an order they have a clearly defined role within the church. Those who work outside, do not. This may help to explain the (sometimes slight) difference in the strength of their reaction to being denied ordination, which I detected during the interviews. Indeed, "women religious" (as they are called) were more likely to underline their sense of commitment to the church.

> I feel that frequently I have directly and indirectly come up against the prejudicial structures of Roman Catholicism, but I personally feel very grateful, and this is grace that the situations that have been pain and obstacles and negative for me . . . that anger-energy, that hurt-energy has been transformed into very creative energy. . . . I'm not bitter. I want to remain within the Roman Catholic Church and be a prophetic voice within. (RC10:13–14)[25]

By contrast, lay interviewees appeared to struggle more for a sense of belonging. "You have to understand, in the Roman Catholic tradition, laywomen are lower in the order of importance. First you have like the bishops and the priests, and then religious sisters and brothers, and then you have single lay people, and then you have married lay women. So it's not only gender, it's also if you're a member of a religious community" (RC8:18).[26]

Even membership in an order, however, cannot afford the same kind of distance from an exclusivistic polity. Religious women, no less than lay women, are locked out on the bureaucratic level or, as one of the respondents noted, "all the holes are plugged" (RC3:19). Indeed, at times the degree of leadership exercised by women in religious orders only seems to exacerbate the outrage felt over the issue of ordination.

> There are a few cases where women, you know, are things like chancellors of dioceses, which is like the chief of administrators, a couple of cases where they edit the diocesan newspaper, something like that. Very often they might run the school system, but at major decision-making levels in dioceses, women are very absent. They just don't do that. Ironically, they do run major church institutions . . . because of the fact that nuns are so prominent. . . . There's this kind of contradiction or irony in the church where we're often hospital administrators or we're very often presidents of universities. In fact, much more frequently than professional women in secular life. Yet, when it comes to the institution of the church *per se* we're very absent from those roles. (RC9:31)

As a result, religious orders appear to function less as a refuge and more as "a base of operations" for efforts of a more "revolutionary" character.[27] One interviewee noted,

> I really like being a part of a group of Roman Catholic sisters, because often there are enough sisters voicing opinions or entering structures that we can challenge the control of the ordained. And I give you as a specific example: for something like nine years the Roman Catholic bishops have been working on a pastoral letter on women and they keep talking about women and about what we should do and about what we should be like. They keep reinforcing the Vatican's opposition to birth control, saying you should only use natural birth control and things like that. . . . Our sisters put out strong statements saying, "You bishops are really not adequately educated in these areas and you're not doing good Christian anthropology." (RC10:12–13)

Redefining Catholicism

However, neither women in religious orders nor the lay women I interviewed are confining themselves to the task of criticizing the establishment. Although women share similar views on the subject of gender, I found that alternative communities, some local, some national, have begun to take shape. Significantly, those communities threaten to supplant the parish church's place in the lives of their participants, sped by a desire to explore the implications of the inclusion of women in the life of the church and a growing unwillingness to "go back to the basic level" with men who persist in their resistance to the ordination of women. (RC2:7) One respondent observes:

> I'm part of a women's Eucharist now where the exclusion is not present, that women are respected, women are okay, women are more than okay but just as good as men. It equalizes it more. . . . When it is [celebrated] with women of other religious communities, I don't go to those places of worship, though I still associate with the people that go there. It's not that I boycott it . . . but it is not a gift to me. It's more of something that I bear, that I tolerate. I don't go because it feels good, or because it seems right, but more that I want to stay in association with people that I know and love. (RC3:9–10)

However, such services are not merely a Roman service conducted by women. Instead, they have become the liturgical center of what can only be described as a redefinition of what it means to be Catholic.

> In my religious community and in this feminist community that I'm a part of, this feminist worshipping community, . . . we as women have been developing a lot of new rituals, which center around Christianity and I find them very exciting. You know, they combine Scripture readings, other kinds of readings, communal reflections and, generally, the sharing of something symbolic—which is sometimes bread and wine, sometimes water, sometimes flowers, sometimes, you know, multicolored ribbons. Many, many different kinds of symbols, to depict either unity or, well, whatever the theme is of the day. You know, it might be contrition or it might be unity or it might be joy in celebration or whatever. Now I don't know whether you'd call—most of them grow out of the Catholic tradition that we do. There ain't a bishop I know

that would sort of own them as a part of the tradition, but this is going on [on] the side, if you will. In fact, it's going on all over the United States. I work in the women's movement in the church rather strongly, and in a lot of major metropolitan areas, especially in the United States, there are groups like I am describing to you. They're often not terribly large, maybe the biggest would be fifty to one hundred, not all of whom come every time, of course. A lot of times they're house churches. I like to think of that as harkened back to the early church tradition where we rotate and go to each other's apartments or homes each time. (RC9:8–9)

There is more than a little irony in this state of affairs. In a recent Gallup survey of the characteristics Roman Catholics most value in their priests, one of the fourteen most important "themes" was "loyalty," i.e., the ability to "identif[y] with the tradition and the history of the Catholic Church" (Rebeck 1993, 672). Yet, clearly, the church's position on the ordination of women is propelling women away from the tradition to which they are otherwise intensely loyal. The result, in the long run, may be salutary for the women involved in alternative communities, with an alternative theology and liturgy, but it is also the diametric opposite of the characteristics the church values most.

Harbingers of Change?

None of what has been said above should be construed to mean that the Catholics I interviewed are entirely without hope. On the contrary, three kinds of anecdotes emerged in the interviews that appear to provide some measure of hope to the women I interviewed.

Three told me about a story that appeared in the *New York Times* on December 8, 1991 ("Czech Hierarchy," 1991b). Evidently, prior to the collapse of the eastern block, the underground Catholic Church in Czechoslovakia ordained at least three women and, reportedly, hundreds of married men.[28] The interviewees were quick to note that Pope Paul VI had sanctioned the ordination of the men. They also pointed out that bishops within Czechoslovakia had taken the initiative to ordain the women. In recounting this story, the respondents stressed the possibility that the same kind of irregular ordination may have taken place elsewhere in eastern Europe and in Latin America.

The respondents seem to have more than one reason for reporting these events. Stories such as these provide a kind of precedent and hold out the hope that something similar may happen again. They appear to provide an occasion for expressing solidarity and for broadening the membership in their cause. Such incidents also appear to implicitly provide an opportunity to challenge the consistency of the hierarchy and, thereby, women's exclusion from ordination. This possibility, at any rate, might explain the interviewees' interest in the episcopal role in the stories described above. One woman attributed yet another significance to the stories I was told:

> What I think is going on . . . is a cultural preparation of the faithful for women in the fullest priestly roles, because vestments and handling of the Eucharist and, in some places, preaching—all of those are things connected with priesthood. So, there is this informal kind of priesthood that is developing . . . that some day is going to be blessed and said "this is holy." . . . They're going to make it official and they're going to actually have ordination ceremonies for women. But that's the way in which I think it is happening in Catholicism right now. (RC9:28–29)

A second kind of anecdote related to the attitude of the laity toward women's ordination. The women I spoke with described their exclusion in hierarchical and clerical terms, but they did not sense the same measure of isolation from the laity. Indeed, the laity even seemed to be willing to overlook the bureaucratic strictures placed upon women at times. This impression appears to be born out by a recent Gallup poll. Of the Catholics surveyed "67% agree that 'it would be a good thing if women were allowed to be ordained as priests'" and a number of interviewees were clearly aware of the shift in lay opinion (*Gallup Survey,* 1992b, 1). Whether such changes occur is, of course, another matter.

The women also told a third series of stories of bishops who occasionally look the other way. One interviewee describes the development as the leading edge of a trend.

> I think we are going to see more and more of this [change] because of the priestless parish situation in the United States. The other thing that I've often thought about is the difference between women theologically, or sacramentally being ordained as priests, and women being . . . perceived in priestly roles by those receiving the ministry. Even though

women may not be officially ordained for a long time, the second is going on all over the place. It is going on with women who are administering parishes, women who are conducting communion services in a lot of parishes, and who will put on an alb when they distribute communion. Some churches vest or partially vest women who do that, or who . . . do the readings. (RC9:29–30)

Whether such changes occur officially is, of course, another matter. The ordination of women in the Eastern bloc can and has been characterized as an aberration, the work of a renegade (or insane) bishop acting without the Vatican's consent (Pomerleau 1992, 3). Lay opinion and behavior, relative to the subject of birth control in the United States has run counter to the position of the Vatican to no avail, and ordination is more easily controlled by the church.[29] Just how much the views of the episcopacy have changed is difficult to assess. If recent reports are to be believed, the pastoral letter failed, not because the Conference favored a more positive description of the role of women, but because a small majority of the bishops assembled simply feared that the statement would scandalize the women of the church.[30]

Clearly, the ambiguities haunt the interviewees:

I think there is some slight change in the right direction, but it is so painfully slow. For me personally, it's worse, because I'm ready to be ordained and I don't know where to go. I mean I don't think I have a real place in the institution. So I let this issue come to a head for me, therefore, I'm in more pain because the institution has not changed enough to accommodate me. (RC6:26)

Notes

1. For a commentary on this canon, see Coriden and others 1985.

2. The Roman Catholic Church traces its establishment in the United States to the second voyage of Columbus to the New World. Ultimate administrative responsibility for the church rests with His Holiness the Pope, Bishop of Rome. The church in the United States is divided into archdioceses and dioceses where responsibility lies with archbishops and bishops, respectively. These appointments are at the discretion of the Pope. The National Conference of Catholic Bishops is a collaborative body engaged in policy formulation and implementation. For this and other information, see Bedell 1992, 108–16.

3. When asked if women are included in the decision-making process on the parish level, only one of ten interviewees answered in the affirmative, but she also admitted that

the parish structure within which she works violates canon law: "Oh yes, at the parish level very much. One of the things about this particular parish is ... its written constitution ... if it was sent to the diocese, it wouldn't be acceptable, but it has operated with that constitution for a number of years and the decision-making in this particular parish is made by the parish council and by the constitutional directives of the parish. The priest is a member of the council and cannot veto what decisions the council makes. Now that's not in accord with canon law" (RC4:19–20).

4. The term "clericalism" might be defined in a number of ways. Thomas Groome defines it as the "expectation of preference ... a stance of 'power over' people ... a hierarchical perspective in which clerics see themselves as ontologically different from and better than other baptized Christians ... a caste group of fellow clerics" and, therefore, "inevitably inverted," a "self-perpetuating" group and a system that is "inherently oppressive" (Groome 1984, 96–97).

5. Only one of the interviewees described the decision-making process differently. She focused on her own parish. She also noted that the constitution of her parish was unacceptable to the diocese and had never been approved.

6. In some Protestant churches, ordination is closely identified with the right to preach. In the Roman Catholic Church, ordination to the priesthood is much more closely identified with sacramental activity. Furthermore, even the reference to preaching made here is made in a narrowly defined sense. Earlier in the interview, the same woman observed: "Many [women] preach and that is provided for in the canon law. Canon law says catechists can preach at masses *with children* and so very many women are catechists and they have every right to preach at masses. After all, there are children present at all masses" (RC1:26–27, emphasis added).

7. Pastoral letters are not legislatively binding, but they are used to shape church policy, its programming, and the content of theological education at the church's seminaries.

8. Considerable optimism was expressed in some quarters when the process of preparing the pastoral letter first began. In 1985, for example, Mary Tobin argued that women were "becoming partners in the dialogue" (1985, 301)."

9. In taking 1975 as something of a watershed for current discussions within the Roman Catholic Church, we follow both Pope Paul VI's reflections and the observations made by Luyckx 1980, 2, 6–7. See also Field-Bibb 1991, 179.

10. Even the Commission established to discuss the larger social issues raised by Women's Year was explicitly barred from discussing women's ordination. See Field-Bibb 1991, 179.

11. The text of the Pope's remarks appears in Luyckx (1980, 6). The interpretation of their significance is mine here and throughout.

12. (Luyckx 1980, 8). Behind the wording of the declaration lies a complex theological debate. Sara Butler notes that when the Declaration was issued she rejected the notion that "the practice of Jesus and the apostles" was decisive and rejected also the argument that the church's long-standing tradition was decisive. Since then she has come to the conclusion that the parties to the controversy do not understand one another (1989, 159). "On the question of method, for example, I could support the declaration. Catholic theology *does* allow the tradition to interpret scriptural evidence, so that a fresh but 'purely historical exegesis of the texts' will not be sufficient to decide the question; and it *does* utilize

arguments from 'fittingness' and accept illustrations by way of analogy with other articles of faith. In other words, the declaration's use of evidence—while some particular judgments may certainly be evaluated critically—does not depart from accepted theological method. Critics had charged the declaration with denying to women the ability to represent or 'Image' Christ. A close examination of the text reveals that this charge is wide of the mark. The declaration does *not* teach that women are incapable of imaging Christ, but only that in this particular capacity—as eucharistic priest—a woman is not an apt symbol. (It is important to note that the argument is made in terms of symbol, not function. It is evident that women are capable of doing what priests *do*. In fact, this is why many women experience their exclusion from this role as painful and arbitrary). . . . A priest is not a God-symbol but a Christ-symbol. . . . It is in his humanity that Christ stands among us as our mediator, and his humanity is male" (pp. 159–60). Butler offers an alternative line of argument as well: "the risen Christ transcends sexuality; . . . baptism suppresses sexual differences (Gal 3:28 'neither male nor female'); . . . in heaven there is neither marrying nor giving in marriage (Mt 22:30); . . . we are Christ's body now, and therefore women as well as men are required to act *in persona Christi*" (p. 160). Her study of "theological anthropology" has also shaped her latest thinking. She sees "the flaws of both the position [she] had rejected ('anatomy is destiny') and the one [she] had espoused ('unisex')." Drawing on the work of Mary F. Rousseau, Butler observes: "the force of her argument for me lies in its ability to give full attention to our embodiment as females or males, accepting the way embodiment conditions and shapes our experience, and simultaneously to underscore the fact of personal freedom to choose and define social roles" (p. 163). As a result, she has come to understand the argument made in the declaration that " 'equality is in no way identity.' " She saw this formula as "ineradicably tied to a vision of the complementarity of male and female which dictates mutually exclusive and non-interchangeable social roles" (p. 163). Rousseau's analysis "broke that connection." According to Rousseau, such assumptions are made " 'on the basis of an abstract, *a priori* definition of femininity.' She proposes that human freedom allows us tremendous latitude in developing appropriate expressions for both female and male persons. The only parameters are the bodily 'givens' of our physical sex and the requirements of intimacy. Beyond that, the full range of behaviors and roles is available to both men and women. We are free to define ourselves, from one culture to another, or within a given culture, or within the course of our lives" (pp. 163–64).

13. See also John Paul II 1988, 89–90.

14. For a summary of the statements made on the subject of women's ordination, see Luyckx 1980; and Field-Bibb 1991, 176–94.

15. Five explicitly cited biblical stories. Two others mentioned Mary, and it may be that they, too, had the Bible in mind. But Mary occupies a place in Roman Catholic life and theology that transcends the stories in the biblical text. Compare van Leeuwen 1984, 105–106. More recently, see Maeckelberghe 1991.

16. According to other researchers, guilt is a common feature of childhood experiences in the Roman Catholic Church. How often that guilt may be directly associated with sex-role stereotyping by adults in leadership positions is difficult to say and lies beyond the scope of this study. Compare Ratcliff 1992. Or is it shame, rather than guilt? See Karen 1992, 46–48.

17. Compare Tobin 1985, 297. Tobin chronicles the experience of women after Vatican II. The engine of frustration for women was their initial engagement in "liberation" or "justice" issues on behalf of *others*. Having recognized that others were disenfranchised, they have finally recognized the extent to which they themselves are disenfranchised. See also, pp. 298–99, where she describes the process as it impacted her own order. The Sisters of Loretto. The growing engagement in issues of justice made sisters "conscious of the contradiction between what they were experiencing as women, increasingly aware of discrimination, and the reality in the church" (pp. 297, 299). See also her book, *Hope is an Open Door,* as well as Getz 1986, 180–81.

18. See, for example, Ruether 1983.

19. One woman reported a measure of change in her own parish, but, just as quickly, she argued that the change was exceptional.

20. The appeal to the "first century" is an interesting one and is, of course, an argument employed by those who oppose the ordination of women. In what she describes as "The First Century Game," Chitra Fernando observes, the "issue is, how do we understand Biblical texts? Do we try to maintain that they are normative for all times, and that the Church continues to be rooted and grounded in the first century or do we try to understand them in accordance with the principles of hermeneutics? In our Biblical interpretation we should be able to distinguish between the compelling demands of the Gospel and the temporary regional regulations which the Apostles considered to be necessary in their particular social context. The new humanity that came into being through Jesus is still being experienced by the Church. The message of the Gospel has to be interpreted by the Church of today and it is up to the Church to work out the Gospel message in relation to women" (1984, 61). The key, Fernando argues, lies with eschatology: "As we know, all theology is ultimately Kingdom theology. So when we discuss the place of women in Church or society it is the place of women in the Kingdom that we should take as our term of reference. If it is the task of the Church to prepare for the coming of God's Kingdom on earth, it must define in no uncertain terms the position of women in it. Since the eschatological vision cannot but include the full and equal participation of all humanity, the full and equal involvement of men and women in building that new society is not merely necessary but vital" (p. 62).

21. Compare Proctor-Smith 1985.

22. See, for example, interview excerpt RC4:8–9; and 7:28–9.

23. I use the word advisedly and was prompted to do so by one of the interviewees' responses cited below. Clearly, however, it is not used here in an accusatory fashion.

24. Compare the comments of Margaret Brennan, herself a member of a religious order, concerned with the independence of those orders: "Women in the Church have become deeply aware of their own persons through a seriously developing feminist theology which seeks a reconstruction of Church history and teaching that will free it from patriarchal and androcentric interpretations which affirm their inferiority and prohibit the full actualization of their gifts and their persons" (Brennan 1985, 47).

25. Citing her 1975 survey of Catholic opinion, Mary Luke Tobin suggests another reason: "Women religious as a group have been reluctant to launch out into the women's movement. Because of their celibate profession, they have not experienced being treated as 'sex objects' in the way other women in the society have, i.e., being the objects of whistles, leering, and overt sexual advances" (Tobin 1985, 298). From her work it might

also be inferred that women who belong to religious orders are, in the nature of the case, more conservative (cf. p. 297).

26. Compare Virginia Sullivan Finn's article, "The Ministerial Aspirations of Catholic Lay Women in the United States," soon to be published by the University of South Carolina under the editorial leadership of Catherine Wessinger (Finn, forthcoming).

27. Compare Ebaugh 1993b, 133–48. At the same time, religious orders are also experiencing a decline, due in part to the greater number of opportunities available to women outside the orders. Recent study suggests that the number of women entering convents has dropped significantly, while the median age is on the rise. See Neal 1984, and Ebaugh 1993a, as well as Neal's article "American Catholic Sisters," soon to be published by the University of South Carolina under the editorial leadership of Catherine Wessinger (Neal, forthcoming).

28. Compare Pomerleau 1992.

29. Compare Seidler and Meyer 1989, 92–108.

30. "In a debate before the vote, the bishops' comments revealed a broad dissatisfaction with the document as incomplete and likely to alienate many women. Bishops who supported the document warned that a rejection would be seen as disloyalty to church precepts, particularly on the question of ordaining women to the priesthood. In fact, however, very few of those who voted against the document wanted to see women as priests; among the bishops, that is the position of a small minority and was never seriously considered" (Steinfels 1992, A1).

7

A Still Small Voice

The goals of the organization are the current preoccupations
and intentions of the dominant organizational coalition. This
conception of organizational goals does not require us to regard them as some ultimate point toward which the entire
organization moves, nor as a steady state characterizing orga-
nization-environment relationships. Instead, organizational
goals may be as fleeting as the membership of the dominant
coalition; as changeable as members' views of what is practical, desirable, or essential. Above all, this view of organizational goals frees us from the need to see such goals as uniform
and stable throughout the organization: they are as varied and
no more stable or rational than the individual.

—Thomas B. Greenfield,
"Organizations as Social Inventions"

Throughout the first six chapters, it
appears clear that I have chosen to organize the interview material available to me in one way rather than another. Each chapter also suggests an
analysis of the dynamics within the five denominations with which others
might disagree, owing either to a difference in data or perspective. I can
hardly argue, therefore, that my own views have been largely absent up
to this point. I have, however, attempted to allow the voices of the
interviewees to be heard and I have also attempted to juxtapose their
voices with my own analysis in a way that allows the reader to test the
latter's accuracy.

Nonetheless, in the course of a study like this, it is necessary to provide some measure of synthesis and analysis for which one must take an even greater measure of responsibility. Here my own voice will admittedly figure more prominently, and it is this task to which I now turn.

I turn to it with a good deal of trepidation. No male can plausibly argue that he understands the experience of women. The potential for oversimplification, and the ease with which one can minimize the obstacles and struggles women encounter, is difficult if not impossible to underestimate. It is even more difficult to suggest how women might respond to those obstacles. At best, one runs the risk of being told, "That's easy for you to say!" At worst, one may appear to belittle those who respond in a particular fashion. I can only plead that I have not knowingly underestimated the challenges that women encounter in the church, and where I have been critical of specific responses, those criticisms are predicated upon certain assumptions about the nature of gender and the church, which at least some women make as well. Ultimately, then, what I offer here is given as a stimulus to conversation and not as part of an all-knowing critique.

Whatever the final limitations of this analysis, it is my hope that, at a minimum, it may help to foster dialogue among those most profoundly affected by the issues discussed throughout this book—women themselves. However, having participated in more than one forum on the subject, at which the audiences have been dominantly female, I admit that I have a still larger goal: to challenge men to accept a measure of responsibility for thinking critically about the way in which women experience the church. For, ultimately, the shortcomings described here do not constitute a "woman's issue" alone. They constitute a challenge to move behind the facade, to ask whether the organizational world we have helped to create is indeed a foretaste of heaven or, instead, a foretaste of hell.

Comparisons and Patterns

As a first step toward providing this analysis, it is important to attempt some comparison of the findings described above along denominational lines. However, the earlier cautions given in chapter 1 regarding the nature of this study continue to apply. Indeed, to some extent those caveats are of even greater relevance here. In addition to the pause the

heuristic character of this study ought to give us, there is now the added
dimension of comparing experiences that are ultimately unique. We grap-
ple not only with the differences in the bureaucratic and cultural character
of each denomination, but with the differences in perception that mark
the outlook of the respondents. With that in mind, I would venture the
following observations.

Cultural Linkages

In studying denominations as theologically diverse as those described
above, one might expect to find a limited number of similarities. However,
when examining those cultures from the vantage point of gender orientation, such diversity proves to be less critical. It is true, for example, that
Roman Catholics had ready answers to questions about icons while, as a
rule, Southern Baptists struggled to apply the question to their experience.
Nonetheless, focused on the issue of gender, the two denominations
proved to have a great deal in common, as did Episcopalians, Methodists,
and Lutherans.

One common thread in the interviews of all five denominations was
an emphasis on the significance of the biblical text and its stories. Notwithstanding the differences in their hermeneutics, most of the women
interviewed continue to reflect on the biblical text and continue to struggle
with its male-dominated character. For this reason, there remain stories
and texts that are repellent to them and have little place in their theology,
except (perhaps) as a catalyst for shaping an alternative.

At the same time, however, I found that women are actively engaged
in a process of reappropriating the Bible's stories. At times this reappro-
priation involves a process of sorting and sifting, saving and discarding.
Some are self-consciously engaged in this process. Others have simply
"bracketed" difficult stories, relying instead on an implicit "canon with in
the canon." Where this does not work well, the respondents indicated
that they rely instead on a cultural and historical reading of the text.

It is interesting to note that although the women I interviewed may
find some parts of the biblical text repellent and, on a rare occasion,
deeply alienating, as a rule they readily made allowances for the time and
place in which it was written. This does not mean, however, that they are
prepared to settle for what it offers. If none of the other strategies described above help them to discover something of value, they look for it
themselves "in between the lines." They do this by reclaiming lost stories

and perspectives, the fragments of which they perceive to be present even yet in the biblical text.

What is striking is the inherent biblicism of what most women have to say about the Bible and about their role in the church. The text remains at the center of the debate over the legitimacy of their ministry; the Bible provides, albeit begrudgingly, the basis of an argument in favor of their ordination; and, although often obscured by the viewpoint of the narrator, a few of its actors serve as examples of courage and faith. In short, for many of the women I interviewed the Bible continues to set "the necessary limits to what the church may believe and teach" concerning the ordination of women and their place in the church.[1] It is, in this sense, that their theology remains biblicistic.[2]

There can be little doubt that this state of affairs is due, in part, to the nature of the controversy that continues to engage a varying number of people from denomination to denomination. Where the ordination of women remains controversial, and a prohibition of that ordination remains a "sacred" value, the Bible plays an important role in the argument that what is at stake is the will of God.[3] Confronted with an assertion of this nature, proponents of women's ordination have gravitated to the same text in an attempt to make their case.[4]

This seemingly intractable measure of biblicism, however, is present as well in much of the hermeneutical theory to which women are introduced in the settings described above. Feminists are widely agreed that the Bible is "thoroughly androcentric and patriarchal" (Anderson 1991), yet most of them continue to place considerable weight upon the effort to reinterpret the text and to reconstruct a picture of the past using the text.[5]

With notable exceptions, the stories of each respondent's denominational history figured less prominently and faired less well than did the Bible. Exactly why this is the case is not entirely clear. Some explicitly noted that they were, at best, indifferent to a tradition history that is largely male dominated. But others simply did not mention anything from their denomination's history. Given the qualitative difference in the place of the Bible and the place of church history in most traditions, this silence may suggest nothing more than a lack of keen interest. I am tempted to believe, however, that the near complete absence of stories from each denomination's history reflects a far more profound disaffection, driven in large part by the absence of female role models.

Where interest was displayed, the women included a few stories about men, particularly stories about the founders of their traditions. Otherwise, however, they tended to focus on the women in their tradition, viewing them as models for their own ministry. At times, personal stories and the stories of their contemporaries took precedence over both the Bible and church history. Some of these stories provided examples or models for ministry. Others illustrated the nature of their own experiences.

Language was very nearly a universal problem according to the interviewees—language about God and about the believing community. There is probably as much or more innovation taking place here than anywhere else—with or without the help of the church. These changes may be due, in part, to the fact that personal choice about language is something over which we all have a higher degree of direct control.

But it is the corporate use of language that impels the women I interviewed to explore alternative ways of expressing themselves. Some are content with the introduction of new language alongside the church's traditional modes of expression. Just how much new language would need to be used is more difficult to say, but according to most of the interviewees, the church has a long way to go. A smaller but significant number of women inclined to revolutionize the church's language are abandoning forms as basic to the church's vocabulary as the traditional Trinitarian formulae.

To the extent that language colored the attitude of the respondents toward the church, there appeared to be some measure of correlation between organized efforts to make the church's language more inclusive and the degree of satisfaction interviewees had with their denomination. The more proactive the denomination was, the more satisfied the women were, and vice versa. This is not to say, however, that they were necessarily satisfied with the speed with which such revisions are being made.

More often than not, if the gender orientation of the church's ritual had an affect on the interviewees, it was due not to the ritualistic act itself, but to the language used. However, the words used in sacramental formulae were not the only factor in shaping their views. Ritual requires actors, and among those of the respondents who struggled with the church's ritual, the frequent presence of a male pastor or priest was mentioned, more often than not, as the feature that gave the greatest offense.

The acts themselves were not entirely devoid of a gender emphasis according to the participants, but their assessment is not what one might have expected. Most of the interviewees who emphasized this point did not argue that the rituals were somehow intrinsically masculine in orientation, but argued instead that they are basically feminine acts that have been expropriated by men. Ritual, then, may be the dimension of ecclesiastical culture around which I detected the greatest range and disparity of responses. For a few of the participants, the gender orientation of ritual was negligible. For others, it has all but driven them from their traditions.

Icons and symbols did not prove to be of great significance for the interviewees. In cases where symbols were important, respondents varied widely in the kinds they found meaningful, typically mentioning both symbols they feel have a gender orientation and symbols they believe might serve as more inclusive alternatives. Here, as in the case of language, some measure of innovation is taking place.

In structuring the interview protocol, I was reasonably sure that the categories I had explicitly identified would not adequately capture all that might be associated with ecclesiastical cultures. So, I was careful to ask participants if there were any other dimensions of their denominational culture they could identify as having a gender orientation of some kind. My surmise proved to be right, and I received a number of interesting answers.

Some of the cultural features were analogous to the dimensions I had already identified. The lectionary, for example, received mention. More striking, however, was the number of times that the respondents focused instead on the largely informal networking patterns, which either limited their opportunities or (far less often) maximized them. Unique, of course, is the situation of Roman Catholics where the culture of the church is perceived, by at least some of the respondents, as intruding in their lives well beyond the walls of the church.

This is not to say, however, that such dynamics affect only the fabric of the church's worship. It is clear from the questions I asked about ecclesiastical culture and informal patterns of association, that such dynamics have the power to redirect the impact of even the most inclusive of bureaucratic provisions. Furthermore, with the exception of the Roman Catholic church, it is here that the shape of in-groups is determined.

In the case of Roman Catholics and Southern Baptists, this exclusion is all but complete, though for very different reasons. In the case of the remaining women, there appears to be a complex interplay of other elements that impact on the level at which women are involved, including regional culture and age. More than one of the respondents, for example, identified the southern United States as an area where churches are more often resistant to the ordination of women. And a significant number of ministers reported that older men, as well as women, tended to resist their ministry.

Nowhere does gender intrude more, however, than it has on the careers of the women I interviewed; and apart from Roman Catholic women, the impact of that intrusion cannot be attributed to bureaucratic linkages alone. Although there are exceptions (and I interviewed some of them), it is generally fair to say that the women I spoke to describe a future with limited horizons. As a rule, women are excluded from the uppermost echelons of power, even in denominations that have been ordaining women for a long time. Where women do appear in upper level positions, they are in a distinct minority, and some of them have only recently achieved their posts.

Furthermore, in the denominations I studied, women continue to serve smaller churches, or as associates in the larger churches. Both the experience and perception of the participants is that women are denied positions on the basis of gender and, for the same reason, are forced to wait a longer period of time before they find a place of service. This dynamic appears to be something of a factor even in the Methodist church, where the polity requires that ordained women be appointed and where, ostensibly, churches are required to accept their appointment. One of the respondents put it well, "ordination is one thing, deployment is another."

I also heard a significant number of stories describing women who were forced by the church's "glass ceiling" into other parts of the denominational structure and out of the church altogether. In the opinion of the interviewees, this has left many parts of the church without the models so badly needed for training women in pastoral leadership. And in denominations where larger responsibilities are given to ministers with longer tenures in the parish, it is a dynamic that further limits the number of women "at the top."

Bureaucratic Linkages

Nonetheless, denominations that clearly provide for the ordination of women and for their full inclusion at all levels of ministry are likely to fair better in the eyes of their clergy than those that do not. For example, the Evangelical Lutherans and United Methodists have provided a single, clear bureaucratic directive: women shall be ordained. Although this message can be compromised at the informal level, it appears to provide a measure of reassurance for the members of both denominations. For that reason, women perceive their future to be secure, even if the way forward is not entirely free of obstacles.

By contrast, the mixed bureaucratic message sent to Episcopal priests has driven at least some women to the fringes of the church. They are convinced that their cause is a question of social justice, and yet they have been left in a bureaucratic limbo where their credentials can be seriously (even if not fairly) questioned. The so-called conscience clause and the provision for episcopal visitors has further exacerbated the situation. As a result, many women have become embittered.

Southern Baptists also contend with a mixed bureaucratic message, but this message is rooted in the church's larger polity. With autonomous congregations, independent state associations, and a national body that cannot legislate policy for the denomination as a whole but exercises considerable bureaucratic influence, the church inevitably speaks with several voices. A local church may ordain, endorse, and nurture the ministry provided by a woman, but as the interviews suggest, the horizons of such nurture may stretch no further than the walls of the church sanctuary. Instead, at nearly every level, power politics appear to shape the bureaucratic life of the church. Certainly a majority of the women I interviewed clearly perceive this to be case, and with women's ordination at the storm center of national debate, it is not difficult to find an explanation.

In addition to the security provided by a clear bureaucratic directive, Evangelical Lutherans are further bolstered by the quota system employed by their denomination. Quotas may be a debatable political commodity, but their impact on the interviewees has a clearly salutary affect. To paraphrase one pastor, there is the sense that, "If I am not directly involved in the decision-making process, there are others like me who are."[6]

A significant variable in three of the four denominations that have an episcopacy is the leadership provided by the bishop. With the exception of, the Roman Catholic Church, if the bishop supports the full involvement of women, so will the diocese. The reverse also holds true.

Women's Response

To this point the study has necessarily focused on the respondents' perceptions of their denominations. From the researcher's standpoint, however, the behavior of the interviewees is of equal interest. I have attempted to categorize that behavior by examining the responses of the interviewees to the culture and bureaucracy of their denominations. I have also reexamined what I believe are their strategies for coping with the church as an institution. Out of this study arises patterns of behavior, which are offered as a means of providing insight into the conduct of the women I interviewed. The categories do not represent discreet types, but strategies and postures, which from time to time anyone of the interviewees might exchange for another.

Outsiders. The outsiders choose not to relate to their denomination at any level, unless it is absolutely necessary. Instead, they focus on ministry in the local church or parish, and it is there that they find their fulfillment. Relating to their denomination is painful, and they often think of it as a hindrance to their ministry. They have withdrawn to work behind the scenes.

Most of the Roman Catholic respondents are active reformers. Frustrated and beleaguered by their church's refusal to ordain them, however, some also fall into this category. The majority of the Southern Baptist respondents fall into this category as well, in large part because they have no choice. Because they are unrecognized by the larger church, women find that the local congregation provides the only context for ministry available to them.

There are, however, "outsiders" in the other denominations. At least one of the Episcopal interviewees was one who, in fact, supplied me with the vocabulary to describe this experience. Frustrated by what she perceives to be her denomination's enslavement to its own political fears and its refusal to take sexism as seriously as it takes racism, she has withdrawn from all but the immediate responsibilities of her ministry.

Disengaged. The women who are disengaged from participation in their denomination, have not chosen to separate themselves completely from the official channels of their denomination, but they are only selectively involved. For example, several Southern Baptist respondents chose to relate at the associational or state levels, while avoiding any contact with the national convention. A number of Roman Catholics choose to relate to their denomination only through their religious orders. A representative number of women from the five denominations are involved only where they feel they can be effective or where such engagement nurtures their ministry.

Threatened. Many of the respondents wonder whether they will be able to continue in ministry, because of the threat posed by those who would have them removed from their positions. At times, they work for wages at or near the poverty line, due to nothing more than their gender. Many of them express doubts about their future, not only in their denomination's ministry, but pastoral ministry in general. Roman Catholics and Southern Baptists can often be found here, but it was an Episcopalian who told me, "I am extremely cognizant that who I am, what I am, and where I am. My next step is very limited—if, indeed, there will be a next step."

Reformers. Reformers are self-consciously engaged in developing alternative styles of worship and leadership. As agents of change, they are sometimes confrontational when they seek to make a place for themselves and for other women. They are not necessarily interested in the well being of women alone, however, and often they are working toward what they would consider to be wholeness.

A significant number of the Roman Catholic respondents fall into this category. They find ways to celebrate the Eucharist outside the sanction of the official church. Several are involved in the development of creative worship services that depict the unity and inclusivity of the gospel, as they understand it, and work through available channels to try to bring about change in the status of women. But the Catholic respondents were not alone. There are a number of United Methodists, Lutherans, and Episcopalians engaged in similar efforts.

Conformists. The conformists choose to comply with denominational expectations and cultural stereotypes in order to insure themselves the freedom needed to continue their ministry. The women in this group sift and sort through literature, liturgies, and hymns, using what they can and sometimes what they must. Whether it is the Lutheran who spoke cautiously about women's issues, the United Methodist who used exclusive language because the denomination suggested that she do so, or the Episcopal priest who made sure she dressed and preached in stereotypically predictable ways, these women felt pressured to conform in order to survive or to advance.

Another Kind of Conformist? In an altogether different sense the vast majority of the women I interviewed were conformists of another kind. Time and again I heard the respondents talk about bringing elements of nurture, care, self-giving, patience, and consensual leadership to their ministry. A significant number suggested that these are, in fact, uniquely feminine attributes and are part of a distinguishable, feminist theology. Similarly, a number of Roman Catholics, Lutherans, Episcopalians, and United Methodists claimed that baptism and communion involve distinctively feminine activities of feeding and washing.[7]

In identifying themselves this way, many of the women appear to have conformed to a cultural stereotype about what it means to be female (and, therefore, male). I was reminded of Susan Faludi's critique of Carol Gilligan's *In A Different Voice* (1982). Gilligan certainly denies that she is stereotyping on the basis of gender. Indeed, she argues that the "different voice" she describes is characterized by theme, rather than by gender.[8]

However, Faludi rightly asserts that Gilligan's work, despite the latter's claims to the contrary, actually generalizes about the behavior of women on the basis of gender (Faludi 1991, 329). In her studies, for example, Gilligan fails to take into consideration factors of social status and power, basing her conclusions instead on gender differences.

As a result, Gilligan left herself open to be used by those eager to focus on differences between men and women. The perceived presence of such a pronounced difference based on gender alone has provided fuel for those who would oppose women's entry into high-level jobs. Some respondents, it seems, have conformed to cultural stereotypes of women without realizing what they had done.[9] In effect, they have constructed a feminist theology and a view of parish ministry, that relies on the same stereotypes used to bar them from ordained ministry.

This state of affairs is not new. Indeed, it is rooted in a much larger phenomenon that has shaped much of the contemporary debate over gender. Arising out of her work on *Women and the Work of Benevolence* during the nineteenth century, Lori Ginzberg observes:

> In her rejection of religion and her insistence that morally expressed gender differences were both ideological and fundamentally dangerous, Elizabeth Cady Stanton placed herself in a small minority of nineteenth-century women. And yet in her discussion can be found virtually all the

threads of one of the most complex debates faced by historians and feminists: how to reconcile the radical and conservative implications of two very different ideologies of gender—one, that the sexes are fundamentally different, the other that they are potentially the same. It is a debate that emerged in the nineteenth century in the context of struggles over political, class, and gender identities in the United States. It remains submerged in, indeed obscured by, those struggles. . . . The conflation of the ideologies of morality and gender played a central role in the emergence of middle-class identity in the nineteenth century. It did so both by adapting revolutionary rhetoric about virtue to an expanding, industrializing, and urbanizing society and by obscuring the interests and identities that informed women's benevolent work. In addition, women's belief in appropriate female behavior undermined radical challenges—ranging from abolitionism to the woman suffrage movement—to the developing class-as well as gender-based authority structure in American society. Finally, the nineteenth century witnessed the emergence of the competing ideologies of gender to which we are the heirs, with many middle-class women persisting in the notion that so-called female traits should set a standard for superior moral behavior and with more urban elite women participating in a process in which an assumption of gender sameness characterized efforts on behalf of their class.[10]

An Auditor's Reflections

As Thomas Greenfield observes, the worlds in which we live are of our own making. It is equally true (as Greenfield himself notes) that powerful coalitions can and do force on others their view of the social realities within which we live.[11]

Before beginning this study, I assumed naively that in some denominations, women were already social architects with influence comparable to that of their male counterparts.[12] That, however, is not the case. They have forged their own forums for conversation and ministry within which they are doing some of the most creative work to be found in the church today. Yet the structure of the church's discourse and ministry clearly indicates that women are still marginalized. Where present, the rhetoric of inclusion is undermined by real-world decisions that shape the culture, procedures, and policy of the church in ways that the rhetoric, unwed to centers of power, is unable to change.

Women are permitted to discuss women's issues, forge a professional identity, and nurture the growth of a few struggling parishes. Occasionally, they are admitted to the second or third tier in larger churches. Less frequently, they are granted the opportunity to make the choices that shape some small part of the "performance" (Greenfield 1984, 152). By and by, however, they are forced to live on the fringes of a church where men discuss the church's theology and its ministry, shape their professional identity in close proximity with centers of ecclesiastical power, and govern the affairs of the largest churches. Indeed, one might argue that women are losing ground in the wake of an ecclesiastical "backlash" not unlike the larger one Susan Faludi detects throughout American culture.[13]

In this sense, the pattern emerging is similar (though certainly not identical) to the one that has frustrated the quest of African Americans for full inclusion. Following an initial drive for civil rights and a handful of legislative concessions, the African-American community was declared a full participant in the nation's life, but found itself largely isolated from the real centers of influence. A combination of weariness and satisfaction dulled the appetites of even the proactive, and, as a result, the cause nurtured by Martin Luther King and Malcolm X has languished now for over a decade or more (Hacker 1992; West 1993).

Women find themselves in an analogous position in the church. Where bureaucratic provisions have been made, complacency has set in and the champions of women continue to be women.[14] To make matters worse, the voice of feminism within the church is increasingly marginalized. Not unlike other players in the larger culture of which we are a part, feminists have paved the way, only to be driven to the fringes of public discourse by the kind of stereotyping that caricatures the rhetoric that made it possible to be heard.[15]

As a result, women in the church's ministry remain "still small voices"—in every sense the phrase suggests. Theirs is a *small* voice, in that it can scarcely be heard above the male voices that dominate the culture and bureaucracy of the church; and theirs is *still* a small voice, in that the changes (where they have been made) have failed to make it easier to be heard.[16]

The Sacred and the Profane

Some would argue that this is as it should be. For them, the debate over the ordination of women is a debate over sacred norms. This view is clearly that of some Roman Catholics and Southern Baptists. It is also the position taken by smaller groups within the other three denominations described above, including, for example, Anglican traditionalists, who argue that there is an absence of so-called catholic consensus on the issue. On one level this state of affairs is not a particularly surprising one.

Every organizational culture, and the church in particular, consists of both the sacred and the profane.

> The 'sacred' is composed of essentially immutable norms; the 'profane' is susceptible to change, with some norms more susceptible than others. The two terms define completely different orders of reality, not just opposite poles of a continuum. . . . The sacred is enduring, efficacious, and gives life its meaning. . . . For that reason, 'the ways in which we can approach the sacred are very limited.' On the other hand, the profane reflects the temporary adjustments to everyday life, the transitory side of existence. It is continually being redefined. As a result, the profane can be debated, altered, planned, and improved; the sacred simply is and unquestionably adhered to. (Rossman and others 1988, 10)

There is little doubt that convictions of this kind limit the involvement of women in their churches. The more closely a denomination associates the ordination of women with a violation of sacred norms, the more resistant its members will be. Both Southern Baptists and Roman Catholics can anticipate a long-term struggle, since the position taken by substantial constituencies within both denominations is rooted in larger sacred norms shaping their world view. The possibility of change is further undermined by strong leadership that is opposed to the ordination of women and is firmly entrenched at the highest levels of their organizations.

Roman Catholics will continue to experience a pervasive and hierarchical measure of control, and, given the character of Catholic bureaucracy, it is clear where and how such change will need to be initiated. By contrast, Southern Baptists will continue to enjoy some measure of insulation from bureaucratic intrusion into their ministries. Long-term security, however, will remain in doubt, and the means of effecting change will remain ill-defined. It is impossible to know how long both groups of women will be forced to wait for widespread recognition of their ministries.

Where the ordination question is less strongly tied to the sacred norms of the church, there is far more immediate hope for change. For Episcopalians, Methodists, and Lutherans, the marginally stronger "will" of some to include women at every level in the fullest way possible is an important variable, just as is strong episcopal leadership, where it favors the ordination of women.

In all five cases, however, it is a mistake to assume that even "sacred" values are immutable, or that behind those values lies more than the will to refuse women a role in the church's ministry. Indeed, it can and should be argued that the sacred facade arrayed against women is the selective defense of prejudices that (unlike others?) the church has refused to renounce. Both "simple sexism" (i.e., a plain prejudice toward women and their full involvement in the church's ministry) and "maintenance sexism" (i.e., the tendency to avoid the issue of inclusion in order to maintain the *status quo*) lie very close to the surface, even where opponents of women's involvement appeal to sacred norms. In denominations where those norms are no longer defended, they lie even closer to the surface.[17] Indeed, there is considerable evidence to suggest that the appeal to sacred norms simply bolsters views that many would hold, with or without divine sanction.[18]

Beyond "Sameness" and "Difference"

As candid as this analysis is, however, it is not enough to re-visit the rhetoric of change. As I noted at the outset, life in the church is unacceptably schizophrenic. Far too little conversation about the church as *ekklesia* moves beyond the theological facade to raise questions about the church as organization or to make recommendations touching the future. This task is left in large part to the church's functionaries, while others theorize at a distance about what might be.

Throughout this work, the observations of Thomas Greenfield, who is an educator and does not write as a member of the church, have figured prominently. In a sense, his anarchic view of organizational life closely approximates the prophetic critique of human institutions. Insistent that we look behind the facade, Greenfield's work underlines the importance of scrutinizing the sheer willfulness shaping the organizations within which we live and work. And unlike some contemporary writers who attempt prophetic critique, he resists reliance on global generalities, insisting instead on confronting the realities and particularities of organizational life. The epigraphs cited throughout the book are intended as a reminder that such confrontation is indispensable.

For this reason I close with a few rather more prosaic, but no less important, observations intended to bring rhetoric to bear more immediately on the task of acting:

1. The will to include women will remain an important variable for the foreseeable future. Strong denominational leadership will need to give attention to "desired values and deliberate role modeling," the interpretation of "stories, myths, mottos, and symbols," and the effort to shape "organization systems to express cultural assumptions" (Rossman and others 1988, 15–16).

2. Women will need to be included in larger numbers at the highest echelons. Questions of seniority will need to be given less weight.

3. At the same time, male leaders will need to be visibly and actively supportive. Such involvement need not be patronizing. The absence of it can be destructive.

4. Quotas need to be instituted and extended to every level of the church in a way that takes the distribution of power seriously. As controversial as they may be,[19] quotas help to underline the church's will to be inclusive; they help to build a sense of involvement, even among those who do not hold positions of leadership; and they promote changes in the attitudes of the laity.[20]

5. Where there are mixed bureaucratic messages, a straightforward and unambiguous directive to ordain women in ministry is indispensable.

6. In taking these and other specific steps, church leaders and those sympathetic to the full involvement of women need to help the church to move beyond the debate over "sameness" and "difference," and the distinctions in opportunity made between the genders on the basis of that debate. A key to this process will be to require that men possess the characteristics, values, and commitments that are often attributed exclusively to women in the task of ministry. These include the capacity for nurture and a commitment to care for one's own spouse and children.

In other words, the church must find new ways to insure that women are full participants in the life and leadership of the church, but no long-term solution rests with that task alone.[21] Long-term solutions lie instead with the task of helping men, as well as women, to see their responsibilities as human beings in an entirely new light.[22] That task can only be accomplished if organizational procedures for ordaining and deploying clerics place a premium on a constellation of characteristics, values, and commitments that are of incalculable value to the life of the church, but which are without basis in the dubious distinctions drawn between the genders.[23] This constellation includes the care, nurture, and emphasis on relationships, that have been identified with women in both their professional and private lives.

Ultimately the debate over "sameness" and "difference" is not the issue, and to insist that it is the issue is to retreat from behind the facade and the choices we must make. Women should not be forced to choose between caring and being fully involved in the church's leadership. Men should not be excused from the task of caring. Instead, the church must insist upon a model of humanity that refuses to separate the two. In helping us to see this, women's voice is not merely "a *still small* voice." As in the old story of the revelation given to Elijah on Mount Horeb, women's voice is also the voice of God.

Notes

1. The definition is adapted from Drive (1981, 82). Compare Sakenfeld 1989, 165–67. Sakenfeld notes that as long as feminists fail to confront the question of authority, they will be forced to choose between ignoring the Bible or abandoning their faith. Calling for interpreters to acknowledge that authority takes shape "in community," Sakenfeld argues that " 'the locus of revelation' is neither in the text or in the history that produced the text, but where *God is at work* in the whole life of the believing community, including its text production and its ongoing reflection on its texts."

2. Compare the observations made by Mary Ann Tolbert concerning the experience of Protestant seminarians and the obstacles they encounter in attempting to appropriate the achievements of feminist scholars (1989, 2–3).

3. Every organizational culture, and the church, in particular, consists of both the sacred and the profane. "The 'sacred' is composed of essentially immutable norms; the 'profane' is susceptible to change, with some norms more susceptible than others. The two terms define completely different orders of reality, not just opposite poles of a continuum. . . . The sacred is enduring, efficacious, and gives life its meaning. . . . For that reason, '. . . the ways in which we can approach the sacred are very limited.' On the other hand,

the profane reflects the temporary adjustments to everyday life, the transitory side of existence. It is continually being redefined. As a result, the profane can be debated, altered, planned, and improved; the sacred simply is and unquestionably adhered to." See Rossman and others 1988.

4. This debate, and the form it has taken, has a long history, dating to the second quarter of the nineteenth century and the efforts of Angelina and Sarah Grimke. See Johnson 1988, 125–27. See also Kraditor 1969; Hersh 1978.

5. For more on the subject, see my forthcoming article, "Beyond a Biblicistic Feminism: Hermeneutics, Women and the Church, to be published in *Feminist Theology* in Jan. 1996."

6. It is interesting to note that even though quotas were declared unconstitutional two years ago, a considerable number of United Methodists mistakenly continue to cite those used earlier in their denomination as grounds for confidence that they and others like them will be included in the leadership of their church.

7. Elizabeth Schüssler Fiorenza identifies this approach as one of three "feminist approaches." Citing the work of Fran Ferder as an example (1978), Fiorenza argues that this approach emphasizes "the unique gifts that feminine persons can offer to leadership and ministry in the church." Starting from "the premise that there is an unchangeable feminine nature that is complementary to masculine nature" (e.g., "sweetness, flexibility, compassion, sensitiveness, intuition, unselfishness, a great natural flair"). It is an approach which, according to Florenza, "could be fatal to the women's struggle, for it rests on a premise which should be called into question. There are no particularly masculine or feminine qualities: very many ways of acting are induced by conditioning that is profoundly rooted in the very domination that is under analysis" (Luyckx 1980, 15).

8. (Gilligan 1982, 2). For a critical discussion of these and other issues arising out of Gilligan's work, see Larrabee 1993. See also Wendy Kaminer on "The Comforts of Gilliganism" (1993).

9. Noting that most religious literature on the subject of gender differences takes the same ("maximalist") position on gender differences, Edward Lehman offers a plausible explanation for the prominence of this view: "Given the prevalence of sexism in the churches, along with the virtually universal experience of resistance among women seeking deeper involvements in church leadership, it is not surprising to see large numbers of women adopting and arguing the maximalist position. The perceptions of superiority in feminine approaches to church life provide meaning, legitimation, and focus to women long frustrated by the churches" (1993b, 5).

10. (Ginzberg 1990, 214). See also Bacchi 1990. Reviewing Ginzberg's work, Sarah Stage raises two vital questions, both of which I believe must be answered in the negative: "Is it possible for feminism to empower women without adopting an essentialist stance? Can a feminism that focuses on difference still fight for equality?" See Stage 1991.

11. (Greenfield 1982, 3; and 1973, 557–58). Both passages are cited at the beginning of the chapter.

12. I take some comfort in the fact that others, who were watching the changes in seminaries far more closely than I was, shared that optimism a scant decade ago, but are now of a similarly pessimistic frame of mind. See, for example Lehman 1985, 3; 1993b; and Carroll and others 1981. See also Ice 1987, 2. As Joy Charlton notes, "the relationship

between [numerical] ratio and effect is not necessarily linear." See Charlton 1987, 313 and compare with Kanter 1977.

13. Such a development is not particularly surprising. See Hunter 1991.

14. This remains true, even in the academy, where in sessions dealing with feminist theology, the participants continue to be women.

15. See especially Hiatt forthcoming. On the same dynamic, as it is manifested in the larger culture, see Kaminer 1993. Ironically, earlier this century, a shift to a less polemical feminism also cost women in their quest for equality. See Verdesi 1976, 177–78.

16. I freely admit that I am exploiting the wording of this phrase, the meaning of which is contested.

17. More than one quantitative study has established that in times of controversy most members are prepared to discriminate against women in the interest of the majority. See, for example Lehman 1987a, 321–22.

18. Edward Lehman observes: "Religious sexism is in many ways but an extension of secular sexism. Persons who harbor misogynistic orientations on the job, at the ballot box, or at home also manifest them in church. Religious sexism shares the same correlates as general misogyny and at least two studies have shown the two types of sexism to be correlated. . . . the theological positions associated with varying attitudes toward women in ministry are largely ideological glosses—theological red herrings or smoke screens that mask underlying and more general orientations. I think they also represent basically social commitments to congregations as organizations at least as much as they indicate theological persuasions *per se*." See Lehman 1981, 116–17; 1987a, 322; and (1987b). See also Nason-Clark 1987. For a historian's assessment of the ideological roots of sexism in fundamentalist circles, see Balmer 1994. For a historical assessment of wider scope, see Heyward 1989, 37–47.

19. On opposition to quotas within the church, see Lehman 1987a, 323. On broader, societal opposition, even among those who endorse affirmative action, see Urofsky 1991, 32–33.

20. Admittedly, quotas will not guarantee immediate change. The research of Edward Lehman and others reveals that although changes in the attitude of the laity are encouraged by experience with female clergy, members do not necessarily generalize from their experience to other female clergy. Nonetheless, as Lehman notes, subsequent female clergy do not start from "scratch" (Lehman 1987a, 324–25).

21. Even in denominations where a substantial number of people are able to imagine women engaged in a variety of ministries, the same people's concept of ministry remains largely masculine in orientation. See Lehman 1987a, 321.

22. On what follows, compare the observations made by Bacchi 1990, 265.

23. Research suggests that even women committed to an ethic of care do not, in fact, implement that ethic on a political or societal level. See Stevens 1989; 1993a; and 1993b, especially 205–6.

Works Cited
Index

Works Cited

Books and Articles

Ammerman, Nancy. 1990. *Baptist Battles, Social Change and Religious Conflict in the Southern Baptist Convention,* New Brunswick, N.J.: Rutgers Univ. Press.

———. 1993. "SBC Moderates and the Making of a Postmodem Denomination." *The Christian Century* (Sept. 22–29): 896–99.

Anders, Sarah Frances, and Marilyn Metcalf-Whittake, 1993. "Women as Lay Leaders and Clergy: A Critical Issue." In *Southern Baptists Observed. Multiple Perspectives on a Changing Denomination,* edited by Nancy Ammerman, 201–21. Knoxville: Univ. of Tennessee Press.

Anderson, Janice Capel. 1991. "Mapping Feminist Biblical Criticism: The American Scene, 1983–1990." In *Critical Review of Books in Religion 1991,* edited by Eldon Jay Epp, 21–44. Atlanta: Scholars.

Anker, Roy M. 1988. "Finding Jesus—A Review Article." *The Reformed Journal* 38, no. 10:20–25.

Bacchi, Carol Lee. 1990. *Same Difference: Feminism and Sexual Difference.* Sydney: Allen and Unwin.

Balmer, Randall. 1994. "American Fundamentalism: The Ideal of Femininity." In *Fundamentalism and Gender,* edited by John Stratton Hawley, 47–62. New York: Oxford Univ. Press.

Bedell, Kenneth, and Alice M. Jones, eds. 1992. *Yearbook of American and Canadian Churches, 1992.* Nashville: Abingdon.

Brennan, Margaret. 1985. "Enclosure: Institutionalizing the Invisibility of Women in Ecclesiastical Communities." Vol. 182 of *Concilium.* London: SCM.

Burton, M. Garlinda, and Brad Motta. 1992. "New *Book of Worship* Boasts Diversity, Flexibility." *Daily Christian Advocate,* May 6, 3.

Butler, Sara. 1989. "Forum: Second Thoughts on Ordaining Women." *Worship* 63 (Mar.): 157–65.

Carroll, Jackson W., Barbara Hargrove, and Adair T. Lummis. 1981. *Women of the Cloth: A New Opportunity for the Churches.* San Francisco: Harper and Row.

Charlton, Joy. 1987. "Women in Seminary: A Review of Current Social Science Research." *Review of Religious Research* 28:305–18.

Childers, Melanie. 1993. "Students Confront Mohler in Forum." *Western Recorder,* Apr. 13, 2.

Coriden, James A., Thomas J. Green, and Donald E. Heintschel, eds. 1985. *The Code of Canon Law: A Text and Commentary.* New York: Paulist.

Cothen, Grady C. 1993. *What Happened to the Southern Baptist Convention? A Memoir of the Controversy.* Macon: Smyth and Helwys.

Daly, Mary. 1968. *The Church and the Second Sex.* Boston: Beacon.

Darling, Pamela W. 1987. *Reaching Toward Wholeness: The Participation of Women in the Episcopal Church.* The Committee for the Full Participation of Women in the Church, The Episcopal Church. New York: Women in Mission and Ministry at the Episcopal Church Center.

Deal, Terrence E., and Allen A. Kennedy. 1982. *Corporate Cultures: The Rites and Rituals of Corporate Life.* Reading, Mass.: Addison-Wesley.

Dennis, Walter D. 1981. "Withholding Consent Cuts Both Ways." *Saint Luke's Journal of Theology* 24, no. 2:138–43.

Doyle, Eric. 1984. "The Ordination of Women in the Roman Catholic Church." In *The Feminine in the Church,* edited by Monica Furlong, 28–43. London: SPCK.

Driver, Tom F. 1981. *Christ in a Changing World. Toward an Ethical Christology,* New York: Crossroad.

Ebaugh, Helen Rose. 1993a. "The Growth and Decline of Catholic Religious Orders of Women Worldwide: The Impact of Women's Opportunity Structures." *Journal for the Scientific Study of Religion* 32, no. 1:68–75.

———. 1993b. *Women in the Vanishing Cloister: Organizational Decline in Catholic Religious Orders in the United States.* New Brunswick, N.J.: Rutgers Univ. Press.

Euzenas, Lynn L. 1989. *C-4 Project Summary: Ethnic Clergywomen, White Clergywomen, and Clergy Couples.* Division of Ordained Ministry, Board of Higher Education and Ministry, The United Methodist Church.

Evans, Gillian R. 1989. "Unity and Autonomy: The Paradox of Lambeth." *Anglican and Episcopal History* 58 (Sep.):364–69.

Faludi, Susan. 1991. *Backlash: The Undeclared War against American Women.* New York: Crown.

Ferder, Fran. 1978. *Called to Break Bread? A Psychological Investigation of 100 Women Who Feel Called to Priesthood in the Catholic Church.* Mt. Rainier, Wash.: Quixote Center.

Fernando, Chitra. 1984. "The Role of the Church in the Oppression of Women."

In *The Emerging Christian Woman: Church and Society Perspectives,* edited by Stella Faria, Anna Vareed Alexander, and Jessie B. Tellis-Nayak, 55–62. Indore, India: Satprakashan Sanchar Kendra.

Field-Bibb, Jacqueline. 1991. *Women Towards Priesthood, Ministerial Politics and Feminist Praxis.* Cambridge: Cambridge Univ. Press.

Finn, Virginia Sullivan. Forthcoming. "The Ministerial Aspirations of Catholic Lay Women in the United States." In *Religious Institutions and Women's Leadership: New Roles Inside the Mainstream,* edited by Catherine Wessinger, Columbia: Univ. of South Carolina Press.

Firestone, William A., and Bruce L. Wilson. 1985. "Using Bureaucratic and Cultural Linkages to Improve Instruction: The Principal's Contribution." *Educational Administration Quarterly* 21, no. 2:7–30.

Fishburn, Peter, Janet Fishburn, and Arthur Hagy. 1992. "Are There Better Ways to Elect Bishops?" *Circuit Rider* 16, (July-Aug.):11–12.

Frizzell, John R. 1988. "Episcopalians' Expediency Sidetracks Unity." *The Christian Century,* (Aug. 17–24): 725.

Getz, Lorine M. 1986. "Women Struggle for an American Catholic Identity." In *Women and Religion in America: 1900–1968,* vol. 3, edited by Rosemary Radford Ruether and Rosemary Skinner Keller, 175–81. San Francisco: Harper and Row.

Gilligan, Carol. 1982. *In a Different Voice: Psychological Theory and Women's Development.* Cambridge, Mass.: Harvard Univ. Press.

Ginzberg, Lori D. 1990. *Women and the Work of Benevolence: Morality, Politics, and Class in the Nineteenth-Century United States.* New Haven, Conn.: Yale Univ. Press.

Greenfield, Thomas B. 1973. "Organizations as Social Inventions: Rethinking Assumptions about Change." *The Journal of Applied Behavioral Science* 9, no. 5:551–74.

———. 1982. "Against Group Mind: An Anarchistic Theory of Education." *McGill Journal of Education* 17, no. 1:3–11.

———. 1984. "Leaders and Schools: Willfulness and Nonnatural Order in Organizations." In *Leadership and Organizational Culture,* edited by Thomas J. Sergiovani, 142–69. Champaign-Urbana: Univ. of Illinois Press.

Grindal, Gracia. Forthcoming. "Women in the Evangelical Lutheran Church in America." In *Religious Institutions and Women's Leadership: New Roles Inside the Mainstream,* edited by Catherine Wessinger. Columbia: Univ. of South Carolina Press.

Groome, Thomas H. 1984. "From Chauvinism and Clericalism to Priesthood: The Long March." In *The Emerging Christian Woman: Church and Society Perspectives,* edited by Stella Farla, Anna Vareed Alexander, and Jessie B. Tellis-Nayak. 90–104. Indore, India: Satprakashan Sanchar Kendra.

Groves, Richard. 1984. "Conservatives Dominate Southern Baptist Meeting." *The Christian Century* (July 18–25): 701–3.

Hacker, Andrew. 1992. *Two Nations: Black and White, Separate, Hostile, Unequal.* New York: Charles Scribner's Sons.

Hames, Jerry. 1993. "Despite Protests, Fort Worth Celebrates a New Bishop." *Episcopal Life,* June, 9.

Harris, Barbara C. 1986. "The 'mind of the house'." *The Witness* 69, no. 11:17.

Hennelly, Alfred T. 1989. *Theology for a Liberating Church: The New Praxis of Freedom.* Washington, D.C.: Georgetown Univ. Press.

Hersh, Blanche Glassman. 1978. *The Slavery of Sex: Feminist-Abolitionists in America.* Champaign-Urbana: Univ. of Illinois Press.

Hewitt, Emily C., and Suzanne R. Hiatt. 1973. *Women Priests: Yes or No?* New York: Seabury.

Heyward, Carter. 1989. *Touching Our Strength: The Erotic as Power and the Love of God.* San Francisco: Harper.

Hiatt, Suzanne. 1986. "The Great Thing about Mary." *The Witness* 69, no. 12:6–8.

———. Forthcoming. "Womens's Ordination in the Anglican Communion: Can this Church be Saved?" In *Religious Institutions and Women's Leadership: New Roles Inside the Mainstream,* edited by Catherine Wessinger. Columbia: Univ. of South Carolina Press.

Hillyer, Philip, ed. 1990. *On the Threshold of the Third Millenium.* Vol. 1 of *Concilium.* London: SCM.

Hirsch, Paul, and John A.Y. Andrews. 1984. "Administrators' Response to Performance and Value Challenges: Stance, Symbol, and Behavior." In *Leadership and Organizational Culture.* edited by Thomas J. Sergiovanni, 170–85. Champaign-Urbana: Univ. of Illinois Press.

Hunter, James Davison. 1991. *Culture Wars: The Struggle to Define America.* New York: Basic Books.

Huyck, Heather. 1992. "Indelible Change: Women Priests in the Episcopal Church." *Historical Magazine of the Protestant Episcopal Church* 51 (Dec.): 385–98.

Ice, Martha Long. 1987. *Clergy Women and Their World Views: Calling for a New Age.* New York: Praeger.

Jacobsen, Douglas, and W.V. Trollinger, Jr. 1994. "Evangelical and Ecumenical: Re-forming a Center." *The Christian Century* (July 13–20): 682–84.

John Paul II. 1988. *Apostolic Letter Mulleris Dignitatem of the Supreme Pontiff: John Paul II on the Dignity and Vocation of Women.* Boston: St. Paul Books and Media.

Johnson, Elizabeth A. 1988. "Feminist Hermeneutics." *Chicago Studies* 27: 123–35.

Kaminer, Wendy. 1993. "Feminism's Identity Crisis." *The Atlantic Monthly,* Oct., 51–68.

Kanter, Rosabeth Moss. 1977. "Some Effects of Proportions on Group Life: Skewed Sex Ratios and Responses to Token Women." *American Journal of Sociology* 82 (Mar.): 965–990.

Karen, Robert. 1992. "Shame." *The Atlantic Monthly.* Feb., 40–70.

Keller, Rosemary Skinner. 1984. "Women and the Nature of Ministry in the United Methodist Tradition." *Methodist History* 22 (Jan.): 99–114.

———. 1986. "Patterns of Laywomen's Leadership in Twentieth Century Protestantism." In *Women and Religion in America: 1900–1968,* vol. 3, edited by Rosemary Radford Ruether and Rosemary Skinner Keller, 266–309. San Francisco: Harper and Row.

Kleinman, Sherryl. 1984. *Equals before God: Seminarians as Humanistic Professionals.* Chicago: Univ. of Chicago Press.

Kraditor, Aileen S. 1969. *Means and Ends in American Abolitionism: Garrison and His Critics on Strategy and Tactics, 1834–1850.* New York: Pantheon.

Larrabee, Mary Jeanne, ed. 1993. *An Ethic of Care: Feminist Interdisciplinary Perspectives.* New York: Routledge.

Lehman, Edward C., Jr. 1981. "Organizational Resistance to Women in Ministry." *Sociological Analysis* 42, no. 2:101–18.

———. 1985. *Women Clergy: Breaking through Gender Barriers.* New Brunswick, N.J.: Transaction.

———. 1987a. "Research on Lay Church Members' Attitudes toward Women Clergy: An Assessment." *Review of Religious Research* 28, no. 4:319–29.

———. 1987b. "Sexism, Organizational Maintenance, and Localism: A Research Note." *Sociological Analysis'* 48, no. 3:274–82.

———. 1993a. "Gender and Ministry Style: Things Not What They Seem." *Sociology of Religion* 54:1–11.

———. 1993b. *Gender and Work: The Case of the Clergy.* Albany, N.Y.: State Univ. of New York Press.

———. 1993c. Review of *Women Priests: An Emerging Ministry in the Episcopal Church,* by John H. Morgan. *Journal for the Scientific Study of Religion* 32, no. 3:289–90.

Leonard, Bill J. 1990. *God's Land and Only Hope.* Grand Rapids, Mich.: William B. Eerdmans.

———. 1993. "When the Denominational Center Doesn't Hold: The Southern Baptist Experience." *The Christian Century* (Sept. 22–29): 905–10.

Lofland, John, and Lyn H. Lofland. 1984. *Analyzing Social Settings: A Guide to Qualitative Observation and Analysis.* 2d ed. Belmont, Cal.: Wadsworth.

Luyckx, Marc. 1980. "The Situation of Women in the Catholic Church: Developments Since International Women's Year." *Pro Mundi Vita Bulletin* 83:2–36.

Maeckelberghe, Els. 1991. *Desperately Seeking Mary: A Feminist Approach to a Traditional Religious Symbol.* Kampen, The Netherlands: Kok Pharos.

McBeth, H. Leon. 1981. "The Ordination of Women." *Review and Expositor* 78 (Fall): 515–30.

Merriam, Sharan B. 1988. *Case Study Research in Education: A Qualitative Approach.* San Francisco: Jossey-Bass.

Morgan, John H. 1985. *Women Priests: An Emerging Ministry in the Episcopal Church.* Bristol: Wyndam Hall.

Moyers, Bill. 1987. "God and Politics: The Battle for the Bible." Show 102, Dec. 16. New York: Public Affairs Television, Inc.

Nason-Clark, Nancy. 1987. "Ordaining Women as Priests: Religious vs. Sexist Explanations for Clerical Attitudes." *Sociological Analysis* 48:259–73.

Neal, Marie Augusta. 1984. *Catholic Sisters in Transition: From the 1960s to the 1980s.* Wilmington, Del.: Michael Glazier.

———. Forthcoming. "American Catholic Sisters." *In Religious Institutions and Women's Leadership: New Roles Inside the Mainstream,* edited by Catherine Wessinger. Columbia: Univ. of South Carolina Press.

Nesbitt, Paula D. 1990. "Feminization of American Clergy: Occupational Life Chances in the Ordained Ministry." Ph.D. diss., Harvard Univ. Press.

———. 1992. "Lamentations: The Politics of Gender and Ministry." In *Society for the Scientific Study of Religion in Washington, D.C.*

———. 1993. "Dual Ordination Tracks: Differential Benefits and Costs for Men and Women Clergy." *Sociology of Religion* 54:13–30.

Nunley, Jan. 1994. "Bishops Reach Uneasy Truce, Urge More Dialogue on Issues Surrounding Women's Ordination." *Episcopal News Service* (Sept. 1): 1–3.

Pellauer, Mary D. 1990. *Twenty Years after the Ordination of Women: Reports on the Participation of Ordained Women.* Commission for Women, Evangelical Lutheran Church in America.

Penn, Jeffrey, and Gustav Spohn. 1993. "Missionary Diocese Defects." *Episcopal Life.* Jan., 1, 4.

Piepkorn, Arthur Carl. 1978. *Profiles in Belief: The Religious Bodies of the United States and Canada.* Vol. 2. San Francisco: Harper and Row.

Pierce, Susan E. 1988. "Doing the Anglican Shuffle." *The Witness* 71 (June-Aug.): 14,16–17.

Pomerleau, Dolly. 1982. *Journey of Hope: A Prophetic Encounter in Czechoslovakia.* Mt. Rainier, Wash.: Quixote Center.

Porterfield, Amanda. 1987. "Feminist Theology as a Revitalization Movement." *Sociological Analysis* 48:234–44.

Prelinger, Catherine M. 1992. "Ordained Women in the Episcopal Church." In *Episcopal Women: Gender, Spirituality and Commitment in an American Mainline*

Denomination, edited by Catherine M. Prelinger, 285–309. New York: Oxford Univ. Press.

Proctor-Smith, Marjorie. 1985. "Images of Women in the Lectionary." *Concilium* 182, no. 6:51–62.

Ranck, Lee. "Social Actions Enable United Methodists 'to Manifest . . . Gospel in the World.' " *The Daily Christian Advocate.* May 16, 6–7.

Ranson, Stewart, Bob Hinings, and Royston Greenwood. "The Structuring of Organizational Structures." 1980. *Administrative Science Quarterly* 25, no. 1:1–15.

Ratcliff, Donald. 1992. "How Children Understand Religious Concepts." *Religion & Public Education* 19:162–72.

Rebeck, Victoria A. 1993. "Gifted for Ministry: Setting up Pastors for Success." *The Christian Century* 110, no. 20: 670–75.

Rosenberg, Ellen M. 1989. *The Southern Baptists: A Subculture in Transition.* Knoxville: Univ. of Tennessee Press.

Rossman, Gretchen B., H. Dickson Corbett, and William A. Firestone. 1988. *Change and Effectiveness in Schools: A Cultural Perspective.* Albany: State Univ. of New York Press.

Ruether, Rosemary Radford. 1972. *Liberation Theology.* New York: Paulist.

———. 1983. *Sexism and God-Talk: Toward a Feminist Theology.* 1st ed., Boston: Beacon,

———. 1989. "Uppity Women & Authentic Ecumenism." *The Witness* 72 (Apr.): 16–17.

Russell, Jean. 1968. *God's Lost Cause: A Study of the Church and the Racial Problem.* Valley Forge, Pa.: Judson.

Sakenfeld, Katharine Doob. 1989. "Feminist Biblical Interpretation." *Theology Today* 46:154–68.

Schaller, Lyle. 1992. "From the Rustbelt to the Sunbelt! Our Church is Moving South." *Circuit Rider* 16, no. 4:4–6.

Schein, Edgar H. 1985. *Organizational Culture and Leadership: A Dynamic View.* San Francisco: Jossey-Bass.

Schreckengost, George E. 1987. "The Effect of Latent Racist, Ethnic and Sexual Biases on Placement." *Review of Religious Research* 28, no. 4:351–66.

Schultz, Rima Lunin. 1992. "Woman's Work and Woman's Calling in the Episcopal Church, 1880–1989." In *Episcopal Women: Gender, Spirituality and Commitment in an American Mainline Denomination.* edited by Catherine M. Prelinger, 19–71. New York: Oxford Univ. Press.

Schwartz, Howard, and Jerry Jacobs. 1979. *Qualitative Sociology: A Method to the Madness.* New York: The Free Press.

Seidler, John, and Katherine Meyer. 1989. *Conflict and Change in the Catholic Church.* New Brunswick, N.J.: Rutgers Univ. Press.

Sergiovanni, Thomas J. 1984. *Leadership and Organizational Culture.* Champaign-Urbana: Univ. of Illinois Press.

Sherrod, Katie. 1993. "Church Hierarchy Keeps Its Women in Pain." *Episcopal Life.* Apr., 23.

Smircich, Linda. 1983. "Concepts of Culture and Organizational Analysis." *Administrative Science Quarterly* 28:339–58.

Snyder, Howard A. 1991. *Models of the Kingdom: Some Say God Rules the Heart; Some Say the Church; Some Say the Cosmos; Some Say Human History; Some Say They Need No King.* Nashville, Tenn.: Abingdon.

Stage, Sarah. 1991. "The Perils of (Post)Feminism: Gender, Class, and Female Benevolence." *Reviews in American History* 19:511–16.

Steed, Mary Lou. 1986. "Church Schism and Secession: A Necessary Sequence?" *Review of Religious Research* 27, no. 4:344–55.

Steinfels, Peter. 1992. "Pastoral Letter on Women's Role Falls in Vote of Catholic Bishops: After 9 Years of Work, No Consensus is Reached." *The New York Times.* Nov. 19, A1, B9.

Stevens, Lesley. 1989. "Different Voice / Different Voices: Anglican Women in Ministry." *Review of Religious Research* 30 (March): 262–75.

Taylor, Steven J., and Robert Bogdan. 1984. *Introduction to Qualitative Research Methods: The Search for Meanings.* 2d ed., New York: John Wiley and Sons.

Tobin, Mary Luke. 1985. "Women in the Church: Vatican II and After." *The Ecumenical Review* 37 (July): 295–305.

Tolbert, Mary Ann. 1989. "Protestant Feminists and the Bible: On the Horns of a Dilemma." *Union Seminary Quarterly Review* 43:1–17.

Urofsky, Melvin I. 1991. *A Conflict of Rights: The Supreme Court and Affirmative Action.* New York: Charles Scribner's Sons.

van Leeuwen, Gerwin. 1984. "Women in Ministries." In *The Emerging Christian Woman: Church and Society Perspectives,* edited by Stella Faria, Anna Vareed Alexander, and Jessie B. Tellis-Nayak, 105–13. Indore, India: Satprakashan Sanchar Kendra.

Verdesi, Elizabeth Howell. 1976. *In but Still Out: Women in the Church.* Philadelphia: Westminster.

Walker, Richard. 1989. "Consecration of Bishop Stirs Episcopal Dissent." *Christianity Today* 33 (Mar. 17): 41, 43.

Wallace, Ruth A. 1992. *They Call Her Pastor: A New Role for Catholic Women.* Albany: State Univ. of New York Press.

Wantland, William C. 1987. "Correspondence." *Saint Luke's Journal of Theology* 31, no. 1:7–9.

Weber, Max. 1946. *Essays in Sociology.* Translated by Hans Gerth and C. Wright Mills. London: Routledge and Kegan Paul.

Weick, Karl E. 1976. "Educational Organizations as Loosely Coupled Systems." *Administrative Science Quarterly* 21 (Mar.): 1–19.

Wessinger, Catherine. "Women's Religious Leadership in America." 1993. In *Parliament of the World's Religions in Chicago.* 25.

————, ed. forthcoming. *Religious Institutions and Women's Leadership: New Roles Inside the Mainstream.* Columbia: Univ. of South Carolina Press.

West, Cornel. 1993. *Race Matters.* Boston: Beacon.

Wilkes, Paul. 1990. "The Hands That Would Shape Our Souls." *The Atlantic,* Dec., 59–88.

Wilson-Kastner, Patricia. 1989. "Women in the Episcopacy: The Process of Reception." *Saint Luke's Journal of Theology* 32, no. 4:269–81.

Wingfield, Mark. 1993. "Baptist Women Quietly Gaining Ground in Ministry Roles." *Western Recorder,* Jan. 26, 1, 7.

Wortman, Julie A. 1992. "High Hurdles Confront Those Seeking Ordination." *Episcopal Life,* Sept., 10.

Wright, Susan Lockwood. 1986. "SBC Women Ministers Break Their Silence." *The Christian Century* (Nov. 12): 998–99.

Other Reference Works

The Book of Common Prayer and Administration of the Sacraments and Other Rites and Ceremonies of the Church. 1979. New York: The Church Hymnal Corporation.

The Book of Discipline of the United Methodist Church. 1992. Nashville, Tenn.: The United Methodist Publishing House.

Constitution and Canons for the Government of the Protestant Episcopal Church in the United States of America, otherwise known as The Episcopal Church adopted in General Conventions, 1789–1991. 1991. New York: The Episcopal Church.

"Constitutions, Bylaws, and Continuing Resolutions." 1989. *Proceedings of the Evangelical Lutheran Church in America.*

"Czech Hierarchy Bars Some Priests: Challenging Status of Many Who Served Underground in Communist Period." 1991. *The New York Times,* Dec. 8, 19.

"England's Bishops Try to Reassure Conservatives." 1993. *Episcopal Life,* Mar. 26.

Gallup Survey Results: Quiet but Massive Revolution in Catholic Opinion on Church Issues. 1992. Mt. Rainier, Wash.: Quixote Center.

"General Conference 1992." 1992. *Interpreter: Program Ideas for United Methodists,* July-Aug., 5–16.

"It Took Just 46 Ballots to Elect a New Bishop." 1993. *Episcopal Life,* Aug., 15.

"One in Christ Jesus: Fourth Draft, Response to Women's Concerns." 1992. *Origins* 22 (Sept. 10): 221–40.

Report of the Executive Council's Committee on the Status of Women. 1991. The Executive Council, The Committee on the Status of Women, The Episcopal Church.

"Reports and Actions." 1970. *Proceedings of the American Lutheran Church.*

"Traditionalist Clears Hurdle to Be Bishop." 1993. *Episcopal Life,* Mar., 2.

"Traditionalists Get Own Bishops." 1994. *Episcopal Life,* Jan., 3.

"U.S. Lutherans Elect First Woman Bishop." 1992. *Episcopal Life,* Aug., 3.

Webster's Ninth New Collegiate Dictionary, 9th ed., Vol 2. 1990. Springfield, Ill.: Merriam-Webster.

"Woman Elected Bishop of Vermont." 1993. *Episcopal Life,* July, 1, 15.

Index